BREAKING MURPHY'S LAW

BREAKING MURPHY'S LAW

How Optimists Get What They Want
from Life—and Pessimists Can Too

SUZANNE C. SEGERSTROM

THE GUILFORD PRESS
New York   London

© 2006 The Guilford Press
A Division of Guilford Publications, Inc.
72 Spring Street, New York, NY 10012
www.guilford.com

The information in this volume is not intended as a substitute for consultation with healthcare professionals. Each individual's health concerns should be evaluated by a qualified professional.

Printed in the United States of America

This book is printed on acid-free paper.

Last digit is print number: 9 8 7 6 5 4 3 2 1

Library of Congress Cataloging-in-Publication Data

Segerstrom, Suzanne C.
  Breaking Murphy's law : how optimists get what they want from life—and pessimists can too / Suzanne C. Segerstrom.
    p. cm.
  Includes bibliographical references and index.
  ISBN-10: 1-59385-209-6   ISBN-13: 978-1-59385-209-2 (trade cloth)
  1. Optimism. 2. Self-actualization (Psychology) I. Title.
  BF698.35.O57S445 2006
  158—dc22
                                        2005035083

To my husband and my lawyer,
who also happen to be my best friends

Contents

Acknowledgments

This book collects the wisdom of a community of optimism and well-being research scientists. I have had the good fortune to know and learn from many of them personally. I particularly acknowledge my mentors at the University of California, Los Angeles, especially Shelley Taylor and Margaret Kemeny; my colleagues who have provided so much intellectual stimulation and inspiration, especially fellow Akumal alumni and the Positive Psychology Network; and my students at the University of Kentucky, especially the graduate students whose hard work and love of learning, research, and the science of optimism have contributed so much to the ideas contained in this book.

Science is not inexpensive, and my optimism research has been supported financially by the National Institutes of Health (NIH), the Norman Cousins Program in Psychoneuroimmunology, the University of Kentucky (UK), and the Templeton Positive Psychology Prize. UK and the NIH jointly supported the sabbatical that made concentrated writing time possible. Thanks are due all of those organizations for their support.

For their parts in the inception and development of this book, I thank the principal players: Jai Giffin for thinking it a good idea, for picking up the slack during the heavy writing times, and for feeding me during the final revisions; Kitty Moore and Chris Benton for believing there was a pony in there somewhere and helping me find it; Liz Large for keeping me legally safe and personally sane; and all the readers of early chapters for their encouraging reactions (including my mom).

Prologue
Stop Trying to Be So Happy

What do you want in life? If you made a list, what would be on it? Would you want a bigger car? A bigger family? More free time? Would you want to be happier?

If one of the items on your list says "be happier" (or something like that), get rid of it. Don't get me wrong; there's nothing wrong with being happy. Happy feels good, for one thing. It feels so good that a lot of what people wish for—things that may have shown up on your list such as friends, power, beauty, money—they wish for because they believe that having those things will make them happy. Not only that, but being happy may also help you get what you wish for. Happy people are more popular (cheerful, lively, and enthusiastic people have more social relationships), are more successful (happy college students have higher incomes after graduation), and may even live longer (happy novitiates were the longest-living nuns). So why not try to be happier?

Imagine that you have had a terrible day at work, and you're feeling very unhappy. On the radio on the way home, you hear about a concert featuring works by your favorite composer, who happens to be Igor Stravinsky. "Egad!" you think, "I'll go to the concert, and Igor will cheer me right up, and then I will be happy." So you buy your ticket, and you sit down, and the music starts, and you wait to get happy.

You might have a long wait.

Surprisingly, if you hadn't gone to the concert expecting to be cheered up, you very well might have been. But your goal to get happier has sabotaged you. An experiment about the effects of trying to be happy showed that both trying to be happy and just monitoring happiness actually prevented happiness. In this experiment, participants listened to Stravinsky's *Rite of Spring*. Some of them just listened to the music, others were told to use the music to cheer themselves up, and others just to keep track of how happy they were as they listened to the music. Surprisingly, the only way that listening to the *Rite of Spring* actually increased happiness was if the listener (1) wasn't trying to cheer up and (2) wasn't even keeping track of how happy she was. As you sit in the concert hall waiting for Igor Stravinsky to cheer you up, you actually guarantee that he won't. By constantly trying to get happy and monitoring whether you're happy, you're keeping yourself from getting happy.

Fun works the same way. Remember the millennium celebrations of 1999? How much fun did you have that New Year's Eve? It was the biggest New Year's Eve of our lifetimes, so shouldn't it have been the most fun? If you're like most people, you'll look back and recall that, even though your preparations and plans may have been more elaborate, you didn't have much more fun than you usually do on New Year's, and you may have had less.[1] Research shows that people who spent more time and money to ensure a fabulous millennial New Year's Eve actually had less fun than people who didn't put much effort into the evening at all. It seems that trying too hard to have fun is a sure way to kill your buzz.

Another reason to cross the happiness goal off your list: happy people often don't list "be more happy" among their goals. A list of goals that includes "be positive," "be happy," "have a good attitude," or the like might indicate that that person is not already very happy or positive. Maybe this is obvious: happy people are already happy, so they don't set a goal to be happy. On the other hand, maybe it's not that obvious. Consider what would happen if you substituted fitness for happiness. Fit people are already fit, but they very often have goals to *remain* fit by doing things like running or working out a certain

---

[1]Depending on how much champagne you had, you may or may not recall that evening. Just work with me here.

number of times a week. Happiness is unlike fitness in that most happy people do not have goals specifically related to remaining happy. They don't wake up in the morning thinking about how they are going to maintain their happiness that day, the way fit people might wake up thinking about how they are going to manage to get in their daily run. The Stravinsky and New Year's Eve research shows that it's a good thing that happy people don't plan their happiness, because if they did, they might actually become less happy. To truly be more happy, you have to stop trying.

KILL YOUR TELEVISION

Right after you stop your pursuit of happiness, you should stop trying to free up your time. People think they'll be happier if they have more free time, but free time is overrated. Look at how American lives have changed over the past century. We have wealth and leisure beyond previous generations' wildest imaginings. The washing machine! The automobile! Air travel! Computers! Television! And we have more years and better health to enjoy our leisure. Expected longevity for children born in the United States increases every year. New drugs control infections, improve our love lives, and even, like the statins that lower cholesterol, compensate for the health effects of our wealthy diet and increased leisure. Still, despite all these improvements, Americans are no happier today on average than they were 50 years ago, when they always had to do the dishes by hand and there was no such thing as permanent press.

Actually, free time is not in and of itself a problem. It's what people do with it, which is in large part watching TV. The average American watches several hours of television every day, and TV is a bigger part of many people's lives than things going on outside the box. For example, about 50 million Americans between the ages of 18 and 44 voted in the 2000 presidential election. About 24 million Americans in roughly the same age group voted for a recent American Idol. When citizens' involvement in a TV show starts gaining on citizens' involvement in their own national government, you have to wonder if TV isn't taking over just a little bit too much of American life.

If I actually killed the television, my husband would probably divorce me.[2] Still, I can't ignore the fact that TV is the refined sugar of daily activities, and Americans consume way too much of both. Here's a problem with sugar: When you eat a candy bar, a large amount of sugar rushes into your bloodstream. A little while later, a large amount of insulin rushes into your bloodstream to process the sugar. Unfortunately, the insulin comes too late, most of the sugar having moved on by then. Insulin ends up having to scavenge whatever leftover sugar remains, and the result is that you get low blood sugar and feel nasty and hungry, which makes you want to eat more candy to get your blood sugar up, and the whole cycle starts over again.

Sugar's effects are ironic; that is, they have the opposite effect from the one you intended. You wanted to feel less hungry and nasty, and you ended up feeling more hungry and nasty. TV has a similar effect, but on happiness instead of hungriness. You watch TV because you want to be entertained, relaxed, involved—you want to feel happy. Unfortunately, although TV can be relaxing, it is only intermittently entertaining and very rarely involving. So, you end up bored, which makes you think you should watch more TV . . . and you can guess the consequences. Everyone needs a little time to watch TV or just do nothing, just like everyone needs a little sugar now and then. A problem arises when you assume that if a little is good, then more must be better. It's not. I guarantee that prolonged periods of sitting in front of the TV and eating sugary snacks will not make you happy in the long run.

THE UNHAPPY MILLIONAIRE

Although many people believe the rich must be happy, we have to add money to the list of things that actually won't make you happy. Although wealth in the United States has tripled over the past 50

---

[2]Lest I seem preachy about TV, I freely admit that there are at least three televisions in my house (I think my husband may have a fourth plugged in down in the basement, but the state of the basement is such that he also might have a pony stabled down there and I wouldn't notice—at least for a while.) We also have a satel-

years, American satisfaction with life has remained level, and the prevalence of depression has increased alarmingly, especially among younger generations. In countries in which per capita gross domestic product is greater than $10,000, wealth has hardly any effect on satisfaction with life. Above subsistence level, then, money truly does not buy happiness. People on *Forbes* magazine's list of richest Americans are, on average, no happier than a group of Pennsylvania Amish, who live without jet planes, designer shoes, plastic surgery, or (for that matter) even television: both average 5.8 on a scale of 1–7, where 7 is the most satisfied with life. An international college student sample (averaging 4.9) is almost exactly as happy as Calcutta slum dwellers (averaging 4.6), despite vast differences in their fortunes.

How can people in such widely different circumstances be equally happy? People have a tremendous ability to adapt to their circumstances, a phenomenon called the "psychological immune system" or the "hedonic treadmill." Two days ago I was ecstatic because I found the last of a particular dress in my size in the country (as far as I can tell). Today, I am not as ecstatic. Although I'm looking forward to wearing the dress and I'm still pleased that I have it, my mood is not particularly elevated.

A much more dramatic demonstration of the "psychological immune system" compared people who had experienced something that should make anyone very happy—winning the lottery—with other people who had experienced something that should make anyone very unhappy, becoming paralyzed in an accident. Their reports of their general happiness are telling. The graph on page 6 shows how they rated their happiness in the past, present, and future and how much pleasure they were getting from everyday activities such as talking with friends, getting a compliment, or buying clothes. The bottom of the scale is "not at all" happy, and the top of the scale is "very much" happy. Not surprisingly, the accident victims saw their present as somewhat less happy than their past (although it looks as though they have a nostalgic view of their past as happier than it probably

---

lite dish, the original purpose of which was to access all 9,412 channels of college football and motorized vehicle races (mostly cars, but also school buses and riding lawn mowers). The purpose has been thwarted somewhat since I discovered the university research channels. It takes all kinds of geeks to make the world go 'round.

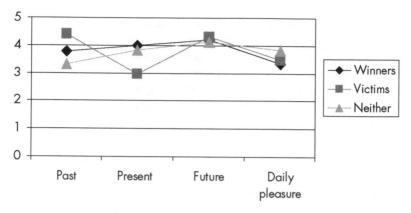

Happiness for lottery winners, paraplegic accident victims, and a group experiencing neither event.

was), and winners saw their present as somewhat happier than their past. However, neither group diverges much from people who didn't win the lottery *or* get paralyzed in an accident. Even the accident victims at their lowest are more happy than not. And although the three groups are very similar, it's revealing that winners get the least pleasure out of everyday activities. The ecstasy of winning the lottery appears to have deadened them to the joys of daily life.

It's no wonder, then, that ability to buy things hasn't increased our happiness. A new sweater will make you feel happier for a while, but not for very long. Two new sweaters won't make you much happier than one new sweater. And a million dollars' worth of new sweaters, in the long run, won't do much at all.

DON'T HATE ME BECAUSE I'M HAPPY

If being happy is good, but trying to get happy either directly through effort or indirectly though free time or income isn't the answer, what should you do? Here is an example of someone who—I think—has found the answer to feeling good. Even though I talked to him for only a few minutes, I remember him and the lesson he taught me very distinctly. A few years ago, I was at a conference in New Orleans, waiting in the bar of the hotel to meet some friends for dinner. Seated next to me was an older gentleman, and he asked me what I was doing in New Orleans (a health conference) and what my work was about (optimism and health). He then shared with me his prescription for happiness. Now, optimism and happiness are not the same thing, but this gentleman hit on exactly what I have come to believe is the key to understanding optimism. The key for him was to *do something*. I forget what it was, but I remember he had hobbies he would pursue when he got home from work, and frankly the details don't matter that much. What does matter is that he specifically said it was important for him to avoid the TV, because watching TV all evening would just make him bored and irritable. This gentleman was *engaged*. He didn't just want to be watching. He wanted to be *doing*, and the doing made him happy.

Now, another possibility is that this guy was a naturally happy person, so it didn't really matter what he was doing. We all know people who are cheerful and happy most of the time and other people for whom a parking ticket can create a black cloud that follows them around all day (or maybe they don't even need the parking ticket). Their happiness or unhappiness seems to come from somewhere inside them, and even though the happy person might be temporarily saddened or upset, he also recovers quickly, and vice versa for the unhappy person. This phenomenon led happiness scientists to propose that everyone has a happiness "set point." A set point implies that most people are pretty stable in their happiness levels. Think of the set point as being like a car's cruise control. Cruise control is a negative feedback loop, in which deviations from the set point are brought back toward the set point. If the car is going too slowly, the cruise control will give it more gas, and if the car is going too fast, the cruise control will ease up on the gas. The system always tries to bring the car's speed back to the set point. Likewise, if your mood strays too far from your "set point," some mechanism will bring it back to its usual level.

One potential mechanism for the set point is genes. It's very clear that a nontrivial part of how happy you are is genetic. If you're generally a happy person, you have genes to thank for some of that happiness, and the same is true if you're generally an unhappy person. Your genes set your happiness "reaction range"—that is, the amount of happiness you are biologically able to produce—in the same way that they set the reaction range for your height. Then, once "nature" has set the boundaries, "nurture" determines where you end up. Experiences make you as happy or as sad as your genes will let you be, in the same way that whether you drink milk or soda as a child will make you as tall or short as your genes will let you be (at least according to Mom).

It is premature, though, to start hating the happy because they happen to be privileged to have this state—happiness—that others can only wish for. There may be an escape from the set point. To escape a set point, there has to be some kind of *positive* feedback loop, that is, some mechanism by which a fast car gets faster.

Optimism is one such mechanism. Many people equate optimism with happiness, but optimism is actually not a feeling. Optimism is a *belief* about the future. Very optimistic people believe that more good things will happen to them than bad, that things will go their way, that the future is positive, and that uncertainty is an opportunity for the best to occur, rather than the worst. Optimistic beliefs set up a positive feedback loop because, as the rest of this book will show, the more optimistic people are, the more they can be expected to experience the positive future they envision. Optimistic people get more joy out of everyday life, they are more resilient to the stressful twists and turns of life, they have better relationships, and they may even be physically healthier. In turn, these positive outcomes naturally feed expectations for an equally if not more positive future—that is, optimism. An optimistic athlete will tend to realize her goals (by processes explained in Chapter 2), leading her to believe even more strongly that she can be successful. An optimistic teacher will tend to have students who (by processes explained in Chapter 4) confirm his belief in his power to educate. Insofar as happiness is a consequence of realizing goals and exercising strengths (a hypothesis addressed in Chapters 2 and 3), optimistic people's happiness may actually grow over time.

It's not entirely wrong to think of optimistic people as happy people, because most optimistic people are happier than most pessimistic people. It may be entirely wrong, however, to think of optimistic people as happy simply because they are positive. For a long time, I thought the most important thing about optimistic people was their positive outlook and specifically that their positive outlook about the future would protect them against present stress, because the present wouldn't seem so bad in light of a positive future to come. Ironically, this viewpoint made me skeptical about whether I was optimistic. When I have published research on the relationship between optimism and the immune system (my primary research area), TV stations, radio programs, and newspapers ranging from the *New York Times* to small local papers and my college alumni newsletter[3] have interviewed me about the results for their stories on psychological well-being and health. I even turned down the opportunity to write the Cosmo Quiz. (I was pretty sure that they wanted a more sensational version than I could provide.) In many of the media interviews I've done, I'm asked about different aspects of the relationship between optimism and health or the immune system, but one question seems to always come up: Are you an optimist?

I had a hard time answering this question. I felt I was too familiar with the scales used to measure optimism to be able to answer honestly. I could see myself confronted with one of these items and thinking to myself, "I think I'm a 4. Should I circle 4? Most people would circle 4 . . . 3 would be acceptable—would that make my score too pessimistic? How many other 4's have I already circled? Any 5's? What's my score so far?"[4] So I couldn't really take the questionnaire because I was too self-conscious about my answers. Imagine that you could decide what number your bathroom scale would show. How accurate would *you* be?

I also had trouble saying that I was a very optimistic person because I am not necessarily a happy-go-lucky, carefree person.[5] I also couldn't in good conscience present myself as consistently cheery and smiley. Though I am often cheery and smiley, I have pronounced grumpy, irritable, and worried aspects. So, when I was asked whether I am an optimist, I would hem and haw, citing my inability to respond honestly to the questionnaires and generally avoiding the question.

That started to change a few years ago. I started to think of other meanings of optimism—meanings that did not imply cheery, smiley, carefree happy-go-luckiness. This was prompted by an unexpected finding: some of the optimists in one of my studies had *lower* immune

---

[3]Lewis and Clark College in Portland, Oregon.

[4]One of my other research interests is rumination. Go figure.

[5]See previous note re rumination.

parameters than their more pessimistic counterparts (a finding described further in Chapter 5). I looked to see whether they were also unhappier, but they usually weren't. I had to find some other explanation for the difference. That led to a line of research that emphasizes something different about optimists: their approach to their goals. Optimists believe their goals are achievable. They are more committed to their goals. They don't give up easily. They will even stress their bodies in the pursuit of their goals. Once I started thinking about optimism this way, I could easily identify with optimists.

Optimism is certainly something that you have. Some people have optimistic beliefs, and others do not. Optimism or pessimism is part of personality, that part of the psychological makeup that is consistent over time and, not incidentally, slow to change if changeable at all. Furthermore, optimism is only one of many personality dimensions associated with being more or less happy and healthy (not to mention successful, tidy, and many other desirable states). Extraverted people are more happy; hostile people are less happy. Secure people are more happy; neurotic people are less happy. This is interesting to know, but if you want to escape the set point, somewhat harder to put into practice. Many personality factors are substantially genetic, and others (such as secure relationship styles) have their sources in early experiences that are unlikely to be repeated in adulthood (such as an infant–caregiver relationship). By adulthood, many aspects of your personality either benefit or harm you just by virtue of being there.

Optimism is no exception to the genes–personality rule, being about 25% heritable. However, the longer I have studied optimism, the more I have come to believe that the benefits of optimism are only partially from *being* optimistic. That is, having optimistic beliefs gets you only so far. You have to get the rest of the way through *doing*. Those optimistic beliefs work to make optimists' lives better because they cause optimistic people to behave in particular ways.

Entry into the positive feedback loop provided by optimism happens through behaving optimistically. If you are looking for a way to escape your set point and move toward the top of where your genes will let you be in psychological and physical well-being, you would do well to attend to what it is to *do* optimism.

Before I delve into the details of how very optimistic people teach the rest of us how to overcome our set points, defeat our psychological immune systems, and get off the hedonic treadmill, a few words about this book. There have been many claims about optimistic thinking over the years. If you took the most extreme of these claims, you might believe that being optimistic means you can never have another unhappy day, and you might just live forever. Cynics, take heart. It's not true.[6] Chapter 6, which separates the potential from the real vulnerabilities that arise from optimism, is just for you.

How does one know what to believe about optimism? This is not the place to go into the theory and philosophy of science or to give a discourse on research design. Those topics require books unto themselves. Suffice it to say that the evidence that I present here is based on scientific studies published in peer-reviewed journals. I think you'll find the science is even more interesting than the extreme claims—it is certainly more complex. Research is like the test kitchen for good ideas. Sure, zucchini bread with dried apricots sounds good, but what happens when you actually make it? And with how many eggs? The *Betty Crocker Cookbook* wouldn't include a cake recipe unless it worked in a variety of home kitchens and was forgiving of a number of cook errors. You can trust in Betty's cake recipe, and you can feel confident that the ideas about optimism presented here reflect its workings in the real world. Maybe even in you.

---

[6]Otherwise, we might expect that a third or so of the population would be perpetually happy and enjoy eternal life, and that's *clearly* not true.

CHAPTER ONE

Glass Half Full, Glass Half Empty, or Glass That Needs to Be Washed?

The Optimistic Character

If a reporter asked you if you were optimistic, what would you say? The bathroom-scale problem aside, it might be a difficult question to answer because different people define optimism in different ways. Like my friend in New Orleans, people sometimes equate optimism with happiness, or they use it to mean a general positivity about life or hopefulness about the future. Psychologists, on the other hand, use a more restricted definition of optimism that refers only to beliefs and not to emotions. Those who study risk estimates (are you more or less likely than the average person to get in an auto accident?) refer to an optimistic bias, those who study causal beliefs (what caused that accident?) refer to optimistic and pessimistic attributions, and, last but not least, those who study personality refer to dispositional optimism. It is this last formulation—optimism as a personality trait—that is the focus of this book.

Everyone has a personality, of course, but how do you know that you have a certain kind of personality, like being an optimist? If you went to a party last Friday night, do you have an outgoing personality? If you cleaned your cabinets last Friday night, do you have an obsessive–compulsive personality? If you got in a bar fight last Friday night, do you have an aggressive personality? Most people would say no, because the concept of personality implies something more than a specific way that you spent a single night. First, personality has to arise from inside the person. If you ordinarily hate parties but went to one last Friday because someone coerced you, then that behavior isn't personality. Second, personality implies a pattern of behavior, not just a specific instance. Maybe you are usually a slob but cleaned your cabinets because your mother was coming to visit on Saturday. We wouldn't call this behavior personality either. On the other hand, if you're cleaning your cabinets three times a day, the possibility of an obsessive–compulsive personality comes to mind. Third, personality implies some influence across a number of situations. If you have a history of picking fights in bars, gesturing and swearing at other drivers, kicking the cat, and arguing with your boss, most people would agree that you have an aggressive personality.

What does it take to have an optimistic personality? First, it takes positive beliefs about what will happen in the future—what psychologists call "positive outcome expectancies." However, you can't just have positive beliefs about the potential outcome of one bar fight next Friday night ("I'm going to kick a**!") to have an optimistic personality, because personality implies a pattern. You have to have optimistic beliefs about several kinds of situations; that is, those "positive outcome expectancies" have to be "generalized" across several domains of life. Finally, to qualify as a personality trait, your optimistic beliefs have to be stable over time. If you're dispositionally optimistic, you're almost certain to have the same generalized optimistic beliefs on Friday that you had on Monday, and your beliefs will probably change very little over weeks, months, or even years.

In fact, on the 10th anniversary of my first major research study of optimism, I decided to try to find out how stable "dispositional" optimism really is by contacting the participants from that study to see whether and how much their optimism had changed. With half of the sample responding so far, the degree of stability is remarkable. The optimism scale used in the study has respectable reliability, a statistic that tells how much overlap you would find between two administrations of the scale if the person didn't change. In this case, if you gave the optimism scale twice and underlying optimism didn't change at all, you could expect the scale to overlap with itself about 72%. The actual overlap between my study participants' optimism scale scores in 1994 and their scores in 2005: 36%. That means that half of the potential overlap was actually maintained over a decade. Looking at these data another way, if we define stability as change of 10% or less on the optimism scale, nearly two-thirds of the sample had stable optimism. If your college roommate was one of those people who envision a future full of accomplishments and successes, she is likely to be doing the same thing at the 10-year reunion. If you had the misfortune to room with an Eeyore, who saw nothing but gray skies ahead (and see Chapter 4 for why this was an unfortunate pairing for you), don't be surprised if he is still forecasting doom and gloom a decade later.

ARE YOU POLLYANNA OR EEYORE (OR BOTH)?

Given the durability of dispositional optimism, you may be encouraged to know you are probably optimistic. When I give people questionnaires that measure their levels of dispositional optimism, around 80% of them could be classified as having optimistic personalities. Very few people are actually pessimistic, and I have seen only one score—in over 1,700 questionnaires—that corresponded to absolute pessimism, meaning the person agreed strongly with all the pessimistic statements (Nothing good will ever happen to me? Of course.) and strongly rejected all the optimistic statements (I usually expect the best? Not at all.). In contrast, I often see scores that correspond to absolute optimism, in which people strongly disagree with all the pessimistic statements and strongly agree with all the optimistic ones. Most people are optimists, just to varying degrees. When you look at the chart on this page, you can see how optimists occupy the biggest piece of the pie.

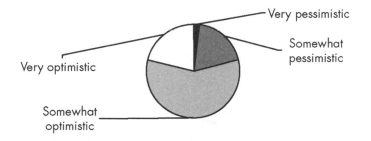

The typical distribution of optimism in my studies. Most people—80%—are somewhat to very optimistic.

Your own degree of dispositional optimism comes from two beliefs:

1. How strongly do you believe that good things will happen in your future?
2. How strongly do you believe that bad things will happen in your future?

If you strongly believe good things are going to happen to you *and* strongly believe bad things are *not* going to happen to you, you are very optimistic. If you strongly believe bad things are going to happen to you *and* strongly believe good things are *not* going to happen to you, you are very pessimistic. Where does your personality fall? If you want, you can assign your answer to each of these questions a number to figure it out. For question #1, give yourself a 1 for "not at all," 3 for "somewhat," and 5 for "extremely." Use the even numbers if you want (2 for somewhere between "not at all" and "somewhat," for example). For question #2, give yourself a 1 for "extremely," 3 for "somewhat," and 5 for "not at all," again using the even numbers if you want. Now take the average of the two numbers. If your average falls between 1 and 2, you are probably very pessimistic. If your average falls between 2 and 3, you are probably somewhat pessimistic. If your average falls between 3 and 4, you are probably somewhat optimistic. If your average falls between 4 and 5, congratulations. You are very optimistic, and probably irritating the heck out of the pessimists around you.

In concrete terms, being very optimistic means that when you think about your life's work, your relationships, your hobbies, and even your goals (like being healthier or more tolerant), you can easily envision yourself accomplishing what you want and, although you can recognize the possibility that not everything will turn out well, you think the odds are in your favor. A woman who scored very high in dispositional optimism perfectly expressed her personality when she wrote to me after moving to a new city, "I'm going to love it here. I miss my friends, but I know I will meet new people here; it's just going to take time. I'm really looking forward to my new job, too."

Conversely, being very pessimistic means that when you think about those important things, you have a hard time envisioning yourself accomplishing the things you want. You can't see how things will go well for you. Compare the previous woman with one who told me,

"Everything seems to be going okay, but I can't shake the feeling that things are going to fall apart. It seems like something is bound to come along to screw things up." She couldn't even believe that things were going all right in her present, much less that they could improve in the future.

Not knowing anything else about you, I will predict that you fall into the "somewhat optimistic" group, only because that's where most people are. A "somewhat optimistic" personality is made up of some greater degree of optimism (good things will happen) and some lesser degree of pessimism (bad things will happen). Most people do recognize that their future holds both good and bad things. However, the relationship between these two kinds of beliefs about the future gets complicated by the fact that the degree to which you expect good things doesn't have to be the opposite of the degree to which you expect bad things. You can have what are essentially unrelated levels of optimism and pessimism, because your answer to question #1 doesn't necessarily dictate your answer to question #2. A small number of people are actually both very optimistic and very pessimistic. These people believe they will both buy a winning lottery ticket at the grocery store and get run over by a tractor trailer on their way home. If you answered *both* question #1 and question #2 with something like "very" or "extremely" strongly, you are that kind of person.

A few other people are simultaneously not very optimistic or very pessimistic. These people apparently believe nothing very interesting will ever happen to them, either positive or negative. They believe they will not get run over by a tractor trailer, but on the other hand, they won't win the lottery either. If you answered *both* question #1 and question #2 with something like "not very" or "not at all" strongly, you are that kind of person.

Most people have a predominantly lottery-expecting personality (more optimism than pessimism) or a predominantly tractor-trailer-expecting personality (more pessimism than optimism), so these exceptions are intriguing. It's particularly interesting to contemplate whether a person who expects both to win the lottery and to be flattened by a tractor trailer is really, down deep, where it counts, an optimist or a pessimist. Because we associate the benefits of optimism with expecting positive events, a lottery-and-tractor-trailer person might expect to reap some of those benefits because he does expect positive events. If you think your kids will make the honor roll, does it matter that you also think they'll probably wreck the car? Perhaps the

PESSIMIST:
"HALF EMPTY"

OPTIMIST:
"HALF FULL"

OPTOMETRIST:
"HALF A GLASS
OF WATER"

Are you an optimist, a pessimist, or an optometrist?
© The New Yorker Collection 2005 Mick Stevens from cartoonbank.com.

positive expectation is more important than the negative expectation. If the expectation of positive events overrides that of negative events, then it is important to be optimistic, regardless of your level of pessimism.

Likewise, the nothing-much person might expect to reap benefits by not expecting negative events. If you don't expect your kids to wreck the car, does it matter that you don't expect them to make the honor roll? If you avoid the cost of expecting negative events, do you even need the benefit of expecting positive events? If the expectation of negative events overrides that of positive events, then it is more important to avoid pessimism, regardless of your level of optimism.

The subtitle of a research article published a few years ago summed up the conundrum with this question: "Is it more important to be optimistic or not to be pessimistic?" The research followed a group of caregivers for patients with Alzheimer's disease. Although many people with Alzheimer's disease end up in professional care facilities when their disease becomes severe, much informal care over the course of the illness is provided by family members and other nonprofessional caregivers. These caregivers save the formal health care system tens of billions of dollars, but at a personal cost. The stress associated with caring for a person with progressive dementia, especially one who has behavioral problems like wandering off and getting lost or getting hostile and agitated, can lead to serious problems such as depression for the caregiver. In this study, lack of pessimism characterized the caregivers who experienced the least anxiety, stress, and depression. Abundant optimism didn't help unless it also paired with lack of pessimism, which was not always the case. It was better to be a nothing-very-interesting-at-all person than a lottery-and-tractor-trailer person.

It seems obvious that this would be true for these caregivers. After all, the progressive nature of their loved ones' illness means their main concern would be the potential for bad things like disease progression to happen. The potential for good things like recovery just isn't that relevant, because Alzheimer's disease is progressive—it gets worse over time. Treatments can only slow the progression of the disease. On the other hand, these researchers also studied a bunch of people who were *not* caring for Alzheimer's patients and therefore were probably not facing a future of irreversible decline for their loved ones. The same results held true: pessimism predicted more anxiety, depression, and stress for people who were not caregivers. More optimism didn't do anything unless it was accompanied by less pessimism.

So, what is the point of even asking question #1? Why do we call it optimism? Why not just ask question #2, call it pessimism, and be done for the day?

Anxiety, stress, and depression are only one side of emotional life. Like optimism and pessimism, positive and negative moods can be independent of each other. How much joy, happiness, and elation you experience in a week isn't necessarily related to how much dejection, anxiety, and anger you experience during the same period. Although it seems that a joyful week should also be a nonanxious week, in fact a joyful week can be either anxious or nonanxious, because anxiety and joy arise from different kinds of events. Positive accomplishments and surprises (e.g., buying a winning lottery ticket) create joy, but they may not have anything to do with the worries and threats (e.g., getting run over by a tractor trailer) that create stress and anxiety. Complex emotions over the course of a week are to be expected from the complex series of events and situations that we encounter.[1] Even if you're depressed by your father's struggle with

---

[1]Some psychologists specializing in emotion argue that you can even feel positive and negative emotion at the same time: mixed emotions. They give the tongue-in-cheek example of when your irritating boss drives off a cliff . . . in your new Jaguar. Which emotion predominates will depend on how strongly you feel about your boss and how well your Jaguar is insured, but in theory they can be equally balanced at that particular moment.

Alzheimer's disease, you can feel joy, contentment, and happiness about your family's gathering around the dinner table or about being praised at work for that project you've been working on.

We can't judge the relative virtue of optimism merely by considering anxiety, stress, and depression, because doing so paints an incomplete picture of emotional life. Negative moods such as these reveal only the influence of pessimism and other negative personality traits such as neuroticism, one of pessimism's closest neighbors on the street of personality. People with a lot of neuroticism have feelings that are easily hurt, have a low tolerance for frustration, and feel incapable of dealing with difficult situations. Not surprisingly, given their vulnerabilities, they also experience a lot more negative mood, including anxiety, depression, and hostility. If you know someone who seems so emotionally fragile that you hate to deliver any bad news, that person likely has a lot of neuroticism. The predisposition to experience negative moods is so characteristic of neuroticism that neuroticism might effectively be called the "unhappy personality." Pessimism and neuroticism live close to each other because of their common friend, negative mood. Pessimism *should* be the better predictor of negative emotions like depression and anxiety because pessimism means expecting negative events, which are linked to negative moods, which are characteristic of neurotic people.

If you want to know about someone's vulnerability to anxiety, depression, and stress, then knowing how pessimistic and neurotic she is should tell you a great deal. If you want to know about a person's probability of experiencing the other side of emotional life—joy, contentment, and happiness—you would rather know how optimistic the person is. Optimism lives in a different neighborhood from pessimism and neuroticism, next door to a different personality variable called extraversion. Extraverts are warm and affectionate, energetic, and outgoing, and they are typically high-spirited, cheerful, and, yes, optimistic. That person you know who is always laughing and ready to go out and have a good time is loaded with extraversion. If neuroticism is the "unhappy personality," then extraversion is the "happy personality." Optimistic people expect positive events, which are associated with positive emotions, which are characteristic of extraverted people.

If optimism predicts the happy half of our emotional lives, why does research seem to indicate that pessimism is more important than

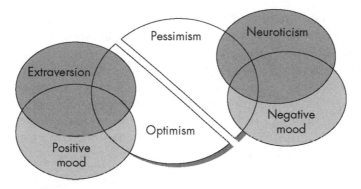

Pessimism overlaps with neuroticism and negative mood, whereas optimism overlaps with extraversion and positive mood.

optimism when it comes to emotional health? It may be only because psychology has deemed negative moods more important than positive moods. Since psychology started to specialize in reactions to trauma during the world wars, the field has become heavily focused on dysfunction, distress, and disease. Positive aspects of life like happiness, although currently making a comeback, have been somewhat neglected. When you look only at threats to mental health—anxiety and stress, for example—it seems that pessimism is more important than optimism. Positive aspects of well-being were not included in the study described above, and they are not included in most psychological studies, which have been aimed at revealing why people feel as bad as they do. Yet "optimism might . . . have been a more significant predictor [of well-being]," the authors of the Alzheimer's caregiver study speculated, "had we examined positive outcomes."

If experiencing positive moods like joy, contentment, and excitement is as important to people as avoiding negative moods like depression, anxiety, and hostility, then optimism is as important as pessimism, and your answers to question #1 and question #2 are both important for your emotional life: Having more optimism should be associated primarily with more positive emotions like happiness, and having less pessimism should be associated primarily with avoiding negative emotions like anxiety. A study of Navy recruits showed just that. When the young recruit expected good things in his future, he also had more positive moods, whereas if he expected bad things, he also had more negative moods. Although in some cases it may look advantageous to be a nothing-much person because you avoid the anxiety associated with pessimism, at the same time you are losing out on the happiness benefits of optimism that are accruing to the lottery-and-tractor-trailer person.[2] Expecting your kids to make the honor roll will increase positive feelings (for example, hope, pride), and expecting them to wreck the car will increase negative feelings (for example, fear, anger). One does not offset the other—they have distinct effects on your emotions.

THE 10-MILLION-DOLLAR QUESTION

If you want to have an emotional life characterized by more positive than negative emotions, you might think winning 10 million dollars in the lottery would be a good start. In truth, having an optimistic personality is a much better choice than winning the lottery. Because of the psychological immune system—hedonic treadmill—set point problem, the 10 million dollars is going to be fun for a while, but the happiness that results will eventually wear off. On the other hand, happiness arising from personality characteristics like dispositional optimism keeps going, and going, and going.

The real 10-million-dollar question is: why? People have shown a tremendous capacity to get used to lots of things, from fairly trivial boosts (buying a new dress or even eating chocolate—the first bite is always the best) to even extreme highs (getting married, the best life event for increasing happiness, makes the average person happier for a couple of years). If the very best things that can happen to you in life don't make you happier in the long run, how is it that you don't get used to having a certain set of beliefs about the future—that is, being optimistic? Why does an optimistic personality make people happy

[2]Having established that both optimism and pessimism are important, I'm going to return to the custom of using the terms optimism, dispositional optimism, and optimistic personality to refer to the combination of optimism and pessimism. Furthermore, in coming chapters the distinction between optimism and pessimism will become less and less important because they seem to contribute equally to the mechanisms responsible for much of the relationship between optimism and well-being.

year after year? Put another way, why is optimism associated with more lasting happiness than 10 million dollars? Surprisingly, psychology has done little to answer this question, despite the fact that the failure to adapt to one's own personality may hold the key to being able to get off the hedonic treadmill. If we could figure out why people don't get desensitized to having optimistic personalities, the same mechanisms could be brought to bear to help people feel better in lasting ways.

The most fatalistic perspective with regard to whether you can have lasting changes in happiness is the set-point perspective, especially when the set-point argument is based primarily on genetic makeup. Most personality characteristics have some substantial genetic component—up to about 50%—so the set-point argument goes like this: if you have the genes to be happy, then you will have a happy personality and be happy, and if you don't, you won't. This argument is supported by research in behavioral genetics, which amasses more and more evidence that genes impact psychological health. One terrific example is a gene that carries the catchy title SLC6A4. This gene affects the serotonin system—the same system targeted by antidepressant drugs such as Prozac. Specifically, SLC6A4 is the runway to a gene system that makes the protein that carries serotonin in and out of cells. As it turns out, some people have short runways and other people have long runways, and just as an airport runway is more useful when it's long than when it's short, this gene is more useful when it's long than when it's short. If you have good fortune (or, more correctly, good parents) and get two long runways, events such as a relationship breakup or stress on the job will result in about half the emotional distress and one-third the probability of thinking about or attempting suicide for you as for someone who has two short runways. (People with one short and one long runway fall somewhere in between.)

Other neurotransmitters can also affect well-being: GABA produces calmness, for example, and dopamine is involved in pleasurable feelings. Personality could be the result of genes that affect long-term differences in levels or functions of such neurotransmitters: serotonin for resilient people, for example, or dopamine for thrill-seeking people. Hence, the set-point perspective would propose that genes determine the way your neurotransmitter systems function, and the nature of that functioning sets your personality and well-being. Although life events may temporarily perturb your set point, eventually you will go back to the brain that nature gave you. No change in genes, no lasting change in well-being.

Still, one wonders if long-term well-being can be reduced to having higher levels of certain neurotransmitters. After all, when these neurotransmitters are administered in the form of drugs, the brain sometimes does get used to them. That is, sometimes the effects of being given a certain amount of neurotransmitter become smaller and smaller with time, so that larger and larger doses become necessary to get the same effect. Consider the person taking amphetamines ("uppers"). Amphetamines have a very pronounced positive effect on emotions because they promote the release of dopamine, which results in pleasure. You could say that dopamine puts the "up" in "uppers." Over time, though, it takes more and more amphetamine to get the same effect: a phenomenon called *tolerance*. Drugs that stimulate other neurotransmitter systems also create tolerance, sometimes unfortunately (the beneficial motor effects of L-dopa, a dopamine medication used to treat Parkinson's disease, wear off over time) but sometimes fortunately (the sexual side effects of antidepressant medications that act on serotonin also tend to go away over time).[3]

Neurotransmitters produced in the brain resemble neurotransmitters administered as drugs about as much as a weather system resembles a sprinkler. Because neurotransmitters in the brain are complex and self-regulated, it's possible that their organization prevents you from developing a tolerance to your own neurotransmitters, and that's why you don't desensitize to your own personality. Nonetheless, the phenomenon of tolerance suggests that having more serotonin is not the sole reason that being optimistic is protective against distress over a lifetime.

Not all of optimism is genetic anyway. In fact, the portion that is genetic—about 25%—is lower than for most personality dimensions, including the "happy" and "unhappy" personalities. Extraversion, the

---

[3]Tolerance does not develop to the actual antidepressant effects, so higher doses of these drugs are typically not necessary to treat or prevent further depression. Something in the brain changes in response to having antidepressant drugs around, because in some cases, abruptly stopping them results in a withdrawal syndrome that includes unpleasant symptoms like dizziness, tingling, irritability, shaking, and diarrhea. Fortunately, the something that develops tolerance and causes withdrawal does not seem to be the same something that affects levels of depression.

"happy personality," is about 54% inherited; neuroticism, the "unhappy personality," is about 48% inherited. Somehow people who are optimistic are happy without necessarily having inherited the genes for happiness, and they still maintain that happiness over long periods of time.

AN EXTREMELY SHORT HISTORY OF OPTIMISM

To find out how optimism might create happiness in people who don't necessarily have happy genes, it's instructive to look at the history of the study of expectancies, which did not begin with the advent of dispositional optimism. Beginning early in the 20th century, psychologists studied the effects of expectancies: not on mood, but on motivation. The more positive a person's expectancy is for an outcome, the more motivated she is to achieve that outcome. Believing you can run faster than anyone else increases your motivation to give your all in a race, for example. Believing you can get promoted increases your motivation to work hard. Sometimes it can require positive expectancies not just to do something better, but to do anything at all: If you believe exposure therapy can cure your snake phobia,[4] you'll have motivation that you otherwise never would to approach or handle a snake in therapy. If you don't believe doing that exposure to a snake is going to help you, it's hard to imagine why you would do it at all.

Furthermore, in this research, expectancies were usually specific to outcomes. If you wanted to know how motivated people were to exercise, you had to know what they expected to happen to them *if they exercised*. For example, did a person have high *outcome efficacy*, a particular type of expectancy linking behaviors to outcomes? That is, did he expect exercise to lead to losing weight or living longer? If so, exercise would be more likely than for someone with low outcome efficacy. In general, the focus of this research was on how beliefs about the future (getting promoted, curing a phobia, losing weight) affect motivation to do something to bring that future about (work harder, touch a snake, exercise).

[4]Which it can in most cases. Exposure treatment for phobia is one of the most effective psychological treatments available.

No one made a big deal about being a positive or negative person in this body of research.

GETTING TO THE BOTTOM OF OPTIMISM

In a way, all this stuff about happy and unhappy, or positive and negative, or optimistic and pessimistic people is beside the point. Whether the glass is half empty or half full, it needs to be washed, dried, and put away in the cupboard, and optimism affects whether or not you are motivated to get that done.

To give you an idea of what I think is at the root of optimism, I give you two first-year law students from my long-term study of how optimism affects psychological well-being and immune function. Please see the footnote for the obligatory lawyer joke.[5] The first year of law school is a very stressful time—many students rate it as the most stressful thing they have ever experienced—and a lot is at stake. First-semester grades have a lot to do with who gets on the law review and who gets a good job the following summer, to name two important outcomes. Optimistic students react differently to this experience than pessimistic students. Here are sections of interviews with two first-year law students:[6]

Q: How has law school been for you so far?

A: At first it was good. It started off and I was on a good pace for studying, but then I started backing off of my studies a little bit and then I kind of got swept away with the competitive atmosphere and just stepped away from everything for a while and didn't really get back into it until 2 weeks before finals. So during finals I felt consumed with law school, but probably 2 months prior to it I didn't feel that law school was

[5]Why psychologists should do research with lawyers instead of lab rats: (a) There are more of them; (b) there are some things a lab rat just won't do; (c) there's a risk that the psychologist will get attached to the lab rat. Apologies to the lawyers. You can substitute your despised profession of choice, including psychologist.

[6]Throughout this book, I will give you examples taken from real optimists and pessimists. Any identifying information has been changed, examples may be composites, and they may be edited for length, but these are based on real reports from real people in the real world. Any names are made up.

even important in my life. As I said, at the beginning of the
semester I was studying a lot, but then when I began to back
off, I began to build more stress on myself because there was
more studying to be done. While I was not studying, I had
more time to think about how stressful law school was and to
question whether or not this was what I wanted to do. But
I'm starting to regret feeling that way now 'cause I didn't do
as well as I had hoped to do. I guess the most stressful part
about law school is just trying to separate myself from the
school itself.

Q: How has law school been for you so far?

A: It's been somewhat stressful, but I think I've always been one
to kind of push myself in all my studies. I'll come home every
night and read probably until I go to bed, and there's always
a feeling that I could be doing more—I could be studying
more and, you know, outlining more and things like that. I
enjoy all my classes. I love learning, so I've never had any
feelings of regret or anything like that. It's just been something that's been constant. It's stimulating but it kind of
tends to wear you out, I guess. If I started feeling like I was
getting behind, then I'd start setting goals for myself and say,
"Okay, now by the end of this week I'm going to have this
much done in preparation for the exam. I'm going to have
this class totally briefed up to what we've been doing." When
I went in and took those exams in December, I came away
with a feeling of satisfaction because it felt like I was actually
being able to apply the concepts that I had learned for the
past 3 months and it made sense to me. I realized what I was
doing and I realized, to a certain extent, how I could apply it
when I got out there and actually practiced. So that was
pretty rewarding.

The first student was in the bottom 10% of optimism scores, and
the second student was in the top 10%. Neither of them was particularly having fun in law school. The first, pessimistic one didn't seem
horribly depressed, and the second, optimistic one didn't seem
happy-go-lucky. Still, there were dramatic differences in their approaches to law school that had to do with how they tackled the diffi-

culties they encountered. The pessimistic student dealt with difficulty by withdrawing, ruminating, disengaging, and eventually underachieving. The optimistic student dealt with difficulty by setting goals, planning, engaging, and eventually reaping the rewards. The essential difference was not between positivity and negativity but between trying harder and trying less.

This is not to say that trying harder and trying less don't affect well-being. In fact, I'm going to argue throughout this book that the path from optimism to well-being in large part goes through engaging, trying harder, participating, and other related states of mind and behavior. Notice that the ways these two students coped with the stress of law school didn't protect one from stress and expose the other one: both of them talked about the stress they experienced. The other day, when I walked into my lab office, this quote had been written on the blackboard: "It takes just as much stress to be a success as to be a failure." Although that quote perfectly describes the fact that these law students both experienced stress, what it does not specify is the differences between the two kinds of stress. One kind of stress—the pessimistic kind—came from rumination and withdrawal and resulted in regret. The other kind—the optimistic kind—came from concerted, prolonged effort and resulted in satisfaction and reward.

Given that it takes just as much stress to succeed as to fail, wouldn't "optimistic" stress be preferable? Why do people ever experience "pessimistic" stress? The unsurprising answer: Because they're pessimists. Looking back at the motivational history of optimism, expectancies are exactly what determine whether you decide to put in more effort or less effort. Positive expectancies—optimism—increase motivation and effort, whereas negative expectancies—pessimism—decrease motivation and effort. It makes perfect sense when put this way: What would be the point of putting a lot of effort toward a future that isn't going to work out anyway? Presumably you will pay out more in effort for something that you think will pay you back in the end. A law student who believes she'll succeed is more willing to put in the hours studying and face intense competition than a law student who doesn't believe he'll succeed. For him, it seems to make more "sense" to withhold effort, although in the end it only ends up in regret. Would you spend a lot of money on a new car if you thought the kids were going to wreck it, or a lot of time exercising if you thought you would never get stronger or leaner? How about spending energy on writing a novel that you don't think will ever get published? Of course you wouldn't do that, and neither do the pessimistic people who have these beliefs. It just doesn't seem rational to them to spend time, money, energy, or effort on a future that looks dim.

THERE ARE MORE WAYS TO BE WELL THAN TO BE HAPPY

My optimistic law student doesn't seem to be brimming with carefree cheerfulness, but does that make her life negative? Is there some other metric for measuring the benefits from being optimistic? A focus on the positivity and negativity associated with optimism, especially emotional positivity and negativity, is too narrow. There is more to well-being than being cheerful, and I think most people would recognize that being cheerful all the time is not really what they are striving for in their lives—there's another whole level of well-being that "happiness" doesn't capture.

Happiness, cheerfulness, and the rest of the positive emotions are often collected under the rubric of emotional or hedonic well-being, it being clear that frequently being in a good mood contributes to emotional health. It feels better (i.e., is more hedonically pleasing) than having negative emotions. However, some psychologists (as well as some nonpsychologists) have argued that there is more to being well than being happy. Aristotle, for one, argued that true happiness was not feeling good but eudaimonia—*eu* meaning "good," and *daimon* meaning "spirit." That is, the road to wellness was not through pleasure but through being true to oneself. People clearly need more than happiness—they need to be engaged with life and with other peo-

---

[7]This is not to say that people need to act independently or even control all aspects of their lives, but that they either retain control or give up control *voluntarily*. Words like *mastery* and *autonomy* are sometimes interpreted to mean "independence," but that interpretation is incorrect because whether you are acting alone or with others is separate from whether you are your own master. You could go along with a group of your own volition and according to your own values and gain mastery and autonomy; conversely, you could be coerced to go it on your own, against your values, to the detriment of your mastery and autonomy.

ple, to grow, and to be masters of their own destiny.[7] Eudaimonic (or sometimes, "psychological") well-being, then, is not reflected in how happy you are, but in how much your life is characterized by doing things well, realizing your potential, good relationships, and personal growth. Eudaimonia literally means being your best self.

Discriminating between happiness and eudaimonia reveals that I was a little disingenuous when I said watching TV won't make you happy. It depends on your definition of happiness. If you are watching something funny, you might laugh until you cry, and that definitely feels good and increases emotional or hedonic well-being. On the other hand, it doesn't offer you much of an opportunity to be your best self or build eudaimonic well-being. Part of your best self might be a good laugher, but hopefully it doesn't stop there. Hopefully, your best self is also creative, or empathic, or wise, and it's hard to exercise that best self when you're watching TV.

Some theorists who advocate eudaimonia emphasize its distinctness from hedonic well-being by asserting that sometimes eudaimonia doesn't feel good in a hedonic sense. Aristotle thought happiness was "vulgar," and psychologist Erich Fromm thought pleasure was potentially harmful. You get the sense from these guys that you're not allowed to have fun while you're being your best self. Fortunately, that idea seems to exist mostly in theory, because in real life being your best self is definitely fun. Although hedonic well-being and eudaimonic well-being are separable, the people who have more aspects of eudaimonic well-being, such as the abilities to relate well to others, meet the demands of everyday life, and learn about themselves, are also the happiest people. They also happen to be the least neurotic and most extraverted people, which makes sense if you figure that neurotic people have a hard time meeting everyday demands and negotiating the emotional side of relationships (tending to diminish eudaimonic well-being) and are beset by negative moods (tending to diminish hedonic well-being), and extraverted people are more social, more turned on by challenges (tending to enhance eudaimonic well-being), and happier (tending to enhance hedonic well-being).

There is another personality trait that also characterizes people who have high eudaimonic and hedonic well-being but doesn't have anything to do with being a "happy" or "sad" personality type: conscientiousness. In the fable about the grasshopper and the ant, *conscientious* people are the ants: competent, organized, ambitious, industrious, and persistent. People who are not conscientious (sometimes called *undirected*) are the grasshoppers: careless, distractible, lazy, and impatient. Conscientiousness doesn't directly incorporate well-being the way neuroticism and extraversion do. Instead, it points to a *way* that people achieve higher well-being, that is, through hard work and stick-to-itiveness. If you look back to the beginning of expectancy and optimism research, back to the motivational roots, it will come as no surprise that conscientiousness is also related to optimism. Optimistic people are like conscientious people in that they are more motivated and goal-directed than the pessimistic and undirected types. What's more, positive expectancies increase motivation, hard work, and effort, and negative expectancies decrease them, so both kinds of expectancy relate to conscientiousness. Optimistic people are more likely to be ants than grasshoppers, more likely to be tortoises than hares.

If asked why optimistic people have higher levels of well-being, I think the obvious reason looks more like extraversion: they are more positive people. The less obvious reason looks more like conscientiousness: they are more persistent people. What optimistic people do seems likely to be as important as what they are in terms of elevating their well-being.

GETTING OFF THE HEDONIC TREADMILL

The realization that optimism is something you do, in addition to something you are, helps explain why optimists, and possibly other happy types as well, don't get used to their own personalities. In general, we get used to things that are static. A new sweater, handbag, TV set, or power boat doesn't give a long-lasting boost to mood because it stays the same all the time. Every day, we get a little more used to what we have. On the other hand, our goals, motivations, and efforts are changing all the time.

An example of how being engaged with a goal results in happiness comes from the study of what has been called "ultimate well-being": the feeling of flow. Flow occurs when a person's skills are fully engaged in the challenges of a task, whether it be building a tower, playing a musical instrument or a sport, analyzing data, or performing surgery. Consciousness falls away and people become fully absorbed in what they are doing. Even though people experience their ultimate well-being during flow, they aren't thinking about it during the task because they are so absorbed by what they are doing.[8] You experience flow when your skills are exactly meeting the challenges of a task or goal. You are not below your ultimate skill level, but you are not in over your head either. A beginning baker will feel anxiety instead of flow if he is trying to make baked Alaska but his skills are only up to the level of chocolate chip cookies. An accomplished pianist will feel boredom instead of flow while playing "Twinkle, Twinkle, Little Star."[9]

You've probably had an experience in which you felt you were using your skills fully and seamlessly, exerting a significant but not overwhelming amount of effort, and becoming completely absorbed in what you were doing. If you are a musician, you may have experienced it while performing a well-practiced piece; if you are an athlete, you may have had a day when you were in a "groove" and seemed not to be able to put a foot wrong. Flow can happen in almost any circumstance where goals and skills are involved—chess, or cooking, or writing. You were gliding through your task and really engaging your skills. You were in flow. Wasn't that great?

The phenomenon of flow is a specific example of the general principle that engagement leads to well-being. There are two subprinciples that follow from this general principle. The first is that the scope of goals and challenges is unlimited. We all have multitudes of pathways we can pursue. For every goal we reach, others are waiting in the wings. It's as if you had a whole closetful of handbags that changed every day, and if you got tired of one, there would be thousands more, of all types, sizes, and colors, waiting to be chosen.[10]

The second principle is that even the same goal can be a lasting source of well-being if its demands can change to keep up with your skills. Consider golf, which many people find fun throughout their entire lifetimes. How does playing golf keep being fun when 10 mil-

---

[8]This lack of self-consciousness actually helps flow to be so positive. As shown in the Prologue, keeping track of how happy you are can actually keep you from being happy.

[9]The Dohnanyi "Variations on a Nursery Tune" notwithstanding.

[10]Substitute power boat if that's your thing.

*If you are doing something unusual,
you might be able to achieve flow while watching TV.*

lion dollars stops being fun? Because golf is a continual challenge. Until you make a hole in one every time at every hole at every course in the world, the demands of golf will always increase to keep up with your skills. The failure of TV to contribute substantially to well-being is completely understandable in this context, because TV demands virtually no skills. Unless you are doing something unusual, like watching a program in a foreign language that challenges your translation skills, you will never be in a state of flow while watching TV.

Optimism leads to increased well-being, because it increases engagement with life's goals, not because of some miracle happy juice that optimists have and others don't. This is why my New Orleans role model mentioned in the Prologue is so important to understanding well-being. He was happier because he was so busy *doing* that he didn't have to worry about *being*.

CHAPTER TWO

....

The Persistence Instinct
Optimists and Their Goals

As related in Chapter 1's Extremely Short History of Optimism, in the "olden" days before optimism was studied as a personality trait, psychologists were interested in how positive or negative expectations affected motivation and persistence. In their research, they would manipulate people's expectancies to make them more or less optimistic or pessimistic and observe how motivation and persistence changed. If you had been in one of those studies, it would have gone something like this: You would be told you were going to perform two tasks. On the first task, you had to unscramble some anagrams to make sensible words (for example, YRIGCN becomes CRYING). You wouldn't do very well (the anagrams were very difficult), which would lead you to conclude you're not very good at anagrams (or so hoped the experimenters). Then you'd be told either that the next task, drawing complex line patterns, was related to anagram skill or that it was unrelated. This was the critical part of the experiment, because if you believed the tasks were related, voilà: you would expect to fail again; that is, you would be pessimistic about the upcoming task. If you believed the tasks were unrelated, you would expect to be more successful, and you would be optimistic about the upcoming task.

If you were a typical participant in these experiments, when you believed that anagrams and line drawing tapped different skills (that is, when you were optimistic), when you got to the second task you

34

would show significantly enhanced motivation and persistence. On average, you would work about 20% longer than people who were led to believe that the task they had bombed (anagrams) tapped the same skills as the new task (line drawing). Furthermore, if the experimenters had led you to believe that anagrams and line drawing were tapping *opposite* skills ("when people do badly on this one, they seem to do *really well* on the next one"), the effects would be even more dramatic: you would probably work 50% longer than people who thought the two tasks were tapping the same skill. This dramatic effect would also occur if you were set up to actually perform well on an initial task that you were then told predicted performance on the second task—you would work about 40% longer than people who performed badly on the initial task.

If you think about how much more you can accomplish by working 40–50% longer at a task, the potential effects of optimistic expectancies are striking. If you do 75 sit-ups instead of 50, your abs are going to get a lot firmer, a lot faster. And this is important: it is going to happen not because you have positive visualizations about your abs. It will happen because your positive thoughts change what you *do*.

PUTTING OPTIMISTIC PERSONALITY TO THE TEST

When I started to realize that optimism might not be about being a positive person but about motivation and persistence, I wanted to return to this kind of experiment. This time, instead of creating optimism and pessimism by manipulating people's beliefs about their skills, I wanted to know: Will people's level of dispositional optimism affect them in the same way? At the time, I had an undergraduate student in the lab named Lise Solberg Nes who wanted to do research on optimism. Lise read a paper that I wrote as a graduate student at UCLA on optimism, and she took it to her faculty advisor to find out how she could learn about this optimism thing that this person at UCLA was working on. Serendipitously, Lise's advisor knew exactly where to send her: around the corner to my new office at the University of Kentucky. Lise got involved in my lab as an undergraduate research assistant. There followed a period of negotiation about the official languages of the lab. Lise is Norwegian and speaks about a zillion languages, including Swedish. My Swedish is decent as long as you stick to pronouns (*you, me*) and common words such as *other* and *like*. I have a very limited vocabulary when it comes to verbs and nouns, which makes conversation, not to mention scientific conversation, difficult. It didn't take long to determine that her English was much better than my Swedish, and we were able to move on to scientific issues. Eventually we decided (in English) that for her honors thesis she would take the persistence studies from 20 years earlier and see if dispositional optimism worked the same way as specific expectancies.

In Lise's study, rather than giving people a first task that endowed them with either positive or negative expectations, we measured their natural optimism using a questionnaire. Then they had a series of impossible or difficult anagrams to unscramble.[1] Because we lack serious sadistic tendencies, we gave only one impossible anagram. The remaining 10 were "merely" difficult (no one solved them all, and most people solved only 5). The question was: Will people who hold *generally* positive expectancies, that is, more optimistic people, work on the anagrams longer than people who hold less generally positive expectancies, that is, more pessimistic people?

They did. People with pessimistic personalities worked on the anagrams for about 9½ minutes, whereas people with optimistic personalities worked for about 11½ minutes. The difference was particularly noticeable for that first, insoluble anagram. On average, the pessimistic people worked on that one for about a minute before giving

---

[1] If you enter "unsolvable anagram" into a web search engine, what you will get is the result of dozens of psychological studies. Why are psychologists so hooked on anagrams? One nice aspect of anagram puzzles, from an experimenter's perspective, is that it's almost impossible to tell by looking at an anagram whether it's solvable or just difficult until you've actually solved it, so unsolvable anagrams can get a persistent person to work a long time without giving themselves away as unsolvable. On the other hand, when you are balancing the desire to measure persistence against the need to avoid excessively frustrating your study participants, you have to let people solve some. In these studies, Lise and I let people solve some, then we adjusted statistically for the effects of language ability (for example, as reflected in standardized test scores) on anagram solutions, as well as the effect of solving anagrams on persistence (after all, you get to stop persisting when you solve it). This technique isolated the effect of optimism on persistence from the effects of verbal ability and number of solutions.

up, moderately optimistic people worked about 50% longer, and very optimistic people worked twice as long, over 2 minutes, before they gave up.

This study, along with the earlier experimental studies, shows that optimists have what might be called a *persistence instinct*. All other things being equal, optimism makes you push ahead and pessimism makes you quit early. This instinct—to persist or to give up—leads to all kinds of psychological and physical consequences for optimists and pessimists. The psychological and social consequences are the target of this chapter and Chapters 3 and 4. The physical consequences, which muddy the waters somewhat, are the subject of Chapter 5.

THE PERSISTENCE INSTINCT, SUCCESS, AND HAPPINESS

Although hedonic well-being—happiness or unhappiness—was not the point of the persistence studies, the persistence instinct is relevant to happiness. Working on difficult anagrams is not experienced by most of my study participants as fun or likely to put them in a good mood. The task is exactly what it is meant to be—difficult. Nonetheless, the same instinct that kept optimists working longer on the difficult task may be responsible for their higher well-being. The relationship between optimism and persistence bodes well for happiness.

To understand why persistence leads to happiness requires a basic understanding of self-regulation, the mechanisms determining why one person goes to work and another goes to the golf course. Self-regulation by humans has much in common with temperature regulation by thermostats. A thermostat has a *goal* (an ideal room temperature) and a *state of being* (an actual room temperature). Stretching the analogy somewhat by endowing thermostats with moti-vation, the thermostat is motivated to take action to reduce any *differ-ence* or *discrepancy* between the ideal and actual room temperatures: to heat the room if it is too cold or cool the room if it is too warm. Mean-while, the thermostat is keeping track of the consequences of its actions through its gauge of room temperature. When the discrep-ancy is small enough, it can reduce its effort; if not, it continues to work to achieve the discrepancy reduction.

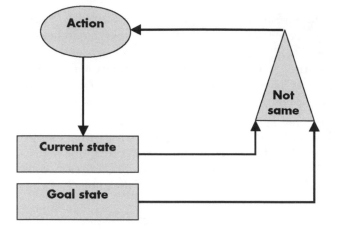

A self-regulatory loop. Thermostats compare room temperature (current state) with their setting (goal state). When not the same, they initiate action to cool or warm the room. Likewise, humans make a comparison to determine whether their current state (say, 90-pound weakling) meets their goal (to stop getting sand kicked in the face) and, if not, take action to get closer to it (sign up for the Charles Atlas program).

Although a thermostat does not resemble a human being at all from a physical perspective, it bears a striking resemblance from a psychological perspective. People have states of being—what they are, have, or feel. They also have goals—some other state of being (fit) or having (rosebushes) or feeling (content) that they don't have now but would like to have in the future or that they have some of now but would like to have more of in the future. They might also have goals focused on avoiding a future state of being (sick) or having (termites) or feeling (despondent) that they don't want. When current states of being and goal states differ, as they frequently do, discrepancies arise. When people notice discrepancies, they become motivated to reduce them and take action to get closer to their goals. If your goal is to advance at work, you might spend a Saturday morning at the office instead of on the golf course; if your goal is to have a better golf game, you might spend a Wednesday morning on the golf course instead of at the office. For you, spending your time working on your career or your golf game is the same as turning the heat on in a cold room: bringing your current state closer to your goal state.

Like a thermostat, you have to be aware and monitoring the situation for discrepancies if goals are to guide your behavior. When you're not paying attention, the various component parts of your internal thermostat—the goal state, the current state, and the discrepancy between them (for example, the difference between your current golf handicap and your goal handicap)—are not salient to you, and you're not motivated to reduce any discrepancy. Self-awareness keeps you tuned in to the feedback loop and on track with your goals. In the various anagram and line drawing studies, optimism increased persistence only when the people were also self-aware (either the experimenter seated them in front of a mirror to do the tasks or they were inherently high in self-awareness). Without self-awareness, optimism did not increase persistence. In fact, when they were not also self-aware, optimistic people often stopped *sooner* than pessimistic people. No one has fully explained this reversal, but one possibility is that optimists were protecting their mood. In general, optimism is associated with more positive mood, and research evidence suggests that people in a positive mood will generally act to preserve that mood. Because difficult tasks are often *not* mood enhancing, someone in a positive mood might be less disposed to work on such a task when not fully aware of the benefits of doing so (that is, reducing a discrepancy and reaching a goal).

The effects of low self-awareness on behavior aren't only obvious in the lab. Ever do something after you had a few drinks that you wondered about later? One effect of alcohol is to decrease self-awareness. It makes a great social lubricant because people who are drinking lose some degree of self-consciousness, which loosens their inhibitions and makes them less stilted in interactions with others. It also makes people less tuned in to their feedback loops and goals. Somehow that resolution about diet or study or dancing *without* a lampshade on our heads fades into the background after a few drinks, and the subsequent pounds, performances, or photos often make us regret having tuned out.

We have one more step to take to make people and thermostats nearly equivalent. We now have to endow people with gauges. Thermostats have temperature gauges to track discrepancies and progress, and people have gauges as well: emotions. One of the main functions, if not *the* main function, of emotions is to alert you to how you are doing. My car sounds a buzzer when something's wrong with it (I'm low on wiper fluid or gas). Emotions are your brain's equivalent of that buzzer, and basic emotions like fear and anger probably developed to signal when something was elementally wrong. For example, fear could signal that the basic goal of staying alive was being threatened by a saber-toothed tiger, and anger could signal that some other prehistoric human was raiding one's store of woolly mammoth hides. Our goals and our lives are more complex now, and so are our emotions, but they still have what is called "signal value"—they tell us how we're doing. In the thermostat sense, they signal the size of the gap between your goal and your present state. When you close that gap—for example, you had wanted to be on the school board, and you were elected—your emotions might range from satisfied to joyful or even elated. When the gap isn't closed—you lost the election by a mile—you might feel dejected, depressed, anxious, or even angry.

THE PERSISTENCE INSTINCT AT WORK IN THE WORLD

Persistence makes it more likely that you are going to succeed at a goal, closing the gap between current state and desired goal and reaping the hedonic rewards. The persistence that optimists showed on anagram and line drawing tasks in the lab bodes well for them in terms of actually achieving their goals. However, lab tasks aren't exactly real-world tests. For one thing, when you're in an experiment, you don't always have a lot on the line. You might not want to appear bad at line drawing in front of the experimenter, but is that as meaningful as not wanting to appear bad at cooking when the object of your affection is coming for dinner? For another thing, you didn't choose to do anagrams or line drawing—those tasks were imposed on you. There may be some things in your life that were imposed on you (doing your taxes), but most important tasks outside the lab are things that you chose yourself. Motivation—and optimism's effects on motivation—might be quite different under those circumstances.

Fortunately, Lise and I soon had an opportunity to extend our laboratory findings to a real-world circumstance. When Lise presented the results of her anagram study at our Psychology Department Honors Day, one of the people who attended was the Dean of

Undergraduate Studies, Phil Kraemer. Phil is a psychologist whose research topic is animal learning but has moved on from studying lab rats to being in charge of undergraduate education at the University of Kentucky.[2] One of Phil's concerns, as well as that of other undergraduate deans, is retention, and when he saw Lise's presentation, he got very interested in whether optimism was related to whether freshman students succeeded in school and returned for their sophomore year or let their dreams of a college education fizzle out. Phil offered to give optimism questionnaires to all the freshmen who attended advising conferences over the summer before they started. Lise and I jumped at the opportunity. This was a chance for us to expand beyond studying a small number of people (albeit very intensely) to testing the effects of optimism on big goals in a very large number of people. As it happened, Lise had been accepted at Kentucky to do her doctoral studies in psychology, and so she adopted the freshman class as the topic of her master's thesis.

True to his word, Phil gave optimism questionnaires to about 1,800 incoming freshmen. A year later we examined whether their optimism before starting school could predict their performance and persistence during the freshman year. Freshman year is probably more challenging to students than any other year. Students leave their families and the familiar social circumstances of high school for college in a strange town with strange people. The demands of college academic work come as a rude surprise to some students who cruised through high school and expected to do the same in college. Not all students weather this transition well, and some fail to manage it at all and don't return for their sophomore year. The University of Kentucky (along with many other universities) perennially struggles with this problem in an effort to reduce the approximately 25% of freshman students lost through attrition.[3]

Because optimism leads to more persistence, we expected that more optimistic students would have the kind of relationship with their goals that they needed to stay in school. Consistent with our

[2]There's got to be another lab rat versus student joke in here somewhere.

[3]This may sound like an abnormally large percentage, but according to statistics gathered by *U.S. News and World Report*, it is typical of many 4-year universities in the United States.

expectations, moderately pessimistic students were *twice* as likely to drop out as highly optimistic students after the freshman year, even after accounting for their academic performance as freshmen. If 99% of success is just showing up—and no one ever got a degree by dropping out of school—optimism gives students a much better chance for success.

Knowing the likely proportions of different levels of optimism among incoming freshmen and how many in each group will drop out, we are able to predict what will happen to the roughly 4,000 freshmen entering the University of Kentucky every fall, as shown in the graph on this page. As in most groups of people, there are many more optimists than pessimists in the freshman class. However, we expect that there will be even more optimists in the sophomore class, because the pessimists are much less likely to come back. For example, we predict that just over 200 pessimists will drop out and that just over 200 high optimists will drop out. This represents almost a third of all pessimists but only a sixth of all high optimists. Put another way, although just over 200 of both groups will drop out, that will leave more than 1,000 high optimists but fewer than 500 pessimists returning the next fall.

Dispositional optimists also had higher GPAs, so it's possible that optimistic students were just smarter, and that's why they didn't drop

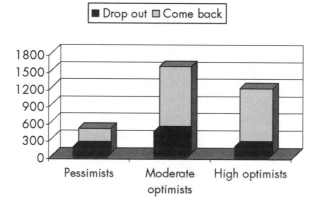

Predicted outcomes for a freshman class of 4,000 students. Almost one-third of pessimists will drop out compared with one-fourth of moderate optimists and one-sixth of high optimists.

out. However, when we statistically held high school GPA and standardized test scores constant, dispositional optimism still predicted whether students stayed in school or dropped out, as well as the increment in college GPA, to the same degree. Academic talent does not tell the whole story of who will be successful in college. In fact, it might be to college administrators' benefit to expand their view of what it means to be academically talented. Psychologist Robert Sternberg has proposed that intelligence should be defined as "the mental abilities necessary for adaptation to, as well as selection and shaping of, any environmental context." Intelligence as we usually think of it, meaning ability to think well and learn, is an important part of adapting to college, but a persistence instinct certainly comes in handy in weathering the challenges of the freshman year. In fact, as it turns out, challenging situations are exactly the sort in which the persistence instinct is most important.

What about hedonism? Was it fun to be optimistic? In addition to being more successful, optimistic students were happier: at the end of the freshman year, they were asked how often they had felt certain emotions over the previous year, and optimistic students were (as one would expect) less stressed, sad, depressed, tired, anxious, and nervous than their pessimistic counterparts. This finding is consistent with the idea that reaching your goals feels good—or, at least, it doesn't feel as bad as giving up on them does.

GETTING THERE IS HALF THE FUN . . . AND ALL THE MEANING

Hedonism is only part of the story of optimism in the freshman year. Optimistic students also reported higher levels of eudaimonia: better social integration, more motivation, more control over their lives, and higher sense of worth. These feelings were unlikely to come from accomplishments per se, such as getting good grades or playing a concert, but rather from the process of getting to those accomplishments, such as learning calculus or practicing the bassoon. When it comes to being your best self, there is something beneficial about having and pursuing goals that falls outside of achieving them, and achieving goals might actually bring this benefit to an end.

Don't get me wrong: reaching goals clearly has benefits of its own. People who graduate from college increase their earning power. People who lose weight increase their health and longevity. People who get involved in their communities help others and make friends. And such benefits of goal attainment may very well be long lasting. Here's the hitch: their effects on hedonic well-being can be short-lived because of the hedonic treadmill and the psychological immune system. Even though a college degree increases earning power, we get used to earning more money and living in a bigger house. The glow wears off. The effects of attaining goals do not accumulate. To keep that glow, you have to keep attaining goals, and that means consistently pursuing new goals. If you rest on your laurels, you will quickly find yourself reclining on wilted greens.

So it's true, what they say about getting there being half the fun, and when it comes to goals it may be even more than half. Although being there is temporarily fun, getting there is more consistently fun. Returning to the process of self-regulation, it turns out that the main function of emotions is not necessarily to signal when you have definitely succeeded or failed at a goal but to indicate the state of your progress toward that goal. Emotions don't just tell you where you are; they also tell you how fast you are moving. If your behavior is getting you closer and closer to your goal, you will feel satisfied even if you are still some distance away.

You can feel happy with even a large discrepancy if you're progressing at a satisfactory *rate*. Imagine you're training for a marathon. When you stop being fatigued after 10 miles, you're going to feel satisfied by your progress, even though you might still be exhausted after 15 miles. If you're trying to learn to play a piano piece, the first time you play it without missing any notes will be satisfying, even though you can't do it every time. The important thing is that you are moving toward your goal. On the other hand, it is possible for you to feel discouraged even when your discrepancy is small. Still combating fatigue at 25 miles after months of training will be more depressing than making progress and overcoming fatigue at 10 miles. Happiness, therefore, may not be as much about achieving goals as progressing toward them.

Furthermore, having goals is one mechanism—some would say *the* mechanism—for achieving challenge and self-definition in life. Your important and meaningful goals form part of what it means to "be yourself" and, especially, to be your best self. Consider parenthood. Although the goal of parenting is to produce a functioning adult human, parenting is not something that people do *because* they want to end up with a functioning adult human.[4] Parenting is something people do because parenting is in itself meaningful and gives them a sense of purpose and connection. In fact, pursuing a goal is sometimes preferable to reaching that goal. Reaching a goal can have negative consequences when being finished with it means a loss of the sense of purpose or self-definition that accompanied it, as in the tough transitions that sometimes occur with the "empty nest" or retirement.

Furthermore, the most important and meaningful goals aren't necessarily fun. There's some suggestion that parenthood decreases marital satisfaction, and being a parent does not always seem to be a happy-go-lucky role. Nonetheless, there's no mad rush to get rid of the kids. Different goals serve different purposes. Goals can provide means to fun, but they also provide integrity when working toward them increases the sense of having a purpose in life, being true to personal standards, or developing as a person. Goals can also lead to accomplishment when working toward them increases challenge and provides opportunity to learn.

So although the most obvious consequence of being more connected to your goals is *benefit*—working toward the goal gets you to the goal, improves your circumstances, and so on—the problem is that this obvious consequence is not the important one. People who work on goals that are aimed at achieving benefit—such as making more money, being thin and beautiful, and becoming famous—do not increase their happiness, their sense of purpose in life, or the amount of meaning they derive from their activities. Why don't people who make more money get any happier? First, you get used to having more money. Second, the goal to have more money doesn't buy you anything except money. You may be richer, but you have not bought happiness, purpose, or meaning. That is not to say that a rich person is as likely to be happy as a camel is to pass through the eye of a needle. Rather, it is to say that the amount of money you have is mostly

---

[4]Can you imagine parents standing around their child's bed asking themselves, "Is it grown up yet? I can't wait!" I'll bet that sometimes this happens, but probably not all the time.

irrelevant to your well-being. Being engaged with and working on goals linked to integrity, accomplishment, and meaning is minimally related to how rich you are, if at all.[5] In fact, it seems likely that you can determine how "good" a goal is by considering whether you think the good that comes from achieving it will accrue to you from the process of pursuing it. If you don't think the goal will enrich you in some way psychologically—at least intermittently—*before* you reach it, you might want to reconsider the goal.

Important goals don't have to be big goals like parenting, either. Most of your ongoing, daily well-being (some of the hedonic and probably all of the eudaimonic) is likely to arise from your daily engagement with goals. These daily goals fall somewhere in between the ridiculous (anagram tasks in the lab) and the sublime (major life decisions like staying in college or becoming a parent). Because optimism was related to persistence at both ridiculous and sublime goals, I wanted to fill in a gap in my research by studying the most common and therefore probably the most important kind of goals: ordinary, everyday goals.

OPTIMISM IN DAILY LIFE: THE SELF-FULFILLING PROPHECY

I—again, with Lise's help—followed a group of college students over the course of a semester. Many research studies of optimism have been done with student samples, usually undergraduates. This is not unique to optimism research but is true of many kinds of psychology, including social, cognitive, personality, health, and so on. As a consequence, psychological research may be slightly distorted in its view of

---

[5]Likewise, thin, popular, blonde, and so on. This is not to say that there isn't a negative effect when a person is seriously lacking along one of these dimensions. Homelessness, morbid obesity, social isolation, and all the extreme opposites of rich, thin, and popular have clearly negative consequences for people. (Blonde seems to be an exception, insofar as brunettes seem to be reasonably well adjusted.) However, many people who do not have to worry about whether they are going to lose their homes are still preoccupied with making more money, and many people who are a normal weight are preoccupied with being rail thin. These are the goals and preoccupations that will likely not make people as happy as they think they will be.

how easily influenced people are (undergraduates are more easily influenced) and how much they rely on thought rather than emotion in daily decision making and behavior (undergraduates have strong cognitive skills and tend to rely on them more). The cynical view of why psychological research tolerates these potential biases cites convenience: most psychologists have access to large numbers of compliant, accessible students on the university campus. To some degree, this is true. We do study students because they are convenient. However, the processes that we study in young students may also apply to different people, like older adults, and so in many cases we hope the knowledge we get from students will apply to other groups of people as well. Often, students' experiences interest researchers because their lives have parallels to what "grown-ups" might call "real life." College students have to figure out exactly what is expected of them, how much work it will take to meet those expectations, and how to get that work done effectively and efficiently, just as in having a new and more challenging job. Students also negotiate social relationships, like friendships and romantic relationships, that are important across the life span.

Students, like "grown-ups," have goals related to important domains in their lives, including doing well in school and at work; initiating, maintaining, or repairing relationships; looking good; working at hobbies or sports; and so on. To study how optimism affected these students' relationships to their goals, we asked them to list all the goals they currently had and tell us their thoughts about them: how likely it was that they would achieve each goal, how important each goal was to them, how committed they were to achieving each goal, how happy they would be if they achieved the goal, and how sad they would be if they didn't achieve it. When you consider the number of students in the study (77), the number of times they told us their goals (6), the number of goals each student typically had (10), and the number of ratings they gave each goal, you get the number of ratings we analyzed: about 80,000 (a number that we did not consider too closely before starting . . . but forging ahead blindly is a topic to come). With this huge amount of information about people's goals, we could draw some conclusions about whether optimism was related to a person's typical day-to-day goal.

It was interesting to find, first of all, that the goals listed by optimists and pessimists weren't particularly different. If you look at two goal lists, one from an optimist and one from a pessimist, you won't readily be able to distinguish them. Here are typical goal lists from an optimistic and a pessimistic person:

Marie's list of goals	Jennifer's list of goals
Have a more positive attitude	Study more for biology
Develop better study habits	Keep in touch with friends at home
Be more attractive	Decide on major
Stay motivated to exercise	Get to know more people
Become organized	Stay physically fit
Let go of worries	Make time for me
Succeed in school	Become more helpful
Become a better Christian	Try different fashions
Be my own person	Read Bible more
Make new friends	Keep strong relationship with my boyfriend

The content of these goals—what the women want to do in their daily lives—doesn't differentiate the optimist from the pessimist very well. The two women have similar goals, including studying better, maintaining relationships, and enhancing faith. The only possible hint as to which is the optimist and which is the pessimist is that Marie feels her attitude and self-image could use improvement and wants to be more positive and feel better about herself. In fact, Marie, a moderate pessimist, is about half as optimistic as Jennifer, a high optimist. The problem that Marie has is that she wants to feel the way Jennifer does, but she goes about it the wrong way. She is trying directly to be more positive and feel better, but those efforts will work against her. She should be more focused on the difference between her and her classmate that isn't obvious from these lists: the attitude each of them has toward her goals.

The difference between optimistic and pessimistic students was not in the goals themselves but in how they approached their goals. First, the more optimistic students were, the more they expected to achieve individual goals in their daily lives. In essence, dispositional optimism led students to be optimistic about individual goals. Dispositional optimism was more than an abstract personality trait that these students had—it infiltrated each of their daily goals, leading to the kind of specific expectancies associated with persistence in the early lab studies. Second, in addition to expecting to achieve their goals, more optimistic students were also more committed to their goals. This combination of attitudes—expecting success and being committed to getting there—is a time-tested recipe for better goal pursuit and progress.

One way optimistic and pessimistic students did *not* differ was in terms of how important their goals were to them. All students said their goals were, on average, important, averaging 4.1 on a 5-point scale. Being pessimistic meant having important goals without committing to them or believing they could be accomplished. As a consequence, pessimists were less likely to actually progress toward their goals and more likely to stop working on them, either temporarily, by postponing their goals, or permanently, by giving up on a goal altogether. In contrast, the more optimistic students were, the more likely they were to retain and, especially, to achieve their goals.

Expecting success is a self-fulfilling prophecy. People who hold optimistic beliefs also believe in their goals, work harder toward their goals, and thereby set themselves up for success. We have found this to be true on every level, from a relatively trivial laboratory task to everyday goals to pursuing a college degree. Optimism may also start people on an upward spiral, whereby optimism leads to more success, which could make people more optimistic, which could lead to more success: a positive feedback loop that *expands* differences rather than reducing them. Unlike the usual psychological processes that tend to bring people back to where they started (the hedonic treadmill and the psychological immune system, for example), optimism creates momentum that may help them escape these processes. Furthermore, having goals, being committed to them, and progressing toward them—that is, doing the optimistic thing—offers not only the hedonic benefit of goal progress but also the eudaimonic opportunity to be your best self.

WHEN THE GOING GETS TOUGH, THE OPTIMISTIC GET GOING

Here is another lesson from the lab studies of optimism and expectancies: you see the biggest differences between optimists and pessimists when the tasks are difficult. To understand why, consider the task in the context of how goals influence behavior. The goal is to solve lots of anagrams, and the current state is how many of the anagrams have been solved. In an easy task, everyone makes good progress toward accomplishing the task, and this rate of progress encourages further effort. There's no roadblock, no decision to make about whether to give up or keep going, and no need to think about what could happen in the future. You just keep going down the road without worrying too much about whether what is waiting at the end will be wonderful—you don't need a great reward to justify the small amount of effort you are putting forth. The effort involved in weeding a small garden bed doesn't require positive visions of a beautiful garden, because you get it done so fast.

What about when you have seven beds to weed, and they're those nasty weeds that you can't pull up because the root breaks off, so you have to get the trowel out and dig them up, and it's hot, and you're tired, and you have five beds left to go? Difficult tasks create different dynamics. There are some natural responses to difficulties and roadblocks: First, emotions turn to irritability, dejection, or anxiety. The discrepancy is still high, and progress is stalled. The emotional buzzer is going off to signal that something is not right. Second, preoccupation with, attention to, and rumination about this problem increases. Roadblocks threaten goals, and any kind of threat results in negative feelings and increased attention to the threatening situation. This is actually a good thing. Here is an illustration of the evolutionary benefit of attending to threats: One caveman saw a saber-toothed tiger earlier in the day. Although that sighting happened a while ago, he still feels threatened by the possibility that the tiger might be lurking in the bushes. He keeps checking the bushes while he collects roots. A second caveman forgets all about the tiger as soon as it's out of sight, and pretty soon the tiger sneaks up on him and has him for lunch.

It's part of our survival mechanism to make sure that threats aren't immediately forgotten, and that tendency to attend to and think about threat can also help with our modern goal pursuit. If progress toward your goal is being threatened, you don't forget about the fact that you're not making progress toward it. Although we generally consider negative emotions and ruminative focus on problems undesirable and try to avoid them, it is exactly this reaction that could lead to an adaptive response to a roadblock. The negative mood provides motivation to resolve the situation and alleviate the emotion. The increased and prolonged attention makes sure you don't forget about it. If you feel anxious that your checkbook doesn't balance and you think about that problem often, you are less likely to stuff your check register in the bottom of a desk drawer and forget about it until you are reminded by a bounced check. If you feel discouraged and you ruminate about your struggle to get past the 15-mile mark in your marathon training, those thoughts about the problem keep you focused on resolving the discrepancy between your current state and your goal.

Having focused your attention on the roadblock and been motivated by your emotions to solve it, you have an important decision to make about *how* you are going to solve it. One possibility is to turn around and go the other way: you can decide that you were never meant to be a marathoner, that you will never get your checkbook balanced, and that you will never make friends with that grumpy coworker or even make her smile. Giving up on a goal is, in many ways, the easier route. If you stop training for the marathon, stamina ceases to be a problem. Giving up certainly takes care of the current state–goal state discrepancy quickly. Take away the goal state, and there will be no more discrepancy.

That doesn't mean your problems are over, however, because a goal typically does not exist in a vacuum. When I teach psychology classes that explore why people act the way they do, I often get my students thinking about their motivations by asking them why they came to class that day. University professors have to accept at some point in their careers that their students do not come to lectures solely because those lectures are so brilliant, pleasing, and entertaining compared with other things that students could be doing.[6] Students come to class because they want to get a good grade (and, ideally, learn something along the way), which in turn will help them accomplish a future state of being (knowledgeable), having (a degree), and feeling (satisfied or proud). That is, coming to class is something they do to help them get closer to those goals.

Goals are often related to other goals, and they tend to be arranged hierarchically, with simple goals feeding into higher, more complex goals. The simple behavioral goal of going to class is tied to the higher goal of graduating from college, and, indeed, without the tie to the higher goal, the simple goal might not have any meaning. Those higher goals (graduate from college) are often themselves tied to very important, self-defining goals (be a competent person). As a

---

[6]I know this for sure because when I asked, my students told me so.

consequence, giving up on simple goals (balancing the checkbook) can threaten higher goals (be financially competent, be an independent adult). Because these higher goals are not easily dismissed, neither are the lower goals. Many of us have broken off romantic relationships with people who turned out to be completely inappropriate for us. We found them emotionally unsuited to our temperaments, or interested in different things than we were, or making out in the coat closet with someone else. So why was it so hard to forget the creep after the breakup? Why is so much emotion and mental energy expended on a relationship that is over? Probably because many romantic relationships tie in to broad, self-defining goals like being a lovable person, spouse, or parent. Even though that particular individual didn't turn out to be the right person to be loved by, married to, or a parent with, his or her loss can threaten those goals.

When a roadblock comes up, therefore, the first option, giving up, can be distressing. Giving up on goals related to relationships might involve resigning yourself to a life on the sofa watching TV with the dog. Don't get me wrong—dogs are wonderful companions, but they are an unsatisfactory solution to the desire for a human partner. Fortunately, giving up is not the only option. Negative mood can motivate you to find a way to negotiate the roadblock, and rumination can keep you thinking about ways to accomplish that negotiation. This is a better choice in one sense, because you are more likely to overcome both the roadblock and, consequently, the negative mood and rumination. In another sense, however, it is a more trying choice because overcoming roadblocks is rarely easy. You might have to hire a personal trainer to help you increase your stamina, and the training regimen prescribed probably will not be easy or pleasant. Spending an hour untangling the snarled mess that is your bookkeeping system will probably not be your most contented and happy hour ever. You might have to kiss a lot of frogs before you find your handsome prince. Although potentially less distressing, it often can be harder to try to overcome a roadblock than to just give up.

The problem with roadblocks is that there is no good solution in the short term. Giving up on a goal does not eliminate the negative mood and preoccupation that arose with the roadblock because of the goal's relationships to other important, self-defining goals. Instead, the failure to overcome the roadblock and resume progress toward those goals maintains that depression and preoccupation. On the other hand, continuing to try to achieve a goal is less emotionally difficult, but it may tax both mind and, especially, body—a possibility addressed in Chapter 5.

Looking into the future, however, you may find that the cost-benefit ratio changes. Keeping at a goal is no guarantee that you will reach it. On the other hand, rejecting it almost ensures that you will not. This is where optimism comes in. Looking into the future is exactly the mechanism by which people decide whether they will go the simple but distressing way (give up) or the difficult but potentially rewarding way (keep going). Optimism helps people see beyond the immediate road-block to a potentially positive future, whereas pessimists see only more roadblocks, problems, and failures. For optimistic people, it makes sense to incur the costs of trying to get past a roadblock because they expect rewards in the end. Positive expectancies keep people working on difficult tasks in the lab when it would be easier to just give up, and a positive vision of a beautiful garden will keep the weeder digging when it would be easier to go inside and take a nap. Pessimistic people have no such inspiration and therefore fail to see the point of putting effort toward the negative future they envision.

Many major and desirable transitions in life come hand in hand with difficulties that have to be negotiated. In the past few years, my husband, Jai, and I have been negotiating a couple of major transitions together. We married (in our mid-30s). We bought a house in a state of dishevelment and started working on restoring its luster. My husband quit his job, for various good reasons, and started a new business with a trusted partner. Although there is no question that these were all good decisions, that doesn't mean that there haven't been roadblocks. We have been working out major issues like how two independent-minded people, each used to having his or her own way at home for at least the past 10 years, can create a cooperative household and how to live on a single salary until the business comes into its own, as well as minor issues like what color to paint the bedroom.[7]

---

[7]One of my editors suggested that I replace the bedroom paint example with something that "will be familiar to everyone as the kind of trivial thing that becomes a big deal between spouses but sounds like small stuff to outsiders." Apparently she has never had a protracted negotiation about what color to paint the bedroom. That happened to be our "small stuff"; your results may vary.

I think that we have so far managed to negotiate these simultaneous challenges not by being happy people (one thing my husband claims to have learned in our marriage to date is to make himself scarce when I'm having a bad day) but by being persistent people who believe in the possibility of a positive future. I tend to believe persistence can overcome a multitude of roadblocks, and my husband is so persistent that we have a joke about it. (Every obstacle is characterized like a sporting event: Jai versus the computer; Jai versus the brush pile; Jai versus the local newspaper delivery service. Jai almost always wins.)

Of course, we are not the only people who overcome roadblocks this way. Other new business owners would do well to pay attention to the benefits of optimism for achieving goals. A new business owner can expect a series of challenges and setbacks, not least the loss of income, that last through the first several years. One guideline for entrepreneurs is to expect hard times for at least 3 years before it's clear whether the business is going to succeed or not. And success is not guaranteed by any means: 50% of new businesses fail within 4 years. Jeff Bezos, the founder of Amazon.com, provides an excellent example of the importance of optimism for people who undertake the extremely hazardous route of entrepreneurship. Amazon.com was started in Bezos's Seattle basement in 1995 and did not turn a profit until 8 years later. In the interim, Amazon.com faced numerous challenges, such as stockholder criticism of its focus on growth over profitability and the burst of the Internet "bubble."

Nonetheless, Bezos persevered, and Amazon.com is now one of the world's leading Internet retailers. Not coincidentally, Bezos is also an optimist. He also describes himself as a happy person, but he singles out optimism, not happiness, as the characteristic that has made him successful. The reason? Optimism keeps him focused on realizing the future he envisions, especially when that realization has to take place over a long period of time. As Bezos said, "Optimism is an essential quality for doing anything hard." Jeff Bezos understands what it really means to be an optimist. It doesn't mean pretending to be positive or avoiding difficulty or stress, but persisting in the long term and keeping your eye on the prize while you weather the difficult times.

Getting married, starting a business, buying a house: although you expect roadblocks to arise in the process of these changes, they are only side effects of otherwise positive transitions. Perhaps they are more tolerable because they are the smaller costs that you accept because of the larger rewards in being married, your own boss, and a homeowner. However, sometimes roadblocks arise that are not part of a larger, happier circumstance. In particular, diseases can limit the amount of time and energy that people have to pursue their important goals, and pain and distress associated with illness can make it hard for people to do the things that are important for them. Furthermore, the roadblocks associated with disease might be harder to overcome because they aren't the cost you pay for a larger reward. They're just costs, and often dramatic, life-threatening ones. Nonetheless, research findings illustrate that optimism helps people overcome the roadblocks of fibromyalgia, cancer, and other chronic illnesses.

Fibromyalgia is a syndrome that causes pain throughout the body, as well as fatigue and sleep disturbance. Although no one knows what causes the condition, the downward spiral of fatigue and pain is clear in patients with this illness. Pain keeps them from sleeping well, and, in turn, the lack of sleep causes increased sensitivity to pain. In part because any pathology underlying fibromyalgia is poorly understood, there are no effective, easy treatments. Generally, people with this syndrome have to learn to adapt their lives to the limitations that come along with it, and these limitations, like the pain itself, are widespread. Even simple movements like putting on clothes, carrying packages, or walking can arouse the pain.

Fatigue and pain certainly limit the amount of energy and effort that can be expended to reach goals, and in one study that followed women with fibromyalgia it was clear that on days when the women had higher pain or fatigue there were negative effects on their ability to pursue both their health goals (for example), maintaining an exercise routine) and their social goals (for example, being more patient with coworkers). Women reported that pain and fatigue interfered with their ability to pursue their goals, decreased the amount of effort they aimed at their goals, and prevented them from making as much progress toward their goals as they would have otherwise. Optimism, however, reduced the perception that pain and fatigue were barriers, so that when a woman had higher levels of optimism she didn't think pain and fatigue kept her from pursuing her goals. Furthermore, on days characterized by the highest fatigue, the most optimistic women were least likely to reduce their effort to reach their goals and, naturally, made more progress toward reaching their goals. Optimistic women overcame their increased fatigue with increased effort. The authors of the study concluded that their results provided evidence for "the optimist's superior ability to surmount obstacles to goal accomplishment." As was true of the undergraduates, optimists did not try harder to reach their goals because they felt their goals were more important. Optimistic and pessimistic women valued their goals equally, but optimistic women put more effort toward reaching them, especially when they were challenged by the fatigue that characterizes their disease.

Another group of women who face disruption of goal pursuit are cancer patients. Studies with these patients show that often their social and recreational activities are disrupted by the fatigue and distress caused by adjustment to the illness and its treatment. However, this disruption is less severe for optimistic women, who tend to persist in pursuing social goals such as continuing to visit and be visited by others and recreational goals such as continuing to do volunteer work, go to church, or go out for entertainment.

Of course, it's not always possible to surmount obstacles. One of our students in the daily goals study listed "get straight A's" as a goal, but this might not prove achievable for this student. Even so, it would be a bad idea for him to completely give up on this goal, because that might threaten bigger, more important goals such as "be a good student" or "be accomplished." One way around this problem is to set a new goal, such as "get a 3.5 GPA," that can help maintain the higher-level goals. The person who does this transfers his expectancies and his commitment to achieving to the new goal and, more important, is able to maintain the link between his daily goal of academic accomplishment and his larger, self-defining goals.

Being able to accomplish such a transfer might be particularly important with aging, when the loss of physical capabilities means that some activities and goals might become impossible. Some people probably run 10 miles a day until they die at the age of 110, but that's not going to be possible for most people.[8] The onset of age-related

---

[8]I would guess that for me, the odds are vanishingly small, given that I don't think I could run 10 miles a day right now without my knees and potentially other parts of my body falling apart, and I'm only about a third of the way to 110.

physical health problems, in particular, limits the kinds of things people can do, including sports, travel, long outings, driving, and gardening. However, it is possible to adopt new goals and activities that accommodate physical limitations. The research on goals does not prescribe certain goals, after all. Improving your bridge game is as good a goal for psychological well-being as running 10 miles every day, as long as the goal to improve your bridge game meets criteria for well-being—that is, it allows you to meet the human needs of engaging, growing, and mastering. As limitations take goals away, goal involvement can be maintained by adopting new, meaningful goals.

One study examined a large group of hundreds of people, mostly in their 70s, whose lives were limited by chronic illnesses including arthritis, heart disease, cancer, and sensory loss. Over 85% of the people with illness had to give up an activity—physical activity (like exercise or gardening), social outings, traveling—because of their illness. However, optimism before the illness started turned out to be a good predictor of whether people remained engaged after the illness started by finding new activities to replace the ones that they had to give up. More optimistic participants replaced the old activities like running and traveling with new activities that included gentler sports (walking instead of running, for example), socializing, playing games or music, and writing. This difference in turn had important implications for quality of life. Failure to replace the old activities led to a loss of happiness over the year after the illness started, whereas people who replaced their activities had no loss of happiness. Although the study did not measure eudaimonia, one might expect even larger effects on whether these folks felt they were approaching their best selves in their daily lives, because there are multiple paths to happiness but few to eudaimonia, and those few mostly have to do with goals. Giving up goals severely limits the ways you can achieve eudaimonia.

Together, all these studies point to goals as a critical part of why optimism is psychologically beneficial. In particular, optimism keeps people involved with their goals when challenged by limitations. These roadblocks might be physical (as in fibromyalgia or age-related illnesses), but might equally be logistical or come from some other source. Optimistic people maintain well-being by staying involved with their goals when roadblocks arise, even replacing their goals when necessary.

But don't let me tell you what kind of goals to have, because then the whole thing falls in like a house of cards. Why you have a goal is as important to your well-being as what kind of goal you have, a proposition considered further in Chapter 8. In general, people are happier when pursuing goals that help them grow as people, have meaningful relationships, and contribute to society, and they are less happy when they're pursuing goals that help them be more attractive, rich, popular, or famous. However, prescribed goals ("You should have more meaningful relationships"; "Why don't you go out and make a contribution to society?") lose their positive punch. You know it's not as much fun to go out and play when your mother tells you to as when you decide for yourself to do it. Generally, being told to go play leads to moping around the yard, sulking, and not having fun, much less feeling self-actualized. On the other hand, it is possible to consider what you are all about and compare that to the goals you pursue on a daily basis. Sometimes we lose the intrinsic motivation that got us started on a path, and we start thinking that we do our jobs for the money, that we play tennis to get better muscle tone, and that we have drinks with our friends to "network," and it takes some contemplation to re-connect to our meaningful reasons for doing these things: challenge, flow, and enjoyment.

Giving up on a goal, therefore, means giving up not only on one route to benefit and happiness but also on the main route to eudaimonia and being your best self. Conversely, being more engaged with goals, as optimists are, means more opportunities for happiness and well-being. Goals mean gaining resources, feeling authentic, defining yourself, and giving meaning to life, and the way optimists approach their goals is likely to be the key to those benefits.

CHAPTER THREE

Building (and Rebuilding) for the Future

Optimists and Their Resources

Lately it seems that people particularly want more well-being that arises from favorable thoughts and feelings about the self—that is, self-esteem. In the interest of being all they can be, and helping others do the same, people are increasingly concerned with maintaining their kids' self-esteem, their own self-esteem, their employees' self-esteem, and generally making sure that everyone feels good about themselves. It seems like a good idea, but how to do it? As with optimism, it's easy to envision people with high self-esteem being "positive" and those with low self-esteem being "negative" and to conclude that improving self-esteem is a matter of getting people who have low self-esteem to think more positively about themselves. This should be easy—after all, thinking positively about themselves is one of the things that people usually do best. If you have any doubts, complete the following sentence for yourself:

> Compared to other drivers on the road,
> I am a better driver than ___% of them.

There are very good odds that you put yourself in the top half of all drivers, and there are decent odds that you put yourself in the top 10 or 20%, that is, better than 80 or 90% of the drivers on the road. Now, I don't know you, and you may very well be an excellent driver. However, if you ask enough people, you will find that almost all of them put themselves in the top half. This is logically impossible. Not all of us can be, like the children of Lake Wobegon, above average. Fifty percent of people have to be in the bottom half on driving skills, and 50% have to be in the top half. We can't all be in the top. Nonetheless, in a study that asked a lot of people this question, over 90% of drivers put themselves in the top half. Even when they were hospitalized because of an auto accident, people thought they were better drivers than average (and most of them were at fault for the accident). This phenomenon is known as *self-enhancement.* Self-enhancement for popularity, intelligence, and ability to pick lottery numbers is more modest than that for driving skill, but across a large number of domains, self-enhancement is the rule, not the exception. Most people self-enhance easily and naturally.

For those few who do not naturally self-enhance, couldn't they work on changing their thoughts, practicing thinking a different way? If so, then increasing self-esteem would be a simple matter of finding people whose glass is half empty and encouraging them to see it as half full. The reality is not that simple. One study tried self-enhancement as a means to bolster self-esteem and thereby improve college student well-being and performance. Students who had done poorly on an examination received a weekly e-mail with review questions as well as messages aimed at helping them see themselves in a more positive light. Unfortunately, these students did *worse* on later tests than a comparison group of students who received review questions alone. Although self-esteem does seem to be associated with better performance, seeing yourself in a more positive light apparently isn't enough. As was found to be true for happiness and eudaimonic well-being, self-esteem probably arises from what you are doing in your life, rather than how you see yourself.

FILLING THE GLASS

Self-esteem isn't a function of merely *seeing* the glass as half full. It is a function of *actually filling* the glass or—in anticipation of the next self-regulation metaphor—the gas tank. In case you didn't already feel like some kind of cyborg, I am pleased to tell you that you not only have cruise control and a thermostat; you also have a gas gauge. Research shows that self-esteem is a reliable *meter*—an index of material, social, and psychological resources—and it serves an important purpose in self-regulation.

Consider the goal of driving to Grandmother's house. Feelings, such as happiness or anxiety, are telling you how fast you are progressing toward your goal.[1] As you know, those feelings are working something like your speedometer, telling you how fast you are approaching your destination, but when you are driving a car, you don't just need to know how fast you are going. It's also very important that you know how much gas is in the tank. Feelings can't necessarily be both the speedometer and the gas gauge of your life. For one thing, feelings change from day to day. They have to, in order to provide ongoing feedback about goal progress and resource change. As one emotion researcher pointed out, "If people are still in a state of bliss over yesterday's success, today's dangers and hazards might be more difficult to recognize." In other words, you can't feel good about today's progress forever or you will lose your motivation to keep moving forward.

Still, it would be nice to know today whether you got anywhere yesterday. Because feelings are busy giving ongoing information, you need something different to tell you how full the tank is. This is where a longer lasting sense of psychological well-being, such as self-esteem, comes in. Satisfaction with oneself and one's life reflects the ongoing, cumulative effect of efforts to reach particular goals. When people direct effort toward their goals, they build more resources and are more satisfied with their lives. High levels of energy, many close friends, strong family support, a close and warm romantic relationship, authority, and athletic ability all lead people to judge their lives to be close to their ideals. Conversely, low levels of these resources lead people to wish they could live life over and change something about it—their lives are not as satisfactory, and they don't feel they've achieved the important things they want in life.

Furthermore, if you want to change people's self-esteem and life satisfaction, you don't have to teach them to be positive—you just have to add to their resources. Being chosen to be part of a group for an experiment (the resource of being included by others and gaining

---

[1]There are also eudaimonic consequences: Because you love Grandma and want to visit her, driving to her house is a meaningful and authentic act in which you are acting as your "best self." This would not be true if you were going because Aunt Bertha gives you $20 every time you visit.

acceptance) causes a rise in self-esteem, and being chosen the leader of that group (the resource of being elevated over others and gaining status) raises self-esteem above and beyond being chosen as a member. People in this experiment weren't chosen to be included as group members or elevated to leaders because they had high self-esteem (they were randomly assigned by an experimenter to be "accepted" by the other "subjects" or not); instead, their self-esteem increased *after* they were included or elevated. Self-esteem was the consequence, not the cause.

Being an experimenter means you can dictate to your research team—posing as the other research participants—whether an unsuspecting target person will be accepted and whether the same person will be elevated to group leader. This kind of experimental control allows researchers to carefully tease apart chicken–egg issues, such as whether acceptance leads to a change in self-esteem or vice versa. In real life, you can't arrange another person's life so easily. For one thing, when people know you're just giving them resources, it messes up the whole thing (Chapter 4 discusses this unintended consequence of social support in more detail). For another thing, most of the time you just don't have that kind of power. You can't designate yourself or the people you care about to be accepted or elevated through wanting it to be so or through kidding yourself that acceptance or elevation is the case when it is not. Self-esteem, life satisfaction, and other kinds of long-term well-being are mostly consequences of each person's hard work to build resources from the ground up. If optimists have higher self-esteem and life satisfaction (and they do), it is likely because their persistence instinct and commitment to goals help them build resources better.

TO HAVE OR HAVE NOT: ANTELOPES, BABOONS, HUMANS, AND THEIR RESOURCES

Why would humans be so attuned to their resources, and why would so much of human well-being depend on them? Ask yourself what would happen to you if you didn't care about your resources. Better yet, what would happen if you were a different kind of animal, like an antelope, and you didn't care about your resources? Like the caveman who didn't pay attention to the tiger, you would be lunch. An antelope that wants to survive has to be motivated to maximize its resources to be the best-fed, strongest, healthiest antelope it can be. That motivation would take the form of a desire to accumulate biological and environmental resources such as good food, water, and an environment that is good for avoiding predators (for example, a place to eat where a lion can't sneak up). An antelope should feel good about itself (insofar as antelopes feel good about themselves) only when it's meeting those needs. In humans, the same principle applies, and self-esteem and life satisfaction are how these good feelings manifest themselves for humans.

Now take another phylogenetic step toward *Homo sapiens* and imagine that, instead of an antelope, you are a primate such as a baboon. Strength and health are only a subset of baboon resources. Baboons live in social groups that provide two other resources: acceptance and status. Acceptance comes with being part of a troop of baboons rather than a lone baboon in the wilderness. With group membership comes better protection (more other baboons looking out for bad guys and helping you fight them off if they show up), food sharing, and so on. For primates, there really is strength in numbers. Once within the troop, status comes from position in the social hierarchy. Baboons with more status have more access to resources like food and mates than baboons lower in the hierarchy. In fact, one of the ways that high-status baboons get resources like food and mates is by taking them away from low-status baboons.

All of us—people, antelopes, baboons—need survival resources: food, water, shelter, health. In addition, people and baboons, as primates, need "troop" resources in acceptance and status. Human resources will turn out to differ in some ways from baboon resources, but the basic categories remain the same.

A list of baboon resources might look something like this:

Basic (survival) resources	Acceptance resources	Status resources
Food Water Shelter	Troop membership	High position in hierarchy

Although modern human resources look somewhat different and survival is less likely to be at stake, the basic themes remain:

Basic resources	Acceptance resources	Status resources
Time	Marriage	Objects
Energy	Friendships	Knowledge or skill
	Family relationships	Socioeconomic status

These resource themes—particularly acceptance and status—surface across all domains of psychology that touch on human well-being. In clinical psychology, cognitive therapists think about how dysfunction in either relationships with others (sociotropy) or achievement (autonomy) leads to mental disorders such as depression. Social psychologists discuss how being with others (communion) and having an effect on the world (agency) contribute to well-being. Personality theorists consider the differences between power and intimacy motivations. Finally, development of senses of effectiveness and belonging are major tasks of the growing child. It is not surprising in light of these (near) universals that a close look at goals shows a similar kind of structure.

Robert Emmons, a psychologist specializing in the study of goals, developed a guide to the kinds of goals that people in his research were typically working toward. These goals had to do with:

Achievement: achieve, compete, do well, win
Affiliation: establish relationships, seek approval and acceptance
Intimacy: establish warm, close, communicative, loving relationships
Power: impact, control, or influence others; get fame, attention, position
Growth and health: improve physical, emotional, mental well-being
Self-presentation: make a favorable impression, appear attractive
Independence: avoid being dependent on others
Generativity: provide for the next generation, achieve symbolic immortality
Self-transcendence: affirm something beyond or larger than the self

His list does not group goal types into categories, but it is easy to group most of these types according to the category of resources they will build:[2]

---

[2]The exceptions: generative and self-transcendent goals. I believe that the latter two build a special kind of resource, and so I give them their very own section,

Basic resources	Acceptance resources	Status resources
Growth and health	Affiliation Intimacy Self-presentation	Achievement Power Independence

Goals and resources fit into the same themes because they are virtually inseparable. Progress toward a goal is often defined by resources building up in that area, and resources come from goal-directed behavior. The people who engage in the most goal-directed behavior will build the most resources over time and enjoy the highest levels of self-esteem and life satisfaction. We are better when we have more resources.

Optimistic people are more persistent when working on anagrams, but this is just a special example of their general persistence instinct, which also affects their behavior toward their daily goals and their higher aspirations (like getting a college education). From the very limited cornerstone of persistence on anagram tasks, links can be built from optimism to all levels of well-being. By making progress toward goals, more optimistic people feel hedonically good, and by being engaged with their goals, they feel eudaimonically good. Now, through building resources, optimistic people also achieve the most stable well-being: self-esteem and satisfaction with their lives.

USING IT:
A BLUEPRINT FOR RESOURCE GROWTH

Although resources and houses are both built over time, resource construction isn't like building construction—starting with one brick, putting another one on top of that one, and another one on top of that one. Building resources is more like being a currency broker, trading one resource for another depending on what you need and what the market demands, striving to come out ahead at the end of the day. Resources are, in large part, very fluid. Much of what we do

---

which is coming up. There is also a class of self-defeating goals concerned with avoiding taking chances or accepting challenges (e.g., "Do as little as possible"), which are not so much goals as antigoals.

every day is to convert some resource (especially time or energy) into some other resource. Money can buy a bigger house, knowledge can translate into a better job, and time spent with friends builds "capital" in those friendships. Even social roles, such as that of child, can be converted into resources, such as money.[3] Depending on what our needs and goals are, we marshal our resources toward meeting those needs and reaching those goals, using resources in one area to build resources in another or using momentum in one area to overcome a roadblock in another. Under most circumstances, conversion doesn't result in a net resource loss but ideally results in net resource gain, as when we invest energy in our jobs and relationships. The next day, our jobs and relationships are more durable and resource laden, and we have restored our energy through sleep and a good breakfast: a net gain.

The most efficient resource to convert or "spend" is one that is both plentiful and renewable. Plentiful resources can be spent without going broke. If you have a lot of friends and you've built up a lot of friendship capital by being a good friend to them, helping them in their times of need, and so on, you don't jeopardize your acceptance resources very much by calling on a friend to help you in a time of need. Although acceptance resources are not always easily renewable, if they are plentiful enough, they can be called on without jeopardy. On the other hand, if you have only a couple of friends and you haven't done much to build capital in those friendships, you could risk drying up your shallow pool of acceptance and goodwill by tapping those resources.

Another way to be efficient in spending resources is to use the easy-to-renew and conserve the difficult-to-renew. Some status resources, such as seniority at work, require a prolonged investment of time, energy, and knowledge, and if lost, also have to be rebuilt over a long period of time. Similarly, the intimacy of a long-term relationship cannot be rebuilt overnight.

Energy, on the other hand, literally *can* be rebuilt overnight with a good night's sleep. Energy is an entirely renewable resource if used wisely: bodies convert eating and sleeping into energy all the time. Money is a renewable resource insofar as time, energy, and knowledge can be converted into money through employment. Time is a

---

[3]"Dad, can I have 10 bucks to go to the movies?"

particularly interesting resource because it is entirely renewable in one sense (if you use up time today, you will get more tomorrow) and entirely finite in another sense (failing the invention of a time machine, you will never get back time you spend today). Time is the great equalizing resource because everyone—old, young, rich, poor, optimistic, pessimistic—gets the same amount every day. Although the principle of scarcity (it is least efficient to use what you have the least of) also applies to energy, money, and time, because these resources are renewable, scarcity is less of a problem. If you have only one hour left in the day today, it doesn't do you any good to hoard it for tomorrow. Although time today is scarce, go ahead and spend it! You can't take it with you.

Resources, in addition to being converted, also can, unfortunately, be lost. Sometimes the best outcome is to minimize resource loss by redistributing what remains effectively. In the most challenging circumstances, a single event can cause losses of many resources at once. Consider, for example, a woman who loses her husband. She suffers a profound loss in "acceptance" resources such as companionship and love, as well as the basic and status resources she shared with him: his knowledge (for instance, how to cook linguine con vongole), his income, and so on. This loss is so profound that a quick infusion of other resources will not compensate. Just as we are better when we have more resources, we are worse when we have fewer resources: we are stressed. As a final way of optimizing well-being, optimistic people use the same self-regulation principles when resources wane as they do when resources grow—in this case, persistence and commitment help them preserve what resources they can.

LOSING IT: HOW OPTIMISTS COPE WITH THREATS AND LOSSES

Unfortunately, life stresses like divorce, bereavement, and unemployment, which entail profound resource losses, have equally profound negative consequences for mental and physical health. Losing a loved one—through either death or abandonment—triples a person's risk of an episode of major depression, a debilitating form of depression that lasts weeks and tends to recur, sometimes over a lifetime. Long-term unemployment or conflict with loved ones triples the likelihood of getting a cold when you are exposed to the cold virus. Stress is even associated with a higher risk of death. In one study of over 10,000 American men, unemployment or business failure increased the risk of death by 29–46%, and separation or divorce increased the risk of death by 23%. In a study of Danish mothers whose children had died, bereaved mothers had a 43% higher risk of death than their counterparts whose children were living.

There are two ways to avoid the negative effects of stress such as depression, illness, or even an early death. The first is to avoid experiencing stressful events, that is, losing resources. Good luck. Although some kinds of stress (for example, going to jail) are avoidable (for example, don't commit a crime), it's hard to imagine that you can avoid all kinds of stress. Part of having resources is the risk of losing them: no job, no relationship, no Ming vase is guaranteed to be there for you forever. If you are going to have resources and risk their loss, you will need some way to avoid the negative effects of stress. Those ways are commonly and collectively called *coping*.

Coping is hard to define but can include anything you attempt in order to alleviate the consequences of stress. Although the word *coping* implies that this attempt is effective ("How are you?" "I'm coping"), coping does not have to be effective, and in fact much of coping research has to do with what kinds of coping are ineffective. If we think of stress as the state of resource loss, effective coping means you are focused on retaining resources and efficiently using what resources you still have, minimizing loss and especially rebuilding what has been lost. Ineffective coping means ignoring opportunities to rebuild or preserve resources and perpetuating a downward spiral: if the woman who lost her husband coped by withdrawing from other activities, like seeing her friends, her resource losses would compound, not diminish.

Predictions about optimism and coping emerge naturally from the persistence instinct. In general, people who are more optimistic will pursue goals more tenaciously and build more resources than their pessimistic counterparts. A stress-related corollary of this prediction is that optimists will be more likely to act effectively to rebuild resources during or after resource loss. A second corollary is that although a positive view of the future predisposes a person to do this, there is no reason a person should have to change his nature to adopt this coping strategy.

The relationship of optimism to coping has been examined in dozens of studies of people facing the threat or the reality of resource loss in situations ranging from college exams to cancer diagnosis to rescue work. From all these studies, one theme emerges. Optimists are more likely to *do* something. Sometimes this something is to attack the problem directly (which psychologists call *problem-focused coping*). A good example of the kind of situation that calls for attacking the problem is going away to college. Going to college poses both academic and social challenges, many of which can be met by investing basic resources (primarily time and energy) in activities that will improve academic performance (for example, studying) and social relationships (for example, joining a club). People using this active, problem-focused approach should be the most effective at coping with college and have the highest well-being. Evidence shows that these effective people are more likely to be the optimistic sorts. One study followed hundreds of UCLA freshmen living in the residence halls. These students reported on their levels of optimism, their mood, and the ways they were coping with college during their first few weeks on campus. True to form, optimistic students were more likely to be using problem-focused strategies such as "redoubled my effort to make things work" and "came up with a couple of different solutions."

At the end of their first term, the students also reported on a number of aspects of their well-being, including illness symptoms, doctor visits, how healthy they felt, how they felt about their lives, how stressed they were, and how happy they were. Freshmen who were more optimistic when they started school were better adjusted at the end of their first term, and better-adjusted students were also in better health. Most important, the most optimistic students were better adjusted and in better health in part *because* they attacked their problems head-on.

The "head-on" qualification is particularly important for this equation. Optimistic people adjust better to stress not because they are focused on the problem, but because of the *way* they are focused on the problem. After all, there are two ways of taking care of a problem: try to fix it or walk away from it. Under the rubric of problem-focused coping, trying to fix the problem implies being engaged, and walking away from it implies being disengaged. Because the basic difference between more and less optimistic people involves whether they could be expected to engage or disengage under stress such as a roadblock or resource loss, more optimistic people are more likely to report problem-focused coping that has to do with engagement, not disengagement. Among the many kinds of problem-focused coping assessed by coping questionnaires, optimism is associated with these kinds:

Planning what to do
Getting advice on what to do
Keeping one's focus on what to do

And less associated with this kind:

Giving up

If an optimist moves to a new town and has no friends, the coping studies indicate that she will be thinking about ways to meet new people and taking actions to make new friends, like joining a club or a sports team. Conversely, a pessimist is more likely to decide that having new friends is not going to be a goal and not make an effort to remedy her lack of friends.

This association between optimism and head-on problem solving is especially true when something *can* be done about the problem. After all, doing something via problem-focused coping is not always a beneficial strategy and could present a potential Achilles' heel for optimists. Redoubling your effort to fix an unfixable problem looks more like a path to frustration and wasted effort than a path to well-being. Fortunately for optimists, "doing something" does not necessarily imply doing something about the situation to make it accommodate to them. Sometimes they do things to help themselves accommodate to the situation.

Take, for example, residents of Three Mile Island, the site of the 1979 nuclear power plant accident. This accident involved the release of radioactive material in the town of Middletown, Pennsylvania. Although the typical amount of exposure to radiation turned out to be less than that involved in a chest X-ray, uncertainty about the danger associated with the radiation posed a threat to a very basic resource—health and life—and the stress and anxiety associated with the accident turned out to be more harmful than the accident itself. In 1982 and 1983, cancer rates were 20% higher among those people living closest to the plant, who also perceived the greatest threat and experienced the most distress. This increase in cancer rates was not due to radiation exposure, which was more closely related to what side of the plant people lived on than to how close they lived to the plant. Furthermore, there was nothing that residents of Middletown could do to make the environment accommodate to them. The accident had happened, and it could not be undone. When residents were given a coping checklist, those who checked off items like "changed something so things would turn out all right" had more depression than those who did not, probably because they were engaged in a fruitless pursuit of solutions that didn't exist. Interestingly, the same people were also more likely to check off the item "I refuse to believe what is happening," which implies they may also have been denying the impossibility of solving the problem themselves.

Are optimists more vulnerable to this kind of mistake? If the possibility were limited to nuclear accidents, then it would be a fairly irrelevant question because nuclear accidents are so rare. However, other kinds of stressors pose the same kind of challenge. Coping with trauma, for example, often involves dealing with something that happened in the past. Because the situation itself is over, trying to change it will generally not be effective. Likewise, awaiting the result of a biopsy allows for little control over the situation or the outcome. Even mundane hassles such as sitting in a traffic jam put people in the situation of facing resource loss (in this case, time) with little they can do about it. In these cases, directing resources toward trying to remedy the situation itself will likely waste those resources. If optimists are not wise, they could—like the Three Mile Island residents who tried to undo the past—end up more depressed, anxious, and even sick.

Fortunately for optimists, it seems that they are thoughtful in directing their coping energies. In one study, emergency rescue workers who worked at the site of an airplane crash were followed for up to 12 months after the accident. Optimistic rescue workers were most likely to cope by recruiting social resources to help them process their emotions. Coping strategies like this one, in which people turn to managing their emotions, rather than the situation, are called *emotion-*

focused coping. As is true for problems, there are two ways to approach emotions: try to fix or improve them or try to avoid them. Again, optimists are more likely to choose the engaged strategy over the disengaged strategy. Another example of this choice is found in a study of women awaiting breast cancer diagnosis. In this study, optimistic women were less likely to endorse avoidance strategies such as "wish the situation would go away." As a consequence, women who were more optimistic before breast biopsy were less distressed throughout the biopsy process and, for those women who had positive biopsies, were also less distressed through the process of surgery to remove the cancer.

Overall, among the many kinds of emotion-focused coping assessed by coping questionnaires, optimism is associated with these kinds:

Try to accept what is happening
Try to think about it in a different way
Talk about the emotions it brings up

And less associated with these kinds:

Pretend the situation doesn't exist
Do something to take my mind off the situation (sleeping, drinking, watching TV)
Wish the situation were different

Imagine that an optimist is lonely not because of moving to a new town but because of a job that involves living in a remote region such as Antarctica. Trying to do something about the situation is unlikely to help, since even her best friend is unlikely to relocate to Antarctica just to keep her company. Instead of trying to solve the problem in this circumstance, the optimist is more likely to try to accept the situation and make the most of it, to think of all the good things about having a few months of peace and quiet, or to write about loneliness in her diary as a way of processing those emotions. On the other hand, the pessimist is more likely to use the same avoidance strategies with unsolvable loneliness as with solvable loneliness, perhaps trying to pretend that she is not lonely or trying to distract from those emotions with alcohol, drugs, or sitcom reruns.

Whether the situation can be changed or not, optimists are more likely to take a head-on approach. Furthermore, the relationship between optimism and different kinds of coping—problem-focused or emotion-focused—changes across the kinds of situations in which optimists find themselves. There are dozens of studies that relate optimism to coping strategies under lots of different kinds of circumstances that vary in the degree to which problem focus or emotion focus should be most useful (such as the difference between coping with college and coping with trauma or moving to Albuquerque and moving to Antarctica). Combining the results of all of these studies shows that optimistic coping is sensitive to the kind of situation at hand. When problems were generally amenable to being tackled head-on, as with college exams, optimism was most strongly related to the corresponding strategy (problem-focused coping). When problems were not amenable to being tackled head-on, as with trauma, optimists were not more likely to try to tackle the problem head-on than pessimists; instead, they were more likely to deal with their *emotions* head-on (emotion-focused coping).

This pattern of coping, seen from a resources perspective, is one that will preserve and rebuild resources most effectively. Compare the effects of coping with a solvable problem head-on to the effects of coping with the same problem by burying your head in the sand. Head-in-the-sand might buffer you from the effects of stress in some ways. If you can go to the movies for a few hours, you may be able to temporarily forget that you have a deadline to meet tomorrow, but in the meantime, you could have been using time and energy resources to try to meet your deadline. While you are sitting in the movies with your head in the sand, resources you could be using to solve the problem are slipping away. When you fail to meet your deadline, you might lose even more resources (like your job). How about the unsolvable problem? Head-in-the-sand is equally inefficient even when there's nothing you can do to solve the problem. You might be able to convince yourself for a short period of time that a situation you don't want to be true isn't true, or that you are not feeling sad or angry when you are. However, that strategy is likely to fail, because trying not to think or feel something almost inevitably makes it prey on your mind (to prove this to yourself, for the next minute or two, try not to think about a white bear). When your avoidance strategy fails, you are right back at square one. In the meantime, you might have been accommodating yourself to the situation and learning to love Antarctica.

As was true of goal pursuit, being positive helps when confronting resource loss *because it leads to a different kind of behavior*, in this case acting wisely to rebuild resources. Just as in goal pursuit, it makes sense to invest resources to rebuild other resources only if you believe that it is going to work and that the stress (that is, resource loss) can be alleviated. However, most kinds of effective coping, although they are more likely to be used by optimistic people, do not require you to be an optimist. They require only that you adopt the kind of approach that optimistic people use.

TRANSCENDING MORTALITY

Even in uncontrollable, life-threatening situations, if you haven't buried your head in the sand, you might be busy building different resources of a special kind: existential resources. Existential resources do not have to do with existence per se ("I wish to be"), but with the meaning of that existence. Existential theorists identified a number of problems that threaten the meaning of existence, which include anomie, alienation from others, lack of purpose in life, and groundlessness. Existential resources could be considered those that serve as antidotes to these problems.

Some emotion-focused strategies typical of optimists, particularly optimists facing uncontrollable stressors, include:

"I look for something good in what is happening."
"I try to see it in a different light, to make it seem more positive."
"I changed or grew as a person in a good way."
"I came out of the experience better than when I went in."

These strategies don't look like the deployment or rebuilding of resources. They look like seeing the glass as half full, so one might be forgiven for assuming that when optimists are using this kind of emotion-focused approach to cope with traumas or health threats, they are taking their ability to think positively about the future and applying it to a stressful event, thinking about that event as positively as they can. However, one principle psychologists value is parsimony: the ability to account for the largest number of phenomena with the simplest explanation. So, rather than proposing one mechanism for optimists' greater use of head-on problem focus with more controllable events (their general orientation toward engagement and goal pursuit) and another for their greater use of head-on emotion focus with more uncontrollable events (positive thinking), we should begin with optimists' general tendency toward goal engagement rather than disengagement. We can then generalize this tendency to optimists' orientation toward retaining and rebuilding resources during stress by continuing to pursue goals. We can also note the effective nature of this pursuit in that coping efforts are wisely deployed based on the possibility for change in their circumstances, themselves, or both. But what resource is being built by strategies like those listed above?

People have (at least) one essential feature that differentiates them from other primates: a foreknowledge of death. Everyone will die one day, and we are all pretty much aware of that fact, although ideally we do not think about it constantly. Knowledge of the inevitability of death provides motivation to attach ourselves to things that will outlive us, providing vicarious immortality and reducing our anxiety about death. Think about the importance people put on naming things after themselves. My own environment, the university, is chock full of examples of people attaining vicarious immortality by having buildings or scholarships named after them. Of course, the most obvious examples on campus are the young students, most of whom have at least one name that will provide vicarious immortality to their predecessors.

Another way to cope with the inevitability of death is to skip over vicarious immortality and go straight to personal immortality. Belief in an afterlife goes a long way toward alleviating anxiety about dying, and endorsing a belief system that promises an afterlife to those who are "good" under its precepts provides that way to defeat anxiety about dying.

Foreknowledge of death leads to goals and resources that are unique to humans. These goals and resources reflect the importance for a human to be attached to something larger and longer-lived than that individual: a nation, a church, a family. In the classification of goals, two of the classes identified by Robert Emmons (mentioned earlier in this chapter) reflect that importance: *generativity* and *transcendence*. In subscribing to these goals, people are attaching themselves to larger or longer-lived entities or increasing closeness with a divine being who may promise them a longer life (after death).

Generativity	Transcendence
Create something enduring	Relate to or gain knowledge of the divine
Give of oneself to others	
Make a purposeful, positive contribution to young people	Conform to social or moral ideals
Leave a legacy or positive influence	Become one with a larger unit (a culture, nature, or the universe)

In turn, pursuing these goals leads to existential resources, the connections and contributions that will continue after death. The kinds of emotion-focused strategies used by optimists can be construed as coping that, like generative and transcendent goals, minimizes stress—net resource loss—by building existential resources or, as one set of authors put it, the sense that one is "a person of value in an eternal world of meaning."

As is true of other resources, high levels of existential resources are reflected in high self-esteem. Recall that existential resources provide protection against the stress posed by the threat of mortality. Mortality threats motivate people to confirm and build their existential resources by increasing their connection to institutions that will either continue after their death (for example, their nation or culture) or provide for their ongoing existence (for example, their religion).

This motivation should be strongest when existential resources are lowest. Calling on a plentiful resource should not deplete that resource to the point that it needs to be confirmed or rebuilt. For example, in the acceptance domain, asking your best friend for a ride to the airport does not motivate you to immediately do her a favor in return because the two of you have a deep relationship with a long history of reciprocity. On the other hand, asking an acquaintance might motivate an immediate reciprocal gesture (a gift from the trip, a dinner invitation, a ride to the auto mechanic) because that relationship's resources do not run as deep.

"Of course I hope to find gold. But my real goal is spiritual growth and inner peace."

Transcendent goals include spiritual growth and "inner peace."

Experiments show that people with high self-esteem are less motivated to rally or rebuild their existential resources. In one study, the experimenters increased the salience of death by having people write about their feelings about death and what will happen to them after they die. Those people then rated two essays: one that was strongly positive toward their country (in this case, the United States) and one that was negative. Typically, mortality threat leads people to increase their favoritism toward positive views of their country over negative views, because they are motivated to see their citizenship as including them in something bigger, better, and longer lasting than themselves. However, in this experiment, people with high self-esteem did not show this increase in favoritism toward their own nation. Their high self-esteem reflected existential resources that were high enough that thoughts of mortality didn't provoke immediate confirmation and rebuilding of those resources.

GROWING FROM GRIEF

When people confront mortality, it's not uncommon for them to change, grow, or shift their values—that is, to bolster their existential resources. Here is an example from the father of an acutely ill newborn:

> Right after she was born, I remember having a revelation. Here she was, only a week old, and she was teaching us something—how to keep things in their proper perspective, how to understand what's important and what's not. I've learned that everything is tentative, that you never learn what life is going to bring. I've come to realize that I shouldn't waste any more time worrying about the little things.

This kind of change has many labels. Some people call it *finding meaning* or *finding benefit;* others, *posttraumatic growth.* But no matter what you call it, some people respond to their confrontations with mortality by building existential strength through renewed connection to other people, appreciation of life, examination of goals and values, or spiritual growth.

The death of a loved one affects people as profoundly and often as negatively as almost any life event, as reflected in the increases in depression and mortality that follow bereavement. In addition to the loss of social resources such as companionship, the death of someone close reminds us of our own deaths, challenging existential resources. However, optimists respond to bereavement differently than pessimists do. In one study, optimists mentioned building or confirming social and existential resources after a loved one's death. For example:

> Having your health and living life to its fullest is a real blessing. I appreciate my family, friends, nature, life in general more. I see a goodness in people.

and

> We definitely learned a lot about ourselves and about each other within the family circle. There was a rallying of support, and a camaraderie that I think only shows itself when something like this happens.

Optimists experienced these changes and in turn enjoyed protection from many of the negative consequences of bereavement. Compared with pessimists, optimists experienced a reduction of depression, less negative preoccupation with the death, and greater capacity for emotion, particularly positive emotion. The psychological protection of building existential resources after bereavement lasted over a year after the death (and may have lasted longer, but the study ended). Other studies found similar effects for people who had undergone bone marrow transplant as a treatment for cancer, as well as mothers of children undergoing this procedure. Bone marrow transplant is an intense, risky, and stressful form of treatment that involves long hospital treatment with a rather high risk of dying, followed by long recuperation. Again, patients and mothers who were more optimistic saw the treatment as having more positive effects on their relationships, goals, and values and had greater life satisfaction as a result.

There are many means of attaining generative and transcendent goals and building existential resources. You can leave a lasting legacy in your community by contributing to the local youth center or planting trees, you can aspire to another form of existence after death by becoming closer to the divine, or you can create something lasting such as an artwork or a family. Even confirming one's connection to other people in whose memory one might live on can accomplish the task. Again, the advantage of being optimistic is in the likelihood of engaging and building rather than disengaging and risking further resource loss.

Here's the problem. Some of these strategies that build existential resources don't seem to work very well for pessimists. When a group of women with early-stage breast cancer were divided into those who were naturally hopeful and optimistic and those who were not, some coping strategies worked for the optimists but not for the pessimists. One of those strategies was *positive reinterpretation*, or coping with cancer by trying to gain something from the experience, grow as a person, or see it in a more positive light. That strategy, which helped optimistic women, did not help pessimistic women. Likewise, pessimistic mothers of children getting transplants got more distressed over time if they reported early after the transplant that there were positive consequences of the experience for the family; only optimistic mothers felt better after they had initially looked for and found positive aspects of the experience. If your natural tendency is to see things in a negative light, engaging in wishful thinking or forcing yourself to endorse benefits that you don't actually believe in will not help you.

One difference between existential resources and other kinds of resources is that the former are, for the most part, invisible. Basic, social, and status resources are often tangible or at least quantifiable. If you say you hold a certain amount of basic resources, a social scientist could confirm that easily by using objective measures of your health and energy. The scientist could confirm your report of social resources against objective measures of how large or strong your social network is. Your status resources could be confirmed against objective measures such as socioeconomic status (education, income, and so on). But how does the scientist confirm spiritual capital objectively? More important, how does the person who holds existential resources confirm them? These resources exist only to the degree that the people who hold them *believe* they exist. As a consequence, having blind faith in resource growth is a prerequisite for existential resources in a way that it is not for other resources.

Optimistic people have the easiest time building existential resources because they have a long history of seeing their efforts to build resources result in the tangible growth of those resources. Their efforts toward building a career, for example, may have been reflected in promotions, earnings, or awards; their efforts toward building a relationship may have been reflected in expressions of affection. Optimists have seen the self-fulfilling prophecy of positive expectations manifested over and over again in their own lives, so it is not a stretch for them to believe that the same will be true for existential resources. It is consistent with their experience.

Because they have not had the same kind of experience, however, pessimists may have more difficulty believing that their efforts to build resources will pay off. With concrete, observable resources, such faith might not matter. Pessimistic people can reap the benefits of optimistic behavior, because effortful persistence to be healthier or wealthier or wiser will pay off to the same degree whether or not you believe deep in your heart that it will. If you exercise more, you will become fitter whether or not you believe in that increasing fitness. The positive belief increases your odds of exercising, not the effectiveness of the exercise itself. On the other hand, efforts to build existen-

tial resources depend on faith in the upward spiral of effort, engagement, and attainment. That faith may depend on a history of seeing
optimistic beliefs and effortful engagement play themselves out: a history that pessimists just don't have.

Not to say that a temperamental pessimist couldn't achieve that
history. The effects of optimism on coping and coping on resources
indicate otherwise. The evidence so far shows that optimistic people
pursue their goals more doggedly, leading them to build resources
through either goal pursuit or effective coping with stress. It seems
likely that optimists are happier and have higher self-esteem and life
satisfaction because they are building available resources, not because
they are positive people per se. The route from optimism to self-
esteem and life satisfaction in this perspective must pass through
goals and resources. Forcing self-enhancement, happiness, or benefit
finding through positive thinking tries to bypass the work of goals and
the accumulation of resources and may even put people on the wrong
track to improving well-being. The consequences of forcing yourself
to be positive are likely to misfire, as when students do worse on
exams when enticed to think more positively about themselves or
when pessimistic women with breast cancer don't benefit from trying
to view their illness in a positive light or to grow personally from it.
The bad news is, there's no shortcut to the benefits of being optimistic. The good news is, you don't have to be optimistic to take the long
way around, and with enough round trips, doing so might even
cause new routes—such as transcendental goal pursuit and existential
resources—to open up. When it comes to optimists and well-being,
again, it is better to try to do as they do than to be as they are.

CHAPTER FOUR

So Happy Together
Optimists and Their Relationships

It seems technically possible that a resource is a resource is a resource, meaning you could have a lot of one and little or none of the others and be just fine. You can have a lot of dollars and not very many Euros, after all, and still be rich. On the other hand, it's difficult to imagine a person who could be happy with only one resource, or at least one who would be considered normal. Parables like the story of King Midas even warn against what happens when one resource, like gold, is valued more than another resource, like a family member. Although a family member made entirely of gold appears to be the perfect solution to the problem of gaining status and social resources simultaneously, it turns out that gold that is also a family member is not very useful as convertible currency, and a family member that is also gold is not very useful as a social resource.

It's important to have a diverse "portfolio" of goals, resources, and the like, but some are more important than others. This idea is captured nicely in psychologist Abraham Maslow's "hierarchy of needs." A need has elements of both goal and resource. As a verb, needing is an imperative way of saying "having as a goal"; as a noun, a need is a necessary resource. Maslow proposed that some needs, like some resources, are more basic than others. At the very least, we need our most basic resources, such as food, water, sleep, shelter, and security. Meeting these needs means staying alive and having physical energy, which are prerequisites to pursuing almost all other goals and building almost all other resources.

"So, does anyone else feel that their needs aren't being met?"

Social resources have always been important for human survival.

After basic needs are met, the next most important need for humans is belonging.[1] Social interaction is inherent to human existence, and social resources are necessary for human survival. We are creatures who have always lived in groups and have always relied on each other. Human interaction is critical to the development of children, as we've seen in the mercifully few cases where children have grown up without human contact and never developed normal language or behavior. Even among adult humans, those who are isolated die sooner than those with more social contacts.

One reason that belonging is so important is that historically we've been sources of basic resources for each other, providing food, shelter, and protection from enemies. However, times have changed. Although the caveman wasn't able to live alone, the accountant can. Why, then, are social networks still essential to well-being? Our spe-

---

[1]Following the need to belong are esteem needs, which roughly correspond to status, and self-actualization needs, which roughly correspond to existential resources.

cies is meant to be social, to interact with others. Even if we can provide financially for our own food and shelter, we can't buy happiness. Money doesn't make us happy, but relationships do. When you look at the resources associated with greater happiness and well-being, you find family support, close friends, and a strong relationship with a significant other at the very top. Resources like money, intelligence, knowledge, connections, and even health are much farther down the list. The gain in social resources from getting married increases happiness for much longer than the gain in financial resources from winning the lottery. Although a variety of resources is important, apparently it's just as important that at least some of them be social. Other people have to be part of the picture for true well-being; to quote a well-known social psychologist, "You can't be yourself by yourself."

MOVING TARGETS:
OTHER PEOPLE AS GOALS AND RESOURCES

Having abundant friendship capital or social resources is a healthy place to be. People who have more social relationships have all kinds of better health outcomes, from lower susceptibility to the common cold to lower risk of death. Curiously, studies of social networks often stop at a snapshot of the quality of social networks and their relationship to future mortality: at some particular point in time, some people have good or large networks and end up living longer, and others have bad or small ones and end up dying sooner. This static, snapshot view of social resources is appropriate for other qualities of people, like gender: some people are women and live longer, and others are men and die sooner.[2] However, the truth of social relationships is dynamic. Social networks are not something you *have* so much as something you *do*—they are the reflection of your actions to build, maintain, or even prune back your social relationships.

---

[2]According to the National Vital Statistics Report from the Centers for Disease Control and Prevention, the expected difference is more than 5 years: girls born in 2002 can expect to live to 80, but boys, only to 74½. Sorry, guys. The good news for you is that men are gaining on women; at one time in the 1970s, women had an 8-year advantage.

Surprisingly little research has been done on how people build large social networks. Personality characteristics like extraversion predict larger social networks, but this analysis jumps straight from what extraverts *are* to what they *have*, skipping over what they *do*. Still, you don't need a degree in social psychology to figure out why some people have larger networks than other people. The more effort you put into your social relationships, the more social relationships you have. One study of daily events logged the number of phone calls and letters participants received (the study was done in the 1970s, when the physical rather than electronic mailbox yielded communications from friends and family.) The best predictors: number of phone calls made and letters written. Another study of residents of university married-student housing found that those who attended more events in the housing complex, knew more of their neighbors, and chatted with and visited other residents more also knew people who would help them with both personal problems and everyday needs. Reaching out to someone doesn't guarantee that that person will reach back out to you, but failing to reach out to someone certainly makes it less likely. If you don't invest in friendships, you won't build social resources.

Building social resources is not as simple as making a bank deposit, however, because social interaction is a two-way street. Social resources are other human beings who are pursuing their own goals and accumulating their own resources at the same time as you are pursuing them as the targets of your goals and the repositories of your resources. Status resources such as money and education don't particularly care to whom they belong. Neither do basic resources such as time and energy. Although it's hard to say for sure, it's possible that even existential resources don't care who you are. Social resources, however, may have very definite feelings about whether they want to be *your* social resource, as anyone who has ever experienced unrequited love knows all too well.

Because social resources are dynamic, all these extra factors have to be considered. From the perspective of the resource builder, there's the question of whether the same strategies used to build static resources like money can also be used to build dynamic resources like friendships. Does the optimistic strategy of persistence work well, or is it perceived by its target as stalking? From the perspective of said target, there's also the question of whether that persistent optimist will make a good partner in building social capital or whether someone else might do just as well. Is there an advantage to having optimistic friends? There's also the question of how two people trade social resources such as favors or sympathetic ears back and forth with the reciprocity that characterizes good relationships; if, when, and where it's a good idea to draw on social resources; and how optimism might affect how social resources are spent or saved. When pursuing social goals, self-regulation (that is, an individual's own goal-directed behavior) is important, but the interactive behavior of the dyad or group of people, which might be called *social regulation,* is even more important.

Finally, because having social resources generally means close contact with other people, there is also the question of how that contact affects how you approach and appraise your other goals. The time you spend with your money doesn't necessarily change the way you think about your other goals and whether you are progressing toward them at a satisfactory rate. Your money is not doing better or worse than you are—in fact, it isn't doing much of anything. It's money. On the other hand, your friends, family, and neighbors aren't just repositories for social resources. In a sense, they're also the competition. Spending time with other people influences the goals and standards that you set for yourself. In fact, just having another person in mind can affect your goals. It doesn't even have to be conscious: studies that subliminally present the name of someone important (for example, your mother, your friend) increase commitment to the goals connected to those people (for example, clean your room, go out for a beer). On top of that, how other people are doing, how much progress they're making, and how many resources they have influence the standards you hold for your own progress and resources. Social comparison—the process of "keeping up with the Joneses"—can be inspiring, dejecting, relieving, or anxiety provoking, depending on how you go about it.

A lot of things happen at once when you spend time with someone else. You may be pursuing your acceptance goal to make a new friend, while at the same time the other person is evaluating you in light of his own goals to make friends and considering whether you'll make a good friend. You may also be aware of how this person makes you feel about yourself and your goals, and that will influence whether he seems like a good prospect for friendship. Building social resources is particularly tricky because you have to be successful on all of these levels to make social relationships work. On the other hand, when the people involved are successful on all of these levels, they pursue closer and closer relationships with each other, and they may make faster progress than is possible when one person pursues a goal alone. If one of your goals is to read *War and Peace,* you can be sure *War and Peace* is not going to help you get there any faster. On the other hand, if both you and your neighbor want to become friends, an upward spiral can ensue. Social regulation involves more potential pitfalls, but also more potential benefits.

WON'T YOU BE MY NEIGHBOR?: OPTIMISM AND FRIENDSHIPS

As you might expect from the importance of social and acceptance resources, most—if not all—people have social goals. Both Marie's and Jennifer's goal lists in Chapter 2 contained social goals, including making new friends, getting to know more people, and keeping a strong relationship with a boyfriend. When I categorized students' goals, many of the goals (39%) were related to status resources like getting good grades, graduating, or going to graduate or professional school. On the other hand, getting ahead wasn't the only theme. Getting along was also important: the students had a lot of goals (22%) related to building acceptance and affiliation—that is, establishing, maintaining, or repairing relationships.

In addition to querying undergraduates, I've also asked law students about their goals. Like the undergraduates, the law students listed status goals like getting good grades and excelling in law school. Also like the undergraduates, the majority of them had at least one social goal such as making new friends, keeping in touch with old friends, or spending time with friends and family. More so than the undergraduates, however, the law students were facing a roadblock with regard to their social goals. Law school severely limits students' free time, causing problems for maintaining a social life. One student even said it was hard to enjoy the free time he did have with friends outside law school because of his near-constant preoccupation with the law (a conversational nonstarter with almost anyone other than other law students). On the other hand, getting over these hurdles and putting effort toward social relationships is almost guaranteed to pay off later because of the strong relationship of social resources to physical and psychological well-being. This is not a resource you want to let run dry.

Optimists' attitudes toward their goals—their higher expectations, their greater commitment—suggest that more optimistic law students will extend themselves to maintain their extramural goals despite the roadblocks that law school presents. As was true of the undergraduates, optimistic law students didn't have different goals from pessimistic law students. Almost every law student had a social goal of some sort. The question is, what does the pressure of law school do to those goals? Are they at the top of the "to do" list, or have they been neglected and shuffled to the bottom?

Because I didn't assign my research team to follow the law students around all day, watching for evidence of goal activity, I had to infer goal activity indirectly. As it happens, if you make a list of goals, the one that comes to mind first is likely to be one you're actively concerned with or working on and will therefore appear somewhere near the top of the list. Conversely, if you have to mentally hunt goals down and blow the dust off them, they are probably not your most active goals. These less active goals, which come to mind only after some thought, will appear closer to the bottom of the list. In the law students, optimism was not necessarily associated with *having* a social goal, but the likelihood of *top* goals being social was very much associated with optimism. The odds that any given goal on a pessimistic student's list was social were 1 in 5. Those odds for any one of the top three goals dropped to 1 in 7, indicating that social goals were not uppermost in pessimists' minds. Instead, pessimists seemed to be more narrowly focused on their achievement in law school. Law school goals are more likely to show up at the top of all law students' lists than other goals (after all, that is a big part of what they do every day), but they seemed to show up to the exclusion of other kinds of goals for the pessimistic students.[3]

On the other hand, the odds that any given goal on an optimistic student's list was social were 1 in 6 (about the same as the pessimist's), but the odds for any one of the top three was higher, about 1 in 3

---

[3]For pessimists, the odds of any given goal being related to law school were 1 in 5; the odds of a goal in the top three being related to law school were 2 in 3.

(twice as likely as the pessimist's). Social goals were very much uppermost in optimistic law students' minds. In fact, the large difference between pessimists and optimists suggests that optimists keep problems (such as how to maintain relationships during law school) uppermost in their minds, where those problems can be active targets for solution. Because pessimists aren't as interested in actively solving problems, they don't keep problems active in their minds either. Instead, they let goals slide off their to-do lists and into the realm of the things you later wish you had done when you had the chance. If you look back into the mists of time, there's probably someone you wish you had asked out on a date when you had the chance, but there was some kind of barrier—it didn't seem like the right time. Pessimistic people are going to have lots of memories like that. Whenever the circumstances are difficult, it will be the wrong time for them. Instead of taking advantage of opportunities despite difficulties, they tend to let social relationships and opportunities slide out of their minds and into the mists.

Optimists, on the other hand, pay more attention to social goals, even—or perhaps especially—when time and effort are at a premium, and the consequences of paying attention to social goals are clear. Optimists are more likely to actually put the time and effort into friendships and other social relationships and to have more friends as a result. In a study of Finnish college students, those who expected positive social relationships—social optimists—were more likely to seek out social interactions and less likely to avoid interacting with others. The consequence was that students who were socially optimistic were less lonely. Furthermore, when students were asked to nominate three people they knew well and would call their friends, as well as three students they did not know well and had not interacted with, optimistic students were more likely to be nominated as friends. This effect occurred because of social behavior: social optimism led to social interaction, which led to popularity; in contrast, social pessimism led to social withdrawal, which led to social neglect. Pessimistic students were not unpopular, that is, not actively disliked. They were just not well known enough to be liked or disliked. Similarly, in one study of college freshmen, optimistic students had more friends at college to whom they felt close and could turn for help and in whom they could confide; they had developed these relationships by the first 3 weeks of their first semester; and they added even more friends by the end of the semester. Although more pessimistic students also made friends during the semester, they never caught up with more optimistic students. You will find more pessimists among the loners in the lounge than among the social butterflies at the keg party.

In addition to having more friendships, optimists have longer friendships. In a study that measured how long friendships lasted, students reported that, on average, their friendships had been going on for almost 6 years. This average varied, of course, and pessimism was one of the things that predicted shorter friendships—for each step of increasing pessimism, average friendship length dropped by over 4 months. Why do optimistic friendships last longer and pessimistic friendships fail over time? One possibility is that, as the evidence about the effects of optimism on social goals and behavior suggests, pessimists stop investing in their friendships, they let barriers interfere with the maintenance of their relationships, they let the "capital" in a friendship wane away, and eventually the friendship ends. This might be particularly true when two pessimists make friends, perhaps through commiserating about where the world is going and in what kind of handbasket. What happens when one of the pessimists gets a new job and starts working more hours? Who's going to go to the effort of figuring out when they can get together? One pessimist is too busy, and the pessimist "left behind" is likely to find the newfound neglect less an obstacle to be overcome than a confirmation of his negative expectations.

THE POPULAR OPTIMIST
MAKES A MORE LOVABLE YOU

The social success that optimists enjoy also implies that optimists are perceived as better potential friends. (After all, friendship takes two. All the persistence in the world won't make or keep friends if they find your persistence aggravating.) The research, in fact, confirms this. A large body of evidence shows that people want to be with happy people more than with unhappy people,[4] probably for myriad

---

[4]With one exception: unhappy or anxious people seem to prefer to be with other unhappy or anxious people. Misery loves company, but mostly if that company is equally miserable.

reasons. One big reason is that they're avoiding "mood contagion," the tendency for one person's mood to affect the other person in an interaction. Optimism is an attitude rather than a mood, but people who have pessimistic attitudes, like those in negative moods, are avoided. When research participants read interviews with "people" who expressed pessimistic views or optimistic views (the interviews were actually made up by the experimenters), they were more interested in interacting socially with the more optimistic "person." For example, when an interview had to do with finding a new relationship, the person who responded "There are so many people around, I'm sure I'll find someone" was a more desirable social partner than the person who responded "I don't think I'll ever find anyone here." The same effect was found for positive and negative mood, but attitude was more important than mood in determining whether participants were interested in spending time with the "person." An optimist in a temporarily bad mood was more attractive than a pessimist in a temporarily good mood.

As suggested by reactions to the "interviews," real social interactions with optimists are more positive than those with pessimists. A study by a group at the University of Pittsburgh had 50 women and 50 men fill out diaries every half hour over 3 days. Those who did not tear the diary to bits with their teeth because of having to fill it out 20-something times a day reported on whether they had had a positive, negative, or neutral social interaction in the past half hour.[5] Perhaps unsurprisingly, people who were more pessimistic had more negative social interactions. Furthermore, even though social interactions in general increased happiness, they didn't increase happiness as much for pessimistic people. The preferences of the students who read the "interviews" reflected a real-world phenomenon: interacting with an optimistic person is a more positive, happy, and enjoyable experience than interacting with a pessimistic person.

Interacting with people who are more optimistic is an attractive proposition because they are less likely to be in a bad mood, so there's less risk of negative mood contagion (although the interview study shows that people will risk negative mood contagion in order to avoid

[5]Surprisingly, none of the people tore the diary to bits with their teeth, although they very occasionally failed to fill out the diary (only 161 of 6,211 scheduled times).

interacting with pessimists—you'd rather sit next to the person with a cold than the one with tuberculosis). But there's another, potentially even more rewarding reason to have optimistic friends that goes beyond mood: interacting with an optimist makes *you* more attractive, like looking in a flattering mirror. A classic experiment in social psychology showed that beliefs about what someone is like actually *creates* those qualities in that person. In this experiment, which was ostensibly about nonverbal communication, experimenters used two pictures, one of a woman who was very attractive and the other of a less attractive woman. Each man in the study was shown one of the pictures and told he would be talking to that woman on the telephone. In fact, the picture was not of the woman with whom he later talked on the phone. That woman had been randomly assigned to the man and didn't know that the man had been shown an alleged picture of her.

Attractiveness is a way to manipulate all kinds of expectancies about what a person is like. For better or worse, attractive people are assumed to have numerous other positive traits, so that attractiveness creates a kind of "halo effect." When the men thought they were going to interact with an attractive woman, they expected her to be more sociable, poised, humorous, and socially adept compared with a less attractive woman. The entire plot of *Singin' in the Rain* is based on this effect. If audiences hadn't expected Lina Lamont's beauty to be accompanied by wit, grace, and intelligence, there would have been no need for Kathy Selden. By seeing a picture of an attractive woman, the men became optimistic about her qualities and the positive possibilities for the phone conversation. In contrast, by seeing a picture of a less attractive woman, the men became pessimistic about her and the conversation.

Each pair talked for 10 minutes on the telephone, and then judges rated the woman's qualities based on a recording of *only her side of the conversation*. Despite the fact that each woman was actually assigned randomly (rather than on the basis of attractiveness or personality) and that she didn't know her conversation partner had good or bad expectations for the conversation, there were marked differences in the woman's side of the interaction. When the man thought the woman was attractive, the woman was actually more confident, more animated, and showed more enjoyment of the conversation and more liking for her partner. The *man's* expectations manifested themselves in the *woman's* behavior, even though she didn't know those expectations existed. Men with positive expectancies brought out the best in their partners, whereas men with negative expectancies did not.

Nothing makes you more attractive than falling in love. Why is that? Are you sending off some kind of love pheromone that people suddenly can't get enough of? That is certainly possible, but some of it may be attributable to your own behavior. It's not that you are in love—it's that someone is in love with you. Without knowing it, the new boost to your lovability quotient (that is, your expectation that you will be found lovable) might be causing people to react to you in a way that confirms that expectation.

Optimists may have more friends and more positive interactions in part because they enter relationships with more positive expectations. By approaching social interactions and real or potential friends with positive beliefs about the future (and, particularly, about how the interaction or friendship will go), people who are more optimistic act in a way that brings that positive future about. Furthermore, because people expect more positive interactions with optimists, and optimists expect more positive interactions with others, the possibility for their interactions to fulfill their expectations may be multiplied. The interaction goes more positively, and the positive prophecy is fulfilled. This prophetic effect occurs for all kinds of social relationships, including marriages, teacher–student relationships, and so on.

The fulfillment of this prophecy, like other positive effects of optimism, does not come about just by our wishing it to be so. A study of newlyweds shows that it has to be backed up by optimistic behavior. The study followed newlywed couples for 4 years, tracking their satisfaction with their marriages and linking that satisfaction to their initial expectations for satisfaction with their marriages and with their partners—that is, optimism about their marriages. The good news for optimists: people who were more optimistic about their marriages at the outset were also more satisfied with their marriages. The bad news: satisfaction fell over time, by about 5 points on a 90-point scale, and optimism didn't protect against this fall in satisfaction.

The most interesting effect in this study had to do with behavior in marriage. Although there are a number of potentially nice things that you can do for a partner, like scratch a back or clip toenails, this study focused on two more important things that might happen when there are bumps in the marital road. The first behavior was interacting positively when discussing a disagreement. Do you talk about the in-laws without degenerating into name-calling? The second behavior was giving your spouse the benefit of the doubt. If your spouse starts to spend more time at the office, is it because of being given extra work, or is it a deliberate attempt to get out of washing the dishes? As it turns out, optimism helps maintain marital satisfaction only to the degree that it is backed up by these two behaviors. Optimistic couples who behaved positively in disagreements and tended to give their partners the benefit of the doubt had high, stable satisfaction across the 4 years. Optimism is self-fulfilling if you *act* to fulfill those expectations. A positive vision of the future creates the capability of creating that positive future, but does not automatically bring it about. On the other hand, without that vision, the future does not get realized. People who were capable of being positive and forgiving but were pessimistic about their marriages not only started out more dissatisfied, but they became more dissatisfied over time. It seems that although they were capable of acting in positive ways in their marriages, pessimists probably were not living up to their capabilities. Without the motivation, the *reason* to use those skills in marriage, that is to say, without optimism, the possibility for positive behavior and a more satisfied marriage was not realized.

DRAWING ON THE FRIENDSHIP BANK

Having built up social resources, what is the best way to use them? After all, resources can not only be built up but can also be converted into other resources, depending on what is needed most. When bad things happen, social networks can provide material support (a loan to get you through to the next payday when your car breaks down, a ride to the repair shop or to work), emotional support (sympathy over the failure of your starter motor, reassurance that a bad starter motor does not make a bad person), or both. If stress can be conceptualized as a loss of resources, then other people buffer against stress by filling in when and where resources are threatened.

Because people are moving targets, however, a lot more steps are involved in spending social resources than in spending money. Consequently, social support can be broken down into three steps or stages, and optimism could influence the outcome of each of the different steps. The first stage is *perceived* or *potential* social support. How many people would be available to help you if help were needed? Positive expectancies could lead people to expect more positive responses from more people in their social networks. The second step is *seeking* social support. People don't always try to solve problems by themselves; they recruit their social networks to help them. Positive expectancies could lead people to tap into their social networks to help them solve problems because they believe the problems can be solved. Why recruit others to help you unless you believe you can be helped? The final step is actually *receiving* social support—that is, other people actually providing help. Because people like optimists better and get along with them better, they might be more willing to help an optimist when called upon.

Although there are good reasons to predict that optimists will perceive, seek, and receive more social support, the only consistent finding is that more optimism leads to higher perceived social support, that is, the belief that more social support is available if needed. Optimistic college students expected more emotional (for example, listening to feelings) or tangible (for example, providing a ride) support if they needed it than did their pessistic counterparts; optimistic emergency workers perceived more support from close others; optimistic men caring for their partners with HIV and AIDS perceived more social validation (for example, people approve of the way you do things), love, respect, and support; optimistic adults in cardiac rehabilitation perceived more support in the form of sympathy, information, and tangible help; and optimistic women with breast cancer perceived more love, emotional support, and tangible support. These are vastly different kinds of people and circumstances, but in all of them, people who were more optimistic thought more social support, ranging from emotional validation to a ride to the garage, was available to them.

This is a somewhat unsurprising finding. After all, asking people about their perceived social support is asking them to imagine what would happen if they needed support, and the definition of optimism is expecting a positive future. In this case, optimistic people are imagining a positive future in which other people are ready and willing to help them.

When we come to the next link in the chain of social support, however, a surprise emerges. In general, a large social network and a high level of perceived support should predict drawing on those resources to deal with stress, that is, using social support to cope. This appears *not* to be the case when the person holding those resources is optimistic. Only one study has found that college students who were more optimistic about how their friends would respond to an appeal for help were also more likely to ask for help. Another study with college students found that although students who were more optimistic had more friends and perceived more social support, they were not more likely to cope by asking for social support. Several other studies with diverse groups have concurred with the second college student study: although optimistic people perceived more social support to be available to them, they were not more likely to ask for that support or to receive more support from others. For example, the optimistic AIDS caregivers perceived more social support both before and, particularly, after the partner's death, but optimistic and pessimistic caregivers actually received the same amount of support from their networks.

In fact, perceiving social support but not using it turns out to be the best way to use social resources, because perceiving social support benefits happiness and health more than seeking and receiving social support do. *Perceived* social support goes along with lower stress, less depression and other psychiatric symptoms, higher self-esteem, better sleep, and better health. *Seeking* social support, on the other hand, does not, and *receiving* social support can even lead to *poorer* adjustment. For one thing, when people actually step in and help, they may not give the kind of help that is needed. For example, the helper may empathize with the difficulty of having one's car repaired when what is really needed is a ride to the garage or a loan to help pay for a rental.[6] Conversely, a helper might offer to help solve a problem when what is really needed is a sympathetic ear. If you're feeling put upon at work, the solution might not be a smaller workload but a

---

[6]It seems to me that this kind of misguided helping is especially annoying when the empathy involves the alleged helpers' stories of the time *they* were in an accident, and *their* car was in the shop, and how *horrible* it was, definitely *horrible*, and actually *worse* than what has happened to you because their cars were *newer* than yours. Surely the "helper" feels that by offering a more tragic story, he will make

more appreciative audience. Social support that offers the wrong kind of remedy isn't very good support at all.

For another thing, having someone step in and help might also be a signal to the person being helped that she is not capable of dealing with the problem independently. This deals a blow to the person's self-esteem. Still, people need real help, and just having someone who could be supportive cannot be enough, can it?

It just might be. Recall that stress can be defined as a net loss of resources, and requesting and receiving social support means *using* social resources. That use may offset another need (for example, having a shoulder to cry on, getting help moving your sofa), but receiving social support depletes social resources. Resource depletion is not associated with feeling better—rather, it typically leads to feeling worse.

The difference between having support and calling on support is very important, as psychologist Niall Bolger and his colleagues showed among a group of lawyers and their spouses. Bolger followed the couples daily from a month before the lawyers took the New York state bar exam through a few days after the exam, assessing whether each spouse had supported the other and how distressed they were. Consistent with the idea that spending social resources is not psychologically helpful, on days when the lawyers said their spouses supported them by listening to them, comforting them, or both, they had *more* anxiety and depression the next day. This time course of social support followed by distress is an important aspect of the study design, because otherwise it would be possible that the increased listening and comforting was *caused by* the anxiety and stress, not the other way around.

More unexpected was the fact that on days when the spouses said they listened to and comforted their partners, but the lawyers didn't perceive that it had happened, the lawyers had *less* anxiety and depression the next day. "Invisible support," support given under the radar, is the best kind of support to have. Social support can be helpful, but only when it is not accompanied by the perception of having spent social resources. When we, as psychologists, ask people about the social support they have requested and received, we are really asking

---

you feel better. What actually happens is that you are now annoyed because your problem has been minimized, and you still need a ride to the garage.

the degree to which they perceive themselves to have drawn on their bank of social resources. Put that way, it's not surprising that the answers don't point to tremendous psychological benefit, because benefit comes from building resources, not spending them.

Other intriguing phenomena suggest the benefit of social resources is in the getting, the building, and the having, not in the spending. First, the lower mortality risk associated with a larger social network may be a function of the support *given* within that network rather than the support *received*. In one study, people with more social contacts had a 19% decrease in mortality risk, consistent with all the other findings that larger social networks contribute to better health. What was surprising about this study was that people who *gave* more social support to others had a 43% decrease in mortality risk after holding physical health constant. Receiving social support had no effect—if anything, it increased mortality risk slightly. When it comes to relationships, to give may be better than to receive because it builds rather than depletes social resources. Furthermore, giving leads to the most beneficial kind of social support, the *perception* of social support. Among the residents of married student housing mentioned at the beginning of the chapter, the biggest contributor to perceived social support was the number of people a participant had helped. Helping others, then, might give you the sense of being involved in a network of people who help each other, and this perception buffers you against stress.

That act of perception does more than act as a check on the amount of friendship capital in the bank. Thinking about supportive ties actually protects us from the negative physical effects of stress. Consider your best friend or another person who is supportive of you and answer the following questions:

What do you value or appreciate most about this person?
What does this person value or appreciate most about you?
What does this person do for you that is supportive or helpful?
How do you feel when you see this person after being away from him or her for a few hours or days?

If you were now to go do something stressful, like give a speech, you would have already buffered yourself against its negative effects just by thinking about your relationship and the social resources inherent in it. One study had people think about either a supportive relationship (as you just did) or an acquaintance. Each person then gave a speech in the lab. Compared with people thinking about mere acquaintances, those who thought about meaningful and supportive relationships felt less anxious and had lower heart rates and blood pressures during the speech.

You can't go through life without ever calling on people for help. For one thing, people need to demonstrate dependence on each other, if for no other reason than to affirm the strength of their relationships and give each other an opportunity to do what is most beneficial—to help. There are always times when we need to call on other people to help us. On the other hand, to be like Blanche DuBois, *dependent* on the kindness of strangers without necessarily giving anything back, seems to undermine well-being.

UPWARD INSPIRATION

Optimistic beliefs fulfill themselves in the social domain because they lead to all the necessary steps to accumulate social resources: optimists act in a way that makes relationships grow (being withdrawn or not making an effort would certainly not build relationships), they act in a way that makes them more attractive relationship partners (otherwise, step one might lead to stalking, not friendship), and they use social resources to cope with stress without depleting them.

Social relationships can also help optimistic people fulfill their positive expectancies for other goal domains. When pursuing goals, a major way to judge goal progress is to look at how others are doing. *Social comparison* occurs when you look around you and see other people doing better or worse than you are: they are more or less attractive or productive[7] than you are, or one of you has a BMW and the other doesn't. Every time you check to see whether you are keeping up with the Joneses, you are engaging in social comparison. One

[7]Insert your own relevant adjective here: thinner, smarter, generating higher sales, whatever.

important function of social comparison is to provide a standard against which you evaluate your goals and your progress. When you see that you're doing better than others, that feedback indicates you're doing well, maybe even better than you need to. When you see that you're doing worse than others, that feedback indicates you're doing poorly, maybe worse than you should.

I started playing the violin at age 9, which is considered old in the violin-learning world (although young in the world at large). My memory is that I was a fine violinist as a kid. I could read music better than most of the other budding preteen violinists, and I was making great progress through my workbooks. I had no idea who Isaac Stern or Itzhak Perlman was, and although I had a vague idea that there were "prodigies" out there, I certainly didn't know any, and I had no idea of how good such a person would be. I just kept on playing the violin, and at some point I got to be good enough that my parents and, eventually, even nonrelatives could bear to hear me play.

People who take up instruments like the violin as adults don't have it so easy. Some disadvantages to learning a musical instrument as an adult arise from being an adult per se; for example, it's harder to adjust to what are sometimes awkward physical poses involved in playing an instrument like the violin or flute. However, I think adults' biggest disadvantage is the same as the biggest motivation when trying to learn an instrument: they love to listen to it. Prospective adult violinists have in their mind not the average beginning violinist's performance of "Twinkle, Twinkle, Little Star," but a professional soloist's performance of the Brahms Violin Concerto. In terms of social comparison, it's like living in a hut next door to a mansion—very discouraging.

Upward comparison (in which you are doing worse than others) can result in dejection, because you seem to be falling behind others. You might start to doubt your abilities and personal qualities and ruminate about your lack of progress. Conversely, downward comparison (in which you are doing better than others) can result in happiness, because one of the sources of happiness is the perception that you are progressing quickly toward your goal. In this case, you seem to be racing ahead of others. As a consequence, in many circumstances downward comparisons are preferred to upward comparisons. For example, women with breast cancer generally prefer to compare themselves with others who are worse off[8] rather than others who are better off. Feeling that you're doing well compared with other people could protect against anxiety and provide a sense of hope.

Nonetheless, upward comparisons are not necessarily harmful, and downward comparisons are not necessarily beneficial. In particular, when your own effort is critical to bringing about good or bad outcomes, upward comparisons (Ms. Y sold more widgets than I did) can be more helpful than downward comparisons (I sold more widgets than Mr. X). Upward comparisons do not have to be discouraging. They can be inspirational. Comparing yourself with someone who is doing better than you are can give you ideas about how to do well yourself. In contrast, comparing yourself with someone who is doing worse can make you complacent.

These highly optimistic law students illustrate inspiration from upward comparison:

> All throughout this semester I always looked to see what somebody else was doing to see if I could improve what I was doing. If I thought they were doing something better, then I'd adopt the way that they were doing it. I was most curious about these students who spent all their time in the library, to see if they would do well. They had a better work ethic than I did, and it made me think about how I could be more disciplined about my studying.

> I think there were people who did better than I did in preparing for exams, and they got better grades, and they seem to be getting more job interviews. It doesn't make me feel that I'm not as adequate as they are; I'm just going to do things differently personally in getting ready for exams. I'm going to focus more on preparing.

In contrast, this pessimistic student failed to be inspired:

[8]Interestingly, these women did not need to know someone who was doing worse to make downward social comparisons. If no suitable comparison was available, they would *imagine* someone who was doing worse: an older woman imagined how much worse it would be for a younger woman; a woman who had had a lumpectomy imagined how much worse it would be for a woman who had had a mastectomy.

People who were doing better, they were paying more attention in class and reviewing the material a lot. I didn't feel very competitive with them; I just wanted to get by. I guess I should have felt more competitive with them, because it probably would have helped my grades.

Upward comparisons, although potentially informative, can also be threatening. Especially in the face of stress or failure, they can make you feel inadequate. When people feel their own performance is threateningly bad, they forgo the inspiration of upward comparisons and instead engage in downward comparisons in an attempt to feel better. This is particularly true when the prospects for better performance in the future look dim. Therefore, the combination of poor performance and pessimism about the future leads people to try to feel better about their performances by comparing themselves with people doing even worse. The problem with this strategy is that downward comparison doesn't improve performance and leads to a downward spiral. Pessimistic college students with declining GPAs lowered their comparison levels so they always compared themselves to people doing worse than they were, which led them to get even worse grades. In the long run, downward comparisons provide examples only of how to do worse, not how to do better. At this point in my musical career, I will not make myself a better violinist by listening to recordings of preteen beginner violinists, because they won't give me anything to shoot for in my own playing.

Conversely, upward comparisons can provide examples of how to do better and avoid stress or failure in the future. Optimistic students with declining GPAs continued to compare themselves to students getting better grades than they did, and their GPAs improved. Optimism, therefore, keeps people inspired by making them more inclined to examine and learn from the behavior of people doing better than they are. For an optimistic violinist who is ready to take her playing to the next level, listening to recordings of professional soloists could inspire learning new techniques or using different vibrato or phrasings.

But what about those negative consequences of upward comparison? Is it possible, when comparing yourself with a better-off standard, to feel inadequate ("Why am I not that good?") rather than inspired ("I could be that good")? Absolutely. However, optimists appear to use their comparisons to extract the most beneficial kind of information. Upward comparisons are more likely to yield inspiration to optimists and discouragement to pessimists. When pessimistic students did make upward comparisons, they tended to be depressed rather than inspired.

This phenomenon has also been demonstrated in an experiment in which a student would work alongside a "peer" (actually an experimenter) who did either much better or much worse than the student at solving anagrams. When the student worked next to a slower "peer," she tended to rate her ability higher and was in a better mood after the experiment. The downward comparison was reassuring ("It could be worse"). Reactions to the faster "peer," however, were quite different for optimists and pessimists. Pessimists rated their ability lower and were in a worse mood, because the upward comparison was threatening to them ("Why am I not that good?"). Optimists also rated their ability lower, but optimists who worked next to the fast peer had just as much improvement in mood as the students who worked next to the slow peer. Even though they weren't denying that they might not be good at anagrams, they didn't seem to be discouraged about that. It seems reasonable to conclude that they were inspired rather than threatened by their faster peer ("That could be me").

Optimists can also extract the least depressing information from downward comparisons. Although downward comparisons did not seem to be particularly threatening and could be ego-protective for students, they also have a potential downside that might emerge when the stakes are higher: when life and health, rather than just a GPA, are on the line. For example, multiple sclerosis is a chronic degenerative disease of the nervous system, and downward comparisons (that is, with worse-off others) have potential for threatening meaning ("That could be me"). Pessimistic patients with multiple sclerosis were depressed when they made downward comparisons, probably because they tended to interpret downward comparisons in a threatening and depressive way ("That could be me") rather than in an ego-protective way ("It could be worse"). Optimists, on the other hand, were not depressed by downward comparisons.

In all these studies, optimistic expectations about the future let people look upward for inspiration without being threatened by their current performance and look downward for comfort without being threatened by a potentially negative future. The kinds of information optimistic people get from the way they compare themselves with others helps them stay engaged with their goals and perform better in the future.

Yes, we are a social species, but social relationships can have both positive and negative consequences. We can have negative, conflict-ridden interactions with others, we can feel inferior to them, and their help can even make us feel inadequate to life's tasks. The positive expectancies that come from optimism, however, seem to lead to positive relationships in which believing the best of others brings out the best in them, people who are excelling become sources of inspiration rather than envy, and the perception of support buffers us against stressful events. The mortality data suggest a particularly intriguing possibility: if optimism leads to better social relationships, and better social relationships decrease mortality risk, does optimism actually lead to a longer life? Read on.

CHAPTER FIVE

·····································

Mixed Blessing
Optimists and Their Health

I remember my first exposure to health psychology—in my undergraduate Abnormal Psychology class—vividly. In the course of his lecture on health psychology, the professor, Dr. Tom Schoeneman, described a study in which psychological factors affected surgical recovery. I was astounded that such a thing could be true: states of mind actually affected how fast people's physical bodies healed. It seemed magical, almost improbable, and immensely intriguing. As a consequence, when it came time to choose a graduate school, I chose a place where I could study health psychology, particularly the phenomenon that struck me as an undergraduate: how states of mind affect physiology. Much of my career has been absorbed with that phenomenon, and I hope Tom will forgive my having forgotten much of the rest of the lecture and take credit for starting me on this path.

Almost 20 years later, there are many more people familiar with the "mind–body" phenomenon than there were at that time. Nonetheless, some people are still skeptical. Last year I gave a lecture at a series of educational events for family practitioners. The lecture focused on how "mind–body" phenomena could account for some of the complaints that practitioners see all the time, like chest pain, difficulty breathing, and headache. After every event, at least one evaluation form expressed disbelief. Not scientific, it would say. Not real.

This attitude comes from a long tradition in Western thought that separates mental and physical phenomena. Originally intended to give church and science their own domains—the soul and the physical body—this thinking has come down to us as a skepticism that the "mind" and the "body" can affect each other. In fact, this skepticism is untenable, because we have progressed well beyond the stage when it is possible to believe that anything about the mind is not based in the physical body. We know that thoughts, emotions, attitudes, and states of mind are based in the brain in the same way that walking is based in the legs, breathing is based in the lungs and diaphragm, and circulation is based in the heart and blood vessels. The brain—and therefore the mind—*is* part of the body, and so even the term *mind–body* is weird. It's like saying there's a walking–body connection. Walking is just something the body does, and so are thoughts, emotions, attitudes, and states of mind.

The mind being based in the brain, the "mind–body" connection is really the "brain–body" connection, which turns out not to be mystical but anatomical. Given anatomical connections between the brain and other parts of the body, like the legs, the lungs and diaphragm, the heart and blood vessels, and the immune system, things that the brain does, like thinking or feeling, might affect the function of other parts of the body that are doing other things, like circulating blood or fighting a virus. The ultimate question in the context of this book, of course, is whether the thoughts and feelings that occur in the optimistic brain create an optimistic, healthy body.

MAKING THE CONNECTION

The fact is, the brain is connected to other organ systems in myriad ways. Communications from the brain travel neurologically—that is, directly through nerves—and endocrinologically, through the bloodstream via molecular messengers. We are most aware of the connection between the brain and the rest of the body when we undertake voluntary movement. When I want to type a word, my brain sends a signal via motor neurons to my fingers, and they press the appropriate keys (most of the time). When I want a drink of water, I stand up and go to the sink, and I get a drink of water.

There are also connections from the brain to other body parts that affect involuntary functions (such as what the digestive system and the kidneys do with the water I drank), and the brain controls those systems as well. There is a special branch of the nervous system that sends messages from the brain that control many involuntary functions. This branch, the autonomic nervous system, controls activities such as respiratory rate, heart rate, digestion, blood flow (via constriction and expansion of blood vessels), and perspiration. There are two branches of the autonomic nervous system: one that coordinates these functions to meet short-term demands on the body (the sympathetic branch) and one to foster long-term projects by the body (the parasympathetic branch). To understand the nature of these projects and demands, think about the circumstances under which the sympathetic and parasympathetic branches of the nervous system developed, when goals didn't have to do with meeting deadlines or keeping the house clean, but with survival itself. Long-term goals included finding food, shelter, and mates, for example. Under most circumstances, these goals would take priority. Sometimes, however, you might have had to abandon the pursuit of those goals to meet short-term demands. These demands would take precedence because if you didn't deal with them immediately, you would be dead, and the long-term goals would therefore be superfluous. Dead men not only tell no tales; they also have a very difficult time finding food, shelter, and—perhaps especially—mates. Short-term demands might be imposed by predators who want to make progress toward their food goals by eating you, storms or floods that can drown you, or even other humans who want your food, shelter, and mate and are willing to hit you in the head with a club to get them.

When facing these kinds of short-term demands, you basically have two behavioral options: fight or flee. These options engender the famous term *fight or flight*. The fight-or-flight response occurs when the autonomic nervous system shifts to sympathetic responses to meet short-term demands. Respiration and heart rate increase, blood vessels in the viscera (internal organs such as the intestines and liver) and the distant extremities (like fingers) constrict, blood vessels in the heart and large muscles dilate, and sweating increases. All of these changes occur so the parts of the body you will use to fight or flee—the large muscles—are getting lots of blood carrying oxygen and nutrients, and the parts of the body you don't really need at the moment aren't using up as much. For example, energy can be redirected from digestion to meet the physical demands of fighting or fleeing.

The brain uses the endocrine system to help in fight or flight as well. The endocrine system usually works on long-term physical projects, releasing substances into the bloodstream that direct metabolic rate, sexual development, growth, and so on. When long-term projects are put on hold to meet short-term fight-or-flight demands, the brain instead causes the release of a hormone called *cortisol.* The main effect of cortisol is to cause the liver (among other sites) to provide glucose, the source of energy that the heart and large muscles will burn in fighting or fleeing.

Through these changes in the autonomic nervous system and the endocrine system, the body maintains allostasis. Many people are familiar with the idea of homeostasis, the maintenance of physiological competence through stability—keeping a steady blood pressure, for example. *Allostasis* means maintaining physiological competence through change rather than stability—raising blood pressure to fight or flee, for example, and then lowering blood pressure again when the crisis is over. In a perfect allostatic world, the body responds to short-term demands when needed and reverts to long-term projects otherwise, maintaining allostatic balance. In modern life, however, short-term demands are the exception rather than the rule. Rather than predators or storms, we are more likely to be confronting social conflicts, stressful jobs, or chronic illnesses. Rather than allostatic balance, these demands result in allostatic *load*, in which the body's typical short-term response to short-term demands persists long-term. When the same changes that are helpful in meeting short-term demands occur over long periods of time, they can be damaging to health. For example, higher blood pressure caused by sympathetic nervous system activity can, over long periods of time, damage blood vessels and lead to atherosclerosis (hardening of the arteries), heart attack, and stroke. Higher cortisol over long periods of time suppresses the immune system, damages parts of the brain, and reduces insulin sensitivity, potentially leading to adult-onset diabetes, among other negative consequences.

Optimism comes into the picture because—as I argued in previous chapters—optimism is psychologically beneficial in lots of ways, including its influence on how people deal with stress. When social conflicts, stressful jobs, or chronic illnesses befall them, the optimists are more likely to address those situations actively and therefore lose fewer net resources compared with pessimists—that is, optimists experience less stress. If long-term stress negatively affects health via immune suppression or high blood pressure, and optimism can reduce the amount of stress that people experience, then optimism should be one of those aspects of the mind that positively affect the body.

OPTIMISM EMBODIED

A number of studies have examined whether optimists benefit physically from their beliefs in a positive future. These studies have looked at whether optimism is of benefit when health is challenged by heart disease, cancer, or HIV. That is, does someone who is optimistic live longer with cancer or HIV or recover better from cardiac surgery? Based on folk wisdom, the answer seems obvious. People with a "positive attitude" or "will to live" recover better and survive longer.[1] Scientific wisdom also points to a potential benefit specifically from dispositional optimism. Anatomical connections between the brain and the cardiovascular, endocrine, and immune systems mean that optimistic beliefs that reduce stress—and therefore the stress-related changes in the brain—could also affect allostatic load and health. For example, better-regulated cortisol predicts longer survival with breast cancer. If optimism reduces stress and improves cortisol regulation, perhaps optimistic women with breast cancer will survive longer.

One of the earliest studies to examine the health effects of optimism was published in 1989 and tested whether optimism could predict recovery from surgery—the health outcome that had interested me so much as an undergraduate just a couple of years before. In this case, the surgery was coronary artery bypass graft surgery (CABG, pronounced "cabbage"). CABG surgery becomes necessary when atherosclerotic plaques obstruct the arteries that supply blood to the heart. Surgeons typically take vessels from the leg and, after stopping the heart, use them to reroute blood around the blockage. These bypasses provide better blood flow to the heart. CABG is a major sur-

---

[1]But what about the person who is "too mean to die"? Folk wisdom on this topic seems just as helpful as folk wisdom on the topic of choosing a good partner (do "birds of a feather flock together" or do "opposites attract"?) or how much time to spend with that partner (does "absence make the heart grow fonder" or is it "out of sight, out of mind"?)

gery that lasts several hours, requires several days in the hospital for acute recovery, and takes several months for complete recovery. Nonetheless, it usually offers good relief from cardiac symptoms such as chest pain, and so it is performed rather frequently. Over a half-million CABG operations were performed in the United States in 2001.

This study followed about 50 men undergoing CABG surgery through the surgery and the 6 months afterward. In the short term, during the surgery, optimists showed fewer indications of damage to their hearts—a serious surgical complication—than did pessimists. These indications were limited to subtle changes in a cardiac enzyme, except for the most pessimistic person in the group. He showed more serious indications of heart damage (changes in his EKG during the procedure that indicated a possible heart attack). In the longer term, during the days after the surgery, the more optimistic men were up and walking around their hospital rooms sooner than their more pessimistic counterparts, which is important because it reduces the risk of blood clots, and the staff members in charge of cardiac rehabilitation rated optimists' progress more advanced. (The staff did not know who was an optimist and who was a pessimist in terms of questionnaire scores, although they may have observed signs that a man was optimistic or pessimistic, such as his outlook on the future and attitude toward rehabilitation, while working with him.)

In the even longer term, after 6 months, optimistic men were more likely to have resumed exercise, more quickly returned to their recreational activities, and had fewer cardiac symptoms. From the beginning of the surgical process to the end, men who were more optimistic had advantages over less optimistic men. Very likely, as the preceding chapters have illustrated, their optimistic beliefs helped them to cope better with the challenges of rehabilitation and to make the most of their social networks, social comparisons, and social support. The accompanying reduction in stress would reduce unnecessary demands on the heart (that is, allostatic load). Moreover, because they were the first to start recovery, optimistic men probably worked harder on recovery *goals*, which ranged from walking to participating in recreational activities.

Over the next decade, more studies appeared showing the benefits of optimism after CABG surgery. The initial CABG study was followed by a second study of over 200 patients (this time both men and women) that reported that the most pessimistic quarter of these patients were more than three times more likely than the most optimistic quarter to be rehospitalized for reasons related to coronary artery disease—the reason they had to have CABG surgery in the first place. Another research group found that 8 months after CABG surgery, patients (both men and women) who were more optimistic had less chest pain, experienced less negative mood like anxiety and depression, and were more satisfied with their activity levels, sexual functioning, and life in general.

New studies also showed that optimism could be beneficial after a less invasive kind of cardiac surgery: in this case, "roto-rooter" surgery (also known to the persnickety as *percutaneous transluminal coronary angioplasty*), in which a balloon is inflated inside the coronary arteries to move the blockage aside rather than running a bypass around it. People in the bottom third of an index combining various psychologically beneficial beliefs (including optimism) were three times more likely to have a new coronary event within 6 months of their original surgery than people who were in the top third. That is, optimistic people were less likely to need a repeat of the roto-rooter surgery, to need bypass surgery, to have a heart attack, or to die of coronary artery disease. Furthermore, over the 4 years following the original surgery, people who were more optimistic had fewer coronary events.

Even those who had a heart transplant, the most extreme cardiac surgery, benefited from optimism. Consistent with the CABG and angioplasty studies, transplant recipients who were more optimistic recovered from their surgery better and took medications to prevent rejection of the heart more reliably, and although both optimistic and pessimistic patients developed infections, the average pessimist's first infection occurred 61 days after surgery, whereas the average optimist's first infection was 126 days after surgery.

Although one recent study did not find that optimism was associated with the length of hospital stay after CABG or valve replacement, the bulk of these studies have found that optimistic cardiac patients ultimately do better than pessimistic cardiac patients. A skeptic could argue that those who were in better shape before surgery (for example, as indicated by less pain or fewer blockages of the coronary arteries) would be most optimistic and that being in better health before surgery leads to both optimism and better health after surgery. That is, better health is both cause for optimism and a predictor of better recovery; optimism does not *cause* better recovery.[2] The evidence, however, says otherwise. First, all these studies statistically equated patients on their presurgical status, so the results come from testing the effects of optimism given equal presurgical health. Second, the transplant study takes advantage of a phenomenon called "clean slate." In essence, a heart transplant gives each patient a new start, because the amount of disease in the old heart is not really relevant to how well the patient does *after* the transplant (after all, the diseased heart is now gone). Even with the clean slate, expectations for recovery before the transplant predicted health after the transplant.

Optimism is also associated with better outcomes in a very different domain: pregnancy. As it turns out, stress during pregnancy affects not only the mother's psychological well-being but also the development of her baby. Mothers who have stressful pregnancies produce excess stress hormones like cortisol, and these stress hormones can contribute to early labor, which produces smaller babies, and inhibit fetal growth so that even full-term babies are smaller. Smaller babies, in turn, have a higher risk for health problems.[3] Two studies that included over 300 women found that mothers who were more optimistic benefited in that their pregnancies were longer and, after equating pregnancy length, their babies were bigger.

As in the cardiac surgery studies, optimism benefitted physical health; in this case, it contributed to longer pregnancies and bigger babies. These studies also showed that optimism reduced the amount of stress experienced in the latter part of pregnancy, which could reduce the amount of stress hormones produced. One of the studies

[2]This is the well-known "third-variable problem." The classic example has to do with the positive correlation between the murder rate and ice cream consumption: when the murder rate goes up, so does ice cream consumption. Does ice cream lead people to commit murder? Do people like to have ice cream after they've murdered someone? Well, of course, neither. Heat waves can lead to both higher ice cream consumption and increases in violence, but that doesn't mean one caused the other.

[3]I have also heard that bigger babies are faster to sleep through the night. I don't know if this is definitely true, but it seems to me that sleeping through the night would be a huge bonus to the health protective effects of a higher birth weight. Of course, there is the delivery issue that comes up with big babies, but it's better not to think about that too much.

also showed that optimistic mothers exercised more, which helped contribute to their longer pregnancies. Like the optimistic cardiac patients, optimistic pregnant women were both less stressed and more physically active, and their relaxed, active approaches to pregnancy helped them and their babies be healthier. As in the cardiac literature, an exception exists—optimism and stress didn't predict outcomes in early pregnancy as well as they did in later pregnancy—but the preponderance of the evidence supports optimism as beneficial.

THE OTHER SHOE DROPS

For cardiac patients and pregnant women, optimism seems to make a positive contribution to recovery and health. What about other health problems such as cancer and AIDS? Studies of cancer patients yield much less consistent evidence of a beneficial effect. Three studies have examined whether optimism affects survival with cancer, and each produced different results: one study found that optimism increased survival for some people but not others, one study found that optimism did not increase survival at all, and one study found that optimism did increase survival. The first study, published in 1996, included patients with diverse cancers (breast, lung, head or neck, gynecologic, prostate, colorectal, and gastrointestinal, among others). Eight months after the beginning of the study, almost 30% of these patients had died. The question was, were optimists more likely than pessimists to survive? The answer was yes, but only among the youngest patients, those under 60 years of age. Among these younger patients, survivors were about two-thirds as pessimistic[4] as those who died. However, among older patients, those who died and those who survived over the 8 months of the study were equally pessimistic.

A second study, published in 2003, also suggested that optimism could prolong survival with cancer. This study focused only on head and neck cancer. One year after the study began, almost half of the

---

[4]In this study, pessimism and optimism were studied separately, and only the pessimism scale differentiated between patients who were alive versus dead at 8 months.

original 101 patients had died. The study showed that the most pessimistic patients (those who would be categorized as very to moderately pessimistic) were the most likely to die: 2 out of 3 had died after a year. Patients who were moderately to very optimistic, on the other hand, were less likely to die: only 2 out of 5 had died after a year. These survival rates indicate that pessimists were over 50% more likely to die during the 1-year study period compared with their optimistic counterparts.

The third study, published in 2004, focused on lung cancer patients. The advantage of the study was a very long follow-up period of several years, as opposed to a year or less in the previous studies. Over that period, 96% of the 179 patients in the study died, and the study focused on how *long* people lived. For the first couple of years after the study started, it looked as if very optimistic people had a survival advantage over moderately optimistic or pessimistic people. At year, about 75% of very optimistic people were alive compared with about 60% of moderately optimistic and pessimistic people; at 2 years, about 35% of very optimistic people were alive compared with about 25% of moderately optimistic and pessimistic people. However, by 3 years, only 20–25% of all groups were still alive, so being optimistic did not confer an advantage over the long term.

Apparently some people had been waiting for the other optimism shoe to drop and therefore had what could only be described as gleeful reactions to the results of the lung cancer study. I got a photocopy of an article from the *Wall Street Journal* with a happy note attached from one of my faculty colleagues that proclaimed, "There is hope for curmudgeons like myself." The title of the article: "Fighting Cancer with a Frown: Research Questions Role of Optimism in Beating the Disease: 'The Tyranny of Positive Thinking.' " *Newsweek* weighed in with an article on its website called "The Trouble with Optimism."

Were the tough headlines warranted? On one hand, it would be easy to discount a single study that failed to support a survival advantage for optimists. You will notice that I did exactly that a few pages back with the one cardiac surgery study and the one pregnancy study that failed to show benefits of optimism. Science is like sports in this way: in any given study, like any given game, anything can happen. It usually doesn't, but the possibility of an underdog having a good day against the favorite exists in science as in sports.[5] No one study is perfect, and so no one study reveals the whole truth. So, even given this one finding that optimism doesn't increase cancer survival, there are arguments in favor of optimism being beneficial: First, the study did not show that "fighting cancer with a frown" made pessimists healthier or live longer. It only showed that there was not a large survival benefit to optimism. No study to my knowledge has shown a survival advantage to *pessimism*. Fighting cancer with a frown does not help, although it might not always hurt very much. Second, the earliest study, which studied several different kinds of cancers, suggested that the advantage of optimism is greatest in younger people. Why? It could be that cancer poses a greater threat to younger people's goals and resources (for example, the possibility that they might not see their young children grow up) and is therefore more stressful for them. If stress is a bigger issue for younger people than for older people, optimism may be more important in influencing survival. It could also be that cancer in younger people is biologically different from that in older people and so differently susceptible to stress hormones, for example. Most people (75%) in the head and neck cancer study were under age 65, but only about half of the people in the lung cancer study were under age 65. Perhaps the age difference between the samples affected the outcomes of these two studies. Third, maybe lung cancer is the wrong kind of cancer to study. Cancer is actually not one disease, but dozens of different diseases. Some of them are more influenced by the autonomic nervous system, the endocrine system, and the immune system than others, and perhaps lung cancer is one of those that is not influenced very much.

Despite these very good arguments, it would be premature to dismiss the lung cancer study. You have to take the inconsistency seriously because there is another disease for which optimism has inconsistent results as well: HIV infection. In a way, inconsistency in the HIV literature has to be taken even more seriously than that in the cancer literature because alternative sources of inconsistency in the

[5]Since moving to Kentucky, I have learned not to give up the chance to bet on any gray horse going off at long odds, based on this principle. (The importance of the horse being gray is to prevent you from losing *all* your money betting on long shots. Because fewer thoroughbreds are gray than bay, brown, or chestnut, limiting your crazy bets to gray horses keeps you in the same neighborhood with sane betting.) See Chapter 6 for the effects of optimism on gambling, addiction to solitaire, and other potential problem behaviors.

cancer literature (for example, those arising from the type of cancer studied) are not issues when studying HIV. Although HIV makes people vulnerable to a lot of different diseases, the underlying pathology is the same. HIV infects immune cells called *helper T cells* or *CD4 T cells*, which conduct or direct the immune system. As the disease progresses, fewer and fewer of these cells survive, leaving the rest of the immune system aimlessly sitting around waiting for instructions. As a consequence, infections are able to run rampant and, eventually, kill the infected person.

The argument for why optimism should be protective against HIV progression is the same as for other diseases: optimism leads to less resource loss and therefore less stress, and because stress accelerates HIV progression, optimism should slow HIV progression. However, even more frequently than in cancer studies, dispositional optimism does not seem to benefit health in HIV studies. In one study of HIV-infected men, dispositional optimism was unrelated to how fast helper T cells declined over 2 years. In another study, dispositional optimism was unrelated to how long HIV-infected men survived after they were diagnosed with AIDS.[6]

Most recently, optimism's potential for benefit in HIV has been rehabilitated a little bit. A study of HIV-infected patients in Los Angeles public health clinics found somewhat more promising results in a more heterogeneous group (for example, women were included) that separated out the effects of pessimism and optimism in predicting changes in the amount of HIV virus in the bloodstream (viral load) and the number of helper T cells over about 18 months. In this group, lower pessimism predicted lower viral load. Higher optimism predicted higher numbers of helper T cells, but only up to the point of moderate optimism. Being very optimistic did not offer any advantage over being moderately optimistic. This study was the first to show a health advantage for optimists with HIV; another study has recently

---

[6]An AIDS diagnosis in this study was based on the 1987 diagnostic criteria for AIDS, which included a series of diseases that are uncommon unless severe immunosuppression is present: for example, certain bacterial infections, severe yeast infections in the airway, a pneumonia caused by *pneumocystic carinii*, severe herpes outbreaks, and the like. Newer criteria include severe immunosuppression in the absence of these diseases, known as *opportunistic infections*.

also found higher optimism to predict higher numbers of T cells in a diverse sample.

One rule of thumb for the scientific literature is that the more robust an effect is (for example, the effect of optimism on health), the more often it should show up. To return to the sports analogy, when a team is very strong, although it will occasionally lose, it should beat its opponent most of the time. On the other hand, if the team is not very strong, it should win only occasionally. In sports, one way to judge the strength of a team is by seeing how often it wins. In science, one indicator of the strength of an effect is how often it shows up. In the case of optimism, a benefit shows up more often than not for heart disease, especially in recovery from surgery, and for pregnancy, suggesting that optimism has a fairly strong beneficial effect on these conditions. For cancer, however, the home team won only two out of three games (and one of those might be better characterized as a draw), and for HIV, only two out of four. Because of the work I do, I can't help noticing that the more the immune system gets involved (essentially in HIV, sometimes in cancer, and more peripherally in heart disease and pregnancy), the less beneficial optimism is for you.

CAN OPTIMISM SUPPRESS IMMUNITY?

That brings me to the second reason I could not immediately dismiss the new cancer findings. I study the effects of optimism on the immune system, and I know optimism has unusual effects on immunity. This is not a conclusion I came to easily. When I first began to study optimism and the immune system, I started with the premise that I keep coming back to in this chapter: stress has negative effects on health, including the immune system; optimism predicts less stress; therefore, optimism should protect against negative effects on the immune system.

In my first study on this topic (my dissertation research at UCLA), I found evidence for exactly that. First-year law students who were more optimistic before they started law school had higher numbers of immune cells and more effective cells than students who were more pessimistic. This was mainly true for optimism about law school: the more students thought they would be successful in law school and achieve what they wanted, the more helper T cells they had, the better tumor-killing ability their natural killer cells had, and (to a lesser extent) the more cytotoxic T cells they had.[7] Dispositional optimism was less beneficial than law school optimism, predicting only slightly higher numbers of cytotoxic T cells. This was the first published study to report a relationship between optimism, stress, and the immune system in healthy people, and it was well received in the scientific community and in the popular press.

Flush with this success, when I started as a new faculty member at the University of Kentucky, I was eager to continue in this line of research, so I collected some preliminary data on a class of first-year law students and went to work applying for research funding for a large study of optimism and immunity, using these preliminary data to demonstrate that my ideas were sound and I was capable of collecting this kind of data. Analyzing those data, however, was somewhat dismaying. Optimism and immune function were related in the UK law students, but the relationship was not as strong as in the UCLA law students. I thought about that a lot. Why? Was there some difference between UK students and UCLA students that made optimism more important at UCLA than it was at UK?

My first (and, we shall see, lucky) guess was that perhaps UCLA recruited students nationwide, whereas UK recruited more local students. Maybe when students had to move far away from home, they had to rely more on their own optimism to adjust to law school, because they had left resources like social networks back home. I went back to my UK sample and separated the students into those who had moved away to go to law school and those who were already living nearby. Sure enough, for the students who had moved away, the strong relationship between optimism and the immune system re-emerged. Hooray! I had figured it out. Optimism predicted better immune function—in this case, response to an immune challenge in the skin—but mostly among students who had to rely on their optimism to cope with the stress of law school.

Still waiting for that other shoe? I had imagined that for students with more access to social resources because of their proximity to

---

[7]Natural killer cells and cytotoxic T cells are members of the orchestra directed by the helper T cell. When signaled to do so, these cells kill other "bad" cells, like tumor cells or cells that have been infected by a virus.

friends and family, the relationship between optimism and immunity would be trivial. Pessimistic students would have social resources to make up for their lack of optimism. That would explain the small effects I had found in the entire sample. Good-sized effect (among students who moved) + trivial effect (among students who did not move) = small effect (in the sample as a whole).

Boy, was I wrong. Not only was there an effect among the students who were already living nearby, but it was strong, and it was *negative*. That is, students who went to law school in their hometowns had *worse* immunity when they were *more* optimistic. This, despite the fact that they were not only optimistic but also had social resources close at hand.

Now, the possibility existed that this negative relationship was a fluke. Even the underdog can win the game under the right conditions. So I went back to my original data from UCLA. Surprisingly, there were more students who were already living in Los Angeles than I had remembered, so my initial guess (UK students were more likely to go to law school near home than UCLA students) was wrong (about an equal proportion stayed home in both samples). However, my "fluke" finding turned out to be no fluke at all. At UCLA, dispositionally optimistic students who stayed home had fewer helper T cells than pessimists; and the reverse was true of students who moved away.

I am not the only person to observe diverse effects of optimism on the immune system. Two other studies have found essentially the same thing outside law school. The first study was a laboratory study that was mostly about the ability to *control* stress: in this case, intermittent blasts of white noise. One group in this study could control the noise by pressing a button sequence (which they had to discover for themselves). The second group couldn't control the noise, but they thought they could, because they had the buttons and no one had told them they couldn't. The third group couldn't control the noise, and they had no buttons. They knew they had to, as the experimenters instructed them, "just sit and listen to the noise." The main finding of the study was that when people could control the noise, the noise had no effect on their immune systems. Believing they could control the noise was nearly as good. Only when they could not control the noise did the stress adversely affect their immune systems (in this case, natural killer cells).

Tucked away at the very end of the research report was an interesting tidbit: the way optimism affected these changes. When people had control over the noise, either real or illusory, optimism had the "expected" relationship with the immune system, so that people who were more optimistic had higher natural killer cell numbers than those who were more pessimistic. However, the reverse was true when there was no control—people who were more optimistic had lower natural killer cell numbers than those who were more pessimistic. Optimism was protective against the stress's effect on the immune system, but only when dealing with the stress was easy. When dealing with the stress was difficult, optimism made people more immunologically vulnerable.

Another paper studied the effects of everyday stresses on women's T cell counts. Again, optimism had an unexpected effect. When stresses lasted less than 1 week, optimism had the "usual" effect: more optimism equaled more T cells. However, if the stress lasted more than 1 week, the reverse was again true. Optimistic women had fewer T cells than pessimistic women with this longer-lasting stress. As in the laboratory study, it looked as if optimism was beneficial only when things were easy (that is, stress resolved quickly). When things were hard (that is, stress did not resolve quickly), optimists were vulnerable.

RUNNING ON EMPTY

Both of these papers had an explanation for why optimists were vulnerable: their positive future didn't come true. The researchers thought that when optimistic people encountered difficult situations in which they couldn't control stress or make it end within a short period of time, they basically fell apart and their immune systems suffered.

This explanation made no sense to me for two very basic reasons. First, optimistic people typically do very well psychologically under all kinds of stress. Second, some studies had actually looked at what happens to optimists when things go wrong, typically in the context of bad medical news. In one study, optimism was measured before couples underwent *in vitro* fertilization procedures. Now, usually by the time a couple undergoes infertility treatment, the partners are highly invested, both emotionally and financially, in conceiving a baby. However, the procedures are far from fail-safe, because only one out of three *in vitro* fertilization attempts succeeds and the odds are worse the older the prospective mom is (according to the American Pregnancy Association, less than 1 in 10 if she is over 40 years old). Most important for the question of optimism, it's a basically uncontrollable procedure because little the prospective parents can do will affect their odds of conceiving. If optimists are likely to fall apart under uncontrollable stress, this is the place it should show up. What the study actually found was that optimistic people were *more* resilient when *in vitro* attempts failed. The pessimistic people—those who didn't believe in a positive future to start with—were nonetheless the ones who were most depressed when that positive future failed to manifest.

If disappointment wasn't the answer, I had to figure out why optimistic students close to their friends and family would have *worse* immunity. This effect goes against the whole idea that optimism and social resources provide double protection, because in this case they seemed to cancel each other out. The best clue came from my oldest data. Before I did my dissertation, I collected some questionnaires from law students about what they found most stressful about law school. Here is the Law School Top 7 Most Stressful Things list:

7. Difficulty of subject matter
6. Not enough *time* for recreation
5. Not enough *time* for family and friends
4. Infrequency or lack of feedback
3. Not enough *time* to cover all the material
2. Not knowing how to prepare or study the material
1. Amount of *time* required for studying

Obviously, there are some aspects of law school that are just about law school: the material is hard (#7), and it comes in a form that most students are seeing for the first time (legal documents) and in language that they don't understand (what the heck does *res ipsa loquitor* mean?) (#2). If you want a good description of how unnerving this can be, especially for students who mastered the material in their undergraduate courses with a relative degree of ease and hence got into law school, read Scott Turow's account of his first year at Harvard Law School, *One L*. Here is how he describes the disconcerting experience of trying to learn legal material:

> It's obvious, in looking back, that one of the things which made me feel most at sea initially was the fact that I barely understood much of what I was reading or hearing. . . . What we were going through seemed like a kind of Berlitz assault in "Legal," a language I didn't speak and in which I was being forced to read and think sixteen hours a day.

Another aspect of law school that is particularly difficult for first-semester law students is the fact that they generally don't get any grades until their final exam (#4). Again, most of these students are used to getting almost all A's in their classes (if not straight A's). Now they are struggling with the material, they're not sure if they're getting it right, and they won't find out until it's too late to do anything about their grades (that is, after final exams). Not knowing whether they're going to get a good grade particularly stresses first-year students because first-year grades have a big impact on some stepping stones to a good job after graduation: getting on the law review (the editorial board of the school's legal journal) or getting a good job for the summer between first and second years. Even worse, law school professors grade on a strict curve, which means that only a certain percentage of students will get A's regardless of how well or poorly the class performs as a whole. This causes students to wonder not only about their own mastery of the material, but also about how they stack up against everyone else. As we've seen, sometimes these kinds of social comparisons can be beneficial (upward inspiration or downward consolation), but other times they can be devastating (upward and downward threat).

These are important aspects of why law school is stressful, but the thing that really sticks out about the law school Top 7 list is time. Because the material is difficult and there is a lot of it, law students spend an average of 40 hours a week studying outside class. (To get an idea of just how much time that is, 40 hours translates to 4 hours every weeknight and 10 hours per day on weekends.) Free time is almost unheard of. Hence, a lot of law school stress comes from the fact that there are only so many hours in the day, and it's hard to fit law school time demands (#1, #3) with any kind of life outside law school (#5, #6). Here is how one of the law students in my study described the weeks leading up to finals:

> The most stressful part has, obviously, been preparing for finals, just because for weeks straight, all you do is get up as soon as you can in the morning and open a book. And you read all day long, every day, until you finally actually get to go in and take the test. And I think that's one of the most stressful things because especially at the end of the semester, everybody else is doing other things, getting ready for Christmas, that kind of thing. But you are studying from the time you wake up in the morning until you go to bed at night. That was the most stressful thing.

And here is where the difficulty comes in, because (as you already know) although doing well in law school is often a law student's top goal, it's not his only goal. Especially if the student is optimistic, it's not even his only top goal. Law students, like anyone, want some time to play sports, go to the movies, go out with their friends, or spend time with their families. The result is conflict between law-school goals and non-law-school goals, but the degree of conflict varies depending on whether students move away from home to go to law school. For students who do move away from home to go to law school, that process has already forced them to change a lot about their goals, particularly with regard to spending time with friends and family. Instead of having a goal to go out with friends every weekend, a relocated student's goal might have changed to keeping in contact with old friends via e-mail. Those two goals make very different demands on time. As a result, law students who move away from home escape some of the conflict between their goals that comes from the limited amount of time they have to spend on anything other than law school. Law students who don't move away from home, on the other hand, experience higher levels of conflict, and these were exactly the students for whom optimism seemed to have a negative effect on immunity.

It occurred to me that trying to keep up with both law school and extracurricular goals would be exhausting. Yet that is exactly what you would expect optimists to do. If the critical quality of optimists is engagement with their goals, what I was seeing in these law students was likely to be the physical cost of that engagement and persistence when pursuing conflicting goals.

Imagine being in your first semester of law school. You have your law school demands, but you also have a group of friends who get together every Thursday night to drink beer and throw darts; you play in the community band, which rehearses on Wednesday night (in fact, the reason darts night is on Thursday is to accommodate your rehearsals); and your parents live 30 minutes away and are used to seeing you about every other weekend. What can you do? Here are three options:

1. Just do it. Do as much of these things as you possibly can. Even though you might have to cut back on some of your activities, and you run yourself down sometimes, you do as much as is humanly possible.
2. Don't work so hard at law school. Decide that it isn't really worth it to spend time *every* day in the library, and certainly not every weekend.
3. Give up a lot of your activities. Quit the band, cut back on darts night (sometimes, you might show up for a little while at the very end), and see your parents only once a month. It's the only way to get all that law school studying done and still have downtime.

If you believe a positive future is not only possible but probable, aren't you likely to choose the first option? Optimists have high expectations for their academic achievements, so they are not likely to give up on law school (option #2); they also, as we saw in Chapter 4, prioritize social goals, so they are not likely to give up on their social activities (option #3). They are likely to be profligate with their basic resources—time and energy—in order to protect the resources they have already invested in: status (achievement in law school) and social connection (close ties with friends, family, and fellow musicians). Spend your energetic resources too profligately, however, and your immune system may pay the price.

Not long ago, a woman who heard me speak at a medical school function asked me to explain better how optimists could be immuno-suppressed. I asked her to name the most stressful thing she had done lately, and she said it was remodeling the bathroom. I probably don't have to tell you that remodeling is exactly the kind of thing that you would never undertake if you were not optimistic. Anyone who has been through a remodel knows that it's extremely painful, takes twice as long as it was supposed to, and costs three times as much. Still, if you believe that your new bathroom will be a great thing, you are willing to pay the literal and metaphorical costs in the short run to benefit in the long run with long soaks in your new tub.

Perhaps a less silly example comes from a colleague of mine. During one phone conversation, she apologized for not having been in touch earlier and explained she was a little busy. Well, that was an understatement. It turns out she was teaching a new class (which takes a huge amount of preparation), working on her house (okay, maybe there's a theme there), and trying to change the care situation for her mother, who suffered from dementia, which involved visiting and interviewing a lot of potential facilities. After reciting this litany of demands, she paused for a second, and then she said, "But it's all going to be great when it gets worked out." The ultimate optimistic statement. She shows clearly that an optimist will go to stressful and draining lengths to realize the positive futures she envisions.

On the other hand, if you believe that a positive future is unlikely, you're more likely to try to avoid pursuing goals when the process is, or is likely to be, stressful and draining. If you're a pessimistic law student, you'll give up on law school, extramural activities, or some of both so as not to exhaust yourself. Why would you run yourself down for a negative future? Sure, you give up on your potential success in law school, your social connections, or some of both. But at least your immune system still works well!

OPTIMISM AND HEALTH:
IS THERE AN ENERGY CRISIS?

It begins to look as if the one resource an optimistic law student will willingly part with is energy. If optimists are typically misers when it comes to spending their other resources, they are positively extravagant when it comes to spending energy to keep those other resources going. Unfortunately, the things the body does when it runs low on energy are not always pretty.

For one thing, the immune system is an energy guzzler, and animals from bumblebees to prairie voles suffer decreases in immune function when energy sources (either external, such as food sources, or internal, such as fat stores) are low. When there's not enough energy to go around, essential systems such as the brain and heart take precedence, because, although it's a gamble, you might be able to survive without a fully functional immune system but not without a brain to operate the rest of your body or a heart to pump the blood that keeps it going.

A key term here is *fully* functional. This redirection of energy away from the immune system is presumed to be an evolved mechanism, and so it should occur in circumstances in which it would eventually promote survival and reproduction. Mouse studies confirm this, showing that goals that would promote reproduction and survival—competing for a mate, taking care of pups, and even defending resources like nest boxes and shelves—can take priority over the immune system when it comes to dividing up a finite store of energy. This makes perfect evolutionary sense. After all, just sitting around having a perfect immune system is not a very good strategy for evolutionary fitness, which depends on the number and quality of your offspring. On the other hand, if the immune system is compromised too much and you get sick and die, those pups aren't going to last very long either. Enough energy has to be taken away from the immune system to maximize opportunities, but not so much that it's likely to kill you. Consistent with this balance, even among our optimistic students with high levels of conflict, not one has gotten deathly ill or dropped dead. Maybe the optimistic students are living on the edge, immunologically speaking, but every one has managed to keep a safe distance from the precipice. Immunosuppression might not be the ideal state of affairs, but it might just be the best choice under the circumstances.

For some people, however, this choice might not be as optimal. The bad news about the immune system is that it ages relatively quickly. As we progress through our 50s, 60s, 70s, and, we hope, beyond, our immune systems become less and less responsive. We become more and more vulnerable to infectious diseases such as influenza and pneumonia. Older adults get priority for flu shots for exactly this reason. With regard to optimism, the cancer survival studies suggest that optimism may be healthier for younger than older people. One possible explanation for this difference is that older people's immune systems have a more difficult time absorbing energetic costs and living on the immunological edge. Furthermore, the evolution of the mechanism that diverts energy away from the immune system to pursue other goals could not have been slowed if it was harmful only to older people whose reproductive years were mostly behind them. By the time such a mechanism started to be costly to health, the genes that directed it would have already been passed on to the next generation.

In addition to immunosuppression, low energy may have detrimental effects on the body if it causes cortisol release. Psychophysiologists are accustomed to equating cortisol production with stress, because that's the primary context in which we study cortisol release. Because cortisol is a fight-or-flight hormone, it is also correct to call it a stress hormone. However, this limited definition gets away from the basic function of cortisol, which is not to provide fighting or fleeing per se but to promote glucose release and therefore provide energy. The body needs more energy during stressful times, but there are other such times as well. For example, when experiments varied the number of hours that healthy people slept, higher cortisol production also occurred after sleep restriction. When energy had not been fully restored by sleep, more cortisol was produced to compensate.

The anagram persistence study that Lise and I conducted (see Chapter 2) demonstrated cortisol release in response to energetic demands. Recall that we found that students who were more optimistic worked quite a bit longer on the anagrams than those who were more pessimistic (about 50% longer on the first, unsolvable anagram and about 20% longer on all the anagrams put together). The primary question we hoped the experiment would answer was whether dispositional optimism would predict persistence the way that specific expectancies had in the original persistence studies, which it did. We had another question, though, and that was whether optimistic persistence came at a physiological cost.

By the time we started to plan the anagram study, I had already observed an immunological cost to optimism in the law students and in a laboratory study of law and medical students as well. In that study, two graduate students and I looked at the relationship of optimism to immune function under easy and difficult circumstances. Easy circumstances consisted of a brief resting period, and difficult circumstances consisted of counting backward from ridiculous numbers (like 1,317) by other ridiculous numbers (like 7). Furthermore, the better the participants did at the difficult task, the more ridiculously difficult it got (count backward from 4,672 by 13), so that they were never able to master or control the level of difficulty. As in all the other optimism studies, under easy circumstances optimism was associated with higher immune function, and under difficult circumstances optimism was associated with lower immune function.

I got lucky again[8] in that a colleague and one of his graduate students were interested in the personalities of people who go to law school and medical school, and so they had given a broad personality inventory to all the people in the study. Because we had personality data, we were able to look at two personality characteristics associated with optimism. As you'll recall from Chapter 1, neuroticism is about being negative, and conscientiousness is about being hardworking and engaged with goals. If you think of stress as unhappiness and negativity, then you would predict more signs of stress (such as immune changes) with greater neuroticism. If you think of stress as exertion, on the other hand, you would predict more signs of stress with higher conscientiousness. When we incorporated these other personality data, the evidence said optimism's effects were more like those of conscientiousness than those of neuroticism. The immune systems of optimistic participants appeared to be suppressed by the task because they were working harder at it, not because they were distressed by it.

So, when Lise and I planned the anagram study, we were already thinking about exertion and energy as the reason optimists sometimes showed more immunosuppression than pessimists. We especially wanted to see what the physical cost of goal engagement, exertion, and energy expenditure was. After we had measured how long people worked on the anagrams on their own, we made them go back and keep working on the ones they had skipped or failed until everyone had worked for 20 minutes.[9] Then we measured their physiological recovery from the task. The same people who had shown more

---

[8]You may be starting to think that a successful research program depends on a series of lucky breaks. Mostly it depends on a lot of reading, listening, thinking, and hard work, but serendipity can sure help things move along faster.

[9]We did this because we were interested in the effect of a person's mental state during the anagrams on their physical response, not just the effect of working for a longer period of time. It's not that mind-blowing to show that working longer

engagement with the anagram task—self-aware optimists—also had elevated cortisol following the task, which implies the body was trying to restore the energy spent doing the anagrams.

These laboratory tasks are just snapshots of optimistic behavior, but they point to something very interesting: Optimists, by working harder and using more energy, sometimes increase their cortisol levels and decrease their immune function. When it comes to health effects, it doesn't matter *why* you produce cortisol. Cortisol produced in response to challenging circumstances (effort or exertion) has no different physical effects from cortisol produced in response to threatening circumstances (fight or flight). Both will suppress the immune system, kill brain cells, and so on if produced for long enough periods of time.

Thinking back, then, the apparent inconsistencies in the relationships between optimism and health may not be inconsistencies at all. There are, as it turns out, two pathways at work. The pathway that people (including me) think of first has to do with optimism's effect on psychological stress. Optimism tends to promote active coping, progress toward goals, and maintenance of resources, which in turn prevent negative mood states, promote positive mood states, and keep the sociometer needle on "Full." Avoiding psychological stress can have physiological benefit, reducing sympathetic activation (increased heart rate, blood pressure, and so on, in preparation for fight or flight) and cortisol release. The other pathway has to do with the psychological and behavioral tendencies of optimistic people to be engaged with and try to overcome challenges, conflicts, and stresses. This pathway can be energetically costly. If you're young, healthy, or both, you can probably absorb this cost. If you're not, energetic costs might offset psychological benefits, leading to zero net effect of optimism on health. It all depends on which pathway is acting with the greatest force and the particular vulnerabilities of the people being studied.

---

would lead to more pronounced physical consequences, but it at least starts to approach mind-blowing to show that even after working for the same length of time, the people who were more involved with the task had more pronounced physical responses.

CHAPTER SIX

·····························

Everything Good, Especially the Bad
Optimists and Their Vulnerabilities

> OPTIMISM, n. The doctrine, or belief, that everything is beautiful, including what is ugly, everything good, especially the bad, and everything right that is wrong. . . . Being a blind faith, it is inaccessible to the light of disproof—an intellectual disorder, yielding to no treatment but death. It is hereditary, but fortunately not contagious.
> —*Ambrose Bierce,* The Devil's Dictionary, *1911*

I find it an interesting paradox that most people are optimists, and at the same time, they are incredibly willing to believe that optimism is a setup. The immunosuppression that occurs when optimistic people vigorously pursue difficult goals indicates that some vulnerability goes along with optimism, but in my experience the vulnerability is much less than some people are eager to believe. I try to explain to journalists, for example, that optimists do *not* get more immunosuppressed than pessimists because their positive beliefs set them up for a big letdown. Yet very often the story that comes out includes at least a line or two about how optimistic people *do* end up somewhere between disappointed and devastated when they get, for example, bad medical news—exactly the opposite of what I try to convey and not what the scientific literature says.

On the other hand, no personality characteristic is a magic bullet that will give you an advantage all the time, under every circumstance.

Every kind of personality characteristic has its Achilles' heel. When I look at optimism, I see a set of positive beliefs about the future that lead to engagement and persistence with goals, which in turn lead to well-being. Other people see optimism as a set of positive beliefs about the future that either arise from or lead to denial, ignorance, and vulnerability and believe that, even if you can get past *that* vulnerability and see engagement and persistence, those qualities aren't necessarily good either. Perhaps, they speculate, optimists are not so much persistent as they are stubborn, a quality that can lead to banging your head against a wall and expending energy fruitlessly, maybe even compromising your immune system.

Fortunately, there is research evidence to resolve this paradox. Studies have addressed, first, whether optimistic people pay insufficient attention to negative information—a risk, a threat, or a sign of being stalled—and, second, whether optimists keep going when it would be wiser to stop. These studies mostly show that optimists are not vulnerable in the ways that skeptics seem inclined to believe they are, but they also show that there may be some circumscribed ways in which optimists *are* more vulnerable. Before charging ahead, optimist-like, into the next chapters and the ways in which you could rearrange your life to maximize your optimism and the good qualities that come along with it, it seems prudent to pause and consider whether there are costs that come along for the ride.

DO ROSE-COLORED GLASSES DISTORT YOUR VISION?

To him this is the best of all possible worlds, and the best of all possible times. He refuses to believe in disorder or evil. . . . But such inveterate and persistent optimism, though it may show only its pleasant side in such a character as Emerson's, is dangerous doctrine for a people. It degenerates into fatalistic indifference to moral considerations, and to personal responsibilities. . . .

—*A shipboard companion
of American optimist Ralph Waldo Emerson*

Optimistic people expect positive futures (Chapter 1) and feel good about themselves and their lives (Chapter 4). But is that always the best strategy? Positive beliefs about yourself and your future could

WHAT LEMMINGS BELIEVE

Could positive expectancies lead people astray?

lead you astray. Believing you're a good driver could lead you to drive faster and without a seat belt; believing you're unlikely to have a heart attack could make you think you don't need to exercise or watch what you eat; and believing you're unlikely to become an addict could lead you to experiment with potentially addictive drugs.

More alarming, people are most optimistic about events that can be controlled by their own behavior, such as getting venereal disease, diabetes, or sunstroke. These problems can be averted by practicing safe sex, eating a good diet, exercising, and staying out of the sun. What if optimistic beliefs about the likelihood that you will have these problems make you careless? What if your feelings of invulnerability to sunstroke make you insensible to signs that you're getting over-heated and dehydrated? This would lead to a rather ironic consequence of optimism: optimism makes you more likely to experience exactly the kinds of problems that you could have avoided.

Recall from Chapter 2 that paying attention to a threat and ruminating about a problem can actually protect you. Looking for that tiger in the bushes or spending time thinking about what's going wrong can, in the best case, lead to avoiding a bloody confrontation or coming up with a solution to a problem. Likewise, feeling vulnerable to problems increases your worry about them, and worry can lead to increased interest in changing behavior to reduce the risk (and the worry). In contrast, people who feel least vulnerable to getting a disease like venereal disease or cancer are also least interested in getting written information about how to prevent such diseases. There are lots of examples of things that you really ought to worry about at least a little bit, because that worry can motivate you to do things like fill your gas tank when it's running low, eat better if your pants are getting too tight, or write more papers if your tenure review is coming up.

If optimists don't pay enough attention to signs that their pants are getting too tight, they might keep hitting the cream puffs until they can't get those pants on at all. On the other hand, there are lots of useful things to do with your attention, and not all of them have to do with waistbands. Paying either too little or too much attention to threat can be problematic. Perhaps optimists, although less attentive than pessimists, pay *adequate* attention to risks.

The world is full of things that could draw your attention, but if you paid attention to all the sights and sounds of daily life, you would quickly become overwhelmed. To prevent this, your brain filters out those things that appear to be irrelevant and lets things through that seem important. This is pretty much an unconscious process: you don't look at everything and then consciously decide to pay attention to one thing but not another (dust bunny under sofa, no; bunny under sofa, yes). Instead, those things that your brain "decides" are important get through, and those that are irrelevant don't. Parents learn this when they sleep through traffic noise, TV noise, and thunderstorms, but immediately wake when they hear their child cough in the next room.[1]

Do optimists tune in only to positive input from their environments and filter out all the negative input? Because the attentional fil-

---

[1] In her later years, my grandmother progressively lost her hearing as well as her vision. Nonetheless, if I got a tickle in my throat and started coughing, she could somehow hear me even if I was in the other room and she was "watching" the TV news with the volume turned all the way up. I suspect a parental filter-related phenomenon.

ter is unconscious, you can't just ask people whether they pay more attention to positive or negative things. You have to somehow sneak in the back door and measure biases in their attention (for example, the tendency to attend to positive or negative signals) without their knowledge. There are a number of interesting ways to do this, but one that intrigued me is called the emotional Stroop test.

The *regular* Stroop test is a test of how well you can inhibit automatic impulses, a major task of the frontal lobes of your brain. Without this ability, you would act on every impulse and generally make an ass of yourself.[2] In the regular Stroop test, you are given a list of color words written in different colors of ink. When you look at a word, your automatic response is to say the word—when you see the word *green,* you automatically think *green.* Your charge in the Stroop task, however, is to inhibit saying the word itself ("green") and say the color of the ink the word is printed in ("red"). You have to inhibit your automatic response and perform an alternate response. This is surprisingly hard. You can try it yourself by writing a longish list of three or four repeating color words (like *green, blue,* and *red*) in different-colored pens or crayons, without writing words in the colors to which they refer (don't write *green* in green ink). Then name the ink colors as fast as you can. The faster you can name the ink colors, the better you are at inhibiting your impulse to read the words.

The *emotional* Stroop test is much the same, except that when you devise it, instead of writing color words in different-colored inks, you write words with emotional qualities in different-colored inks. Depending on the nature of your mental filter, when you are trying to name the colors, certain words will automatically draw your attention more than other words, the same way certain sounds (crying or coughing) automatically draw a new parent's attention more than other sounds (thunderstorms or traffic noise). Once your attention is drawn to the word, it will take time—only milliseconds, but time

---

[2]The most famous example of this effect is Phineas Gage, a railroad foreman who was the victim of an accident in which a tamping rod was driven at high velocity all the way through one of his frontal lobes, exiting the top of his head and landing yards away. Although he survived the accident, his personality changed dramatically. His friends described him before the accident as a mild-mannered and hard-working fellow, but afterward he became scatological, irreverent, unreliable, and impulsive. He lost his job with the railroad and died 12 years later, apparently without ever regaining his former character.

nonetheless—to turn your attention away from the word and back to the ink color. Therefore, words that capture your attention will cause you to name the ink colors more slowly. Conversely, if the words don't capture your attention, you can read the ink colors faster.

The emotional Stroop test seemed to be an ideal way to see whether dispositional optimism affected how much attention people pay to positive signals in their environments, such as signs of progress, and negative signals in their environments, such as signs of threat. I had students fill out an optimism questionnaire at the beginning of the semester. Later in the semester and not knowing that the study had to do with optimism, they came to my lab and did a series of emotional Stroop tests: one with negative words like *failure, threat,* and *death*; one with positive words like *succeed, happy,* and *love*; and one with neutral tool words like *hammer, screwdriver,* and *pliers*. I then linked their levels of optimism to how much more slowly they named the colors of positive and negative words than neutral words. Naming the colors of positive words more slowly than neutral words shows an attentional bias toward positive aspects of the environment; naming the colors of negative words more slowly than neutral words shows an attentional bias toward negative aspects of the environment.

The graph on page 136 shows my results.[3] As you might have predicted, people who are more optimistic pay more attention to positive than negative words, and those who are more pessimistic pay more attention to negative than positive words. What's particularly interesting, though, is the absolute amount of bias toward positive and negative words. Even the most optimistic people paid some attention to negative words; it was just that the pessimistic people paid *more* attention.

It's important to pay attention to negative, threatening stimuli in the environment, so skeptics are being reasonable when they say failure to do so could be dangerous. They're wrong, however, to assert that optimists don't do this at all. In fact, you could argue that pessimists do it too much. Ask yourself this: how much attention to the negative is healthy? There is such a thing as too much attention, as when you get fixated and can't disengage from thinking about the

---

[3]Since we published this study, Dr. Andrew Geers and his students at the University of Toledo have found the same effect in their studies. (Score another one for the home team.)

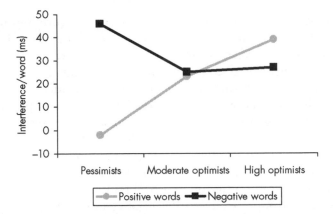

"Interference" (that is, slowing) in ink color naming as a function of word type (positive or negative) and degree of optimism. Optimistic people have some interference from negative words, but the most pessimistic people have virtually no interference from positive words.

negative. People who worry too much don't solve problems and may even be fixated on problems that can't be solved, like things that happened in the past and can't be undone. They can't disengage from their negative thoughts. Pessimists tend to be worriers. They spend much more time than optimists thinking about things they've done wrong, things that are wrong with them, and things that could go wrong in the future. Their pronounced bias toward seeing negative signs in their environment may even convince them they're doing worse than they really are. Disapproving looks, errors, and slights will be noticed more by pessimists and therefore seem more frequent to them, even when they are actually doing just as well as everyone else.

I know several teachers who either don't read the comments on their teaching evaluations anymore or suffer from the one-critic syndrome. This syndrome occurs when you get 110 evaluations, some of which say things like "Great class, I loved it"; "The teacher was very knowledgeable"; or "I never understood this topic before this class—thanks for making it easy" and one of which says "Boring speaker, monotone voice, too repetitive, couldn't stay awake." Because it's impossible to be everything to everyone in large classes or seminars, even very good teachers or speakers get a few negative evaluations. A pronounced attentional bias toward the negative, however, makes the one critic stand out and can prompt prolonged thoughts about why you are so thoroughly hated and what you could have done wrong. The answer is "you're not" and "nothing," but it doesn't seem that way when attention keeps turning back to the negative. The problem gets worse when there is no competition from the positive. Pessimistic people paid virtually no attention to positive words, implying that the positive evaluations and praise wouldn't have the magnetic force for them that the one negative evaluation would. In fact, the positive feedback might not have any more magnetism than evaluations that didn't say anything at all. Sadly, the only way that some teachers have to avoid the sole critic's assault on their attention is to avoid reading evaluations altogether. A consequence of this avoidance is that they don't get feedback that could help them improve or feedback that helps them see when they do well or make progress. Lacking guidance and encouragement, it is no wonder pessimists are pessimistic, give up on their goals, and are less happy.

In contrast with the pessimists, attention to the positive was balanced with attention to the negative among moderately optimistic people, and attention to the positive was even higher among very optimistic people. In terms of being out of touch with reality, then, the evidence points to the pessimists, not the optimists. Optimists, although more attentive to the positive, still attend to the negative; they strike a balance. Although criticism will draw their attention, praise will be just as sticky. Optimists won't get bogged down in the one-critic syndrome because they have some perspective.

Negative attentional bias can lead pessimists to attempt to avoid threatening news, but optimistic beliefs may conversely help people take in potential threats without feeling overwhelmed, helpless, or despondent. The possibility therefore arises that optimists could actually be more willing than pessimists to consciously decide to see or hear threatening information, such as negative teaching evaluations or, in a study that examined this possibility directly, information about health risks. In this study, two groups of students—one that used vitamins and one that sunbathed or used tanning booths—were given the opportunity to read information about potential health risks or benefits of their behavior on a computer. The computer recorded how long each person had information about risks or benefits open on the screen. Overall, people chose to read benefit information (which they had open for an average of 95 seconds) over risk information (which they had open for an average of 86 seconds), but one group chose to read more risk information than benefit information: very optimistic people.

Instead of denying the negative and avoiding threatening information, evidence shows that optimists acknowledge both positive and negative and take in information about their risks (as well as their benefits). The argument that rose-colored glasses are distorting is based on a view of optimism that stops at seeing an optimist as a positive person. However, the argument of this book is that being positive is only the beginning for optimists. Their positive thoughts about the future seed an approach to the world that emphasizes overcoming obstacles. From this perspective, the desire to overcome obstacles should be accompanied by a desire to know exactly what those obstacles entail so as to come up with a better plan to get past them. The evidence that optimists do pay attention to the negative fits with a desire to engage and overcome problems, not to ignore them. Although a good way to accomplish what you want is to play to your strengths, you don't get to be a better teacher, spouse, or poker player by ignoring your weaknesses either.

EXPECTING THE WORST TO ACHIEVE THE BEST: DEFENSIVE PESSIMISM

> Optimistic people expect the best. They believe that things won't go wrong for them. They expect things to go their way. But things do go wrong. The best doesn't always occur. When things go wrong in a big way, the optimist may be particularly vulnerable.
>
> —*Psychologists Howard Tennen and Glenn Affleck, in an article entitled "The Costs and Benefits of Optimistic Explanations and Dispositional Optimism"*

Anticipating potential problems is a wise move, because if you see something bad coming, you can take steps to avoid it. In fact, there are people who anticipate bad things coming *in order to* motivate themselves to prevent those very things from happening. These people are called *defensive pessimists*. Instead of expecting the best, defensive pessimists expect the worst and imagine all the things that can go wrong.

Unlike dispositional pessimism, defensive pessimism can be a very effective strategy for good performance. In one study, dart throwers were told to prepare for a darts test by using a defensive pessimistic strategy, thinking about possible problem throws and their solutions (that is, missing the target and trying to correct those mistakes). Others were told to prepare by using a typically optimistic strategy, thinking about possible good throws (that is, hitting the middle of the target). A final group imagined soothing, relaxing images such as lying on the beach. Performance on the darts test was actually very similar for people using all of these strategies, unless you looked at the *kind* of people who were using them. People who reported that they often used defensive pessimism to deal with problems were most accurate at throwing darts when they were given a pessimistic strategy in which they imagined *missing* the target beforehand. Making them imagine perfect performance or relax before throwing actually made them perform worse. Other people threw darts best when they relaxed. Making them think about the task beforehand—either poor or perfect performance—made them perform worse.

A similar effect occurred in real life among honors college students. Thinking about the possibility of failure in college (that is, worrying) was associated with higher GPA for defensive pessimists. Students who were optimistic about school, on the other hand, had lower GPAs if they worried. Even though anxiety and worry are generally considered detrimental to performance, if you're a defensive pessimist, trying not to worry is exactly the wrong strategy for you.

Right now you should be asking yourself this question about how defensive pessimists overcome their obstacles by imagining the worst: If defensive pessimists are really pessimistic, why do they bother to try to overcome obstacles at all? One characteristic—maybe the most defining characteristic—of *dispositional* pessimists is that they give up. But *defensive* pessimists don't give up. In their responses to potential problems, defensive pessimists resemble dispositional optimists more than dispositional pessimists. Both dispositional optimists and defensive pessimists think about how to overcome problems and keep working toward their goals. Dispositional pessimists prefer to avoid thinking about the problem or to give up altogether. Furthermore, although defensive pessimists think about the possibility of failure as a way of preparing themselves, they do not have the experience of failure that might lead them to conclude that it is inevitable. Both dispositional optimists and defensive pessimists have a history of success, whereas dispositional pessimists have a history of failure.

Consider Amy, a defensive pessimist, and May, a dispositional pessimist. Both are unsure they can be successful at work. Amy considers all the ways her performance might be found lacking, takes steps to improve it, and gets a good review. Although she continues to focus on problems she has at work, she also sees the possibility of overcoming those problems and making successes happen for herself by averting problems. May, like Amy, also considers all the ways in which her work might be found lacking. Unlike Amy, she considers her weaknesses inevitable, so she doesn't take steps to correct them and then gets a poor performance review, which only confirms her belief that bad things are going to happen to her.

I think defensive pessimism is actually a likely strategy for dispositional optimists. How could a dispositional optimist actually be a defensive pessimist? Being generally optimistic doesn't guarantee you'll expect the best in every domain of your life. A lot more than personality disposition goes into what we expect from our relationships, our endeavors at work, or our driving skills. Experiences and feedback from the environment play large parts as well. For example, law students who did well on the LSAT had more confidence in and positive expectations for their success in law school than those who did less well—a rational response, given that this standardized test was designed to predict how well students will do, especially early in law school. Similarly, how optimistic University of Kentucky freshmen were about their academic potential was related not just to their level of dispositional optimism but also to their high school GPA. Students who had been successful in high school expected to be successful in college. The narrower the expectancy, the less dispositional optimism seems to play a role. When students predict their grades in a specific course, dispositional optimism accounts for only 2.3% of their expectation for this very narrow domain.

Even if you are dispositionally pessimistic, you can be confident about specific outcomes—maybe you have a long history of chess championships, for example, that gives you an island of optimism about chess in your sea of pessimism about other things. Likewise, even if you are dispositionally optimistic, you can be skeptical about isolated pockets of your life: that your tennis game will ever improve, that you'll win an election, or that you can get along with difficult people. Our goals data, which assessed degree of optimism about specific daily goals, showed clearly that pessimists had a few goals that they felt confident about and optimists had the occasional goal that they were uncertain they could reach.

Optimistic people are not in denial. The Stroop results indicate that they pay adequate attention to negative and threatening information, so if the future seems to hold potential for things to go wrong, dispositional optimists should be aware of that potential. What is interesting, though, is what dispositional optimists and dispositional pessimists would be expected to do when both anticipate the worst in a very specific area, such as losing weight. There is actually some reason for pessimism in this area, because most people have difficulty losing weight and those who do lose weight are prone to gain most or all of it back. The dispositional pessimist, true to his nature, would be likely to give up on a weight loss goal. But the idea of giving up might rub the dispositional optimist the wrong way. Optimists are generally used to applying engagement and persistence to solve problems. When you combine the tendency to approach and engage with negative expectations, what do you get? A person who not only imagines all the potential pitfalls (Danishes on the coffee cart, cheesecake on the dessert tray) but also imagines ways to avoid or overcome them.

Defensive pessimism: the optimistic approach to pessimistic expectations. In response to a vision of getting hammered by an opponent's cross-court backhand, the dispositional pessimist concedes the game in her mind before it even starts. The defensive pessimist sets up the ball machine and practices returning the shot. Maybe the practice will be effective and maybe it won't, but in the long run, this approach will certainly be more effective than walking off the court before the game even starts. Expecting to lose an election induces a dispositional pessimist to throw in the towel, but a defensive pessimist stays up all night making more campaign posters.

WHEN THE GRASSHOPPER SEEMS WISER THAN THE ANT

The place where optimism most flourishes is the lunatic asylum.
—*Physician Havelock Ellis*

Defensive pessimism addresses the situation that arises when you anticipate problems but feel you can overcome them. What about the opposite situation, when you feel the future *should* be positive, but you can't make that future come true? This could happen if you didn't have the skills to bring it about (no matter how hard I practice, I will probably never dunk a basketball) or if the situation wasn't responsive to your efforts (you can lead a horse to water, but you can't make him drink). The skeptic might say the optimist would try and try to achieve a goal that just isn't achievable, wasting time and energy and getting a whopper of a headache in the process.

The concept of the unreachable goal does not always reflect well on the optimist. Here's another word for persistence: *stubbornness*. Whereas the word *persistence* conjures visions of success, the word *stubbornness* conjures visions of working unproductively on some project that will never pay off. Can you persist too long? And if so, are optimists less persistent than they are stubborn? After all, there can be costs to persistence. Consider the uncontrollable situation or the unsolvable problem. Some people would suggest that the fact that optimists work longer on unsolvable anagrams in experimental studies means they're stubborn rather than persistent. Some problems will never be solved, no matter how long you work at them. Under those circumstances, the time and effort spent trying to solve them never pays off. Giving up is the better part of valor.

Business students learn this idea in terms of "sunk costs," which is the business school equivalent of "throwing good money after bad." Imagine you're designing a new widget. You've invested $200,000 in developing your widget, when another widgeter at your company comes up with a better widget. You need to spend only $20,000 to get the old widget into production. Do you spend it? Are you so compelled by the $200,000 you already spent (the sunk costs) that you have to take it to completion? In fact, the development of the new widget in effect makes the $200,000 in sunk costs "bad money," and persisting in spending the last $20,000 is throwing good money after it. More persistence in developing the old widget isn't going to pay off. You have to know when to give up.

Overpersistence incurs opportunity costs, that is, things you could have done with the $20,000 other than spend it on finishing the development of an obsolete widget. In other contexts, this might mean you've spent time and effort on a problem that you can't solve or a goal you can't achieve. That time and effort could have been spent on some other problem or goal that is solvable or achievable, and by overpersisting you missed the opportunity to solve that other problem or achieve that other goal. The costs of your persistence (stubbornness) include not only the wasted time and effort but also the loss of something else you could have achieved.

Do optimists waste effort and incur opportunity costs? The experimental studies, in which optimists work longer on unsolvable problems, indicate that they do. Or do they? Giving up is not a typically optimistic response in laboratory experiments, but laboratory experiments are strange. Lisa Aspinwall, a psychologist at the University of Utah, pointed out that in experiments in which optimists seemed to be persisting too long, there are some serious problems with interpreting that persistence as unproductive, unwise, or costly. First, in laboratory studies there are no alternatives to working on the "unproductive" task; real life offers both alternative goals and alternative pathways to goals. The only alternative to persisting in the lab is to quit and sit there doing nothing. Second, there is no real opportunity cost to persisting in laboratory studies. The person has committed a certain amount of time to participating in the study, and that time is committed whether she persists or quits. It's not as though she can stop working on the study tasks and study for her chemistry exam instead. It's like being in a mandatory staff meeting that lasts for an hour. Whether you pay attention or contribute to the staff meeting doesn't affect the opportunity costs of that hour. You are stuck there, and you can either participate or not, but you won't get the hour back.

If you set up an experiment to look less like a staff meeting and more like a free hour, the effects of optimism also change. Lisa set up a study in which people could either keep working on the fruitless task or change to something else. Participants in her study were given a set of unsolvable anagrams and 20 minutes to work on them. Some of them were also given an alternative task—a different set of anagrams—to which they could proceed, if they wanted to, by giving up on the unsolvable anagrams. In the group that had only the unsolvable anagrams, almost everyone spent the entire 20 minutes working on them. However, in the group that had the choice to proceed, the average person chose to move on after 12 minutes. This in itself shows that the availability of alternatives affects how people approach nonproductive tasks (for example, you could choose to work on something else instead of participating in the staff meeting—an alternative that in my experience is quite commonly exploited, sometimes discreetly, but sometimes overtly).

What is particularly interesting about the results of the study is that optimists were actually *faster* to move on to the next set of anagrams when they had that alternative available. The most optimistic participants spent about two-thirds of the time that more pessimistic participants spent on the unsolvable anagrams before moving on. That is, optimism led people, in the presence of an alternative, to give up sooner. Maybe reading or using your Blackberry under the table during the staff meeting is actually a sign of optimism. It could also be a sign that staff meetings are not particularly productive, because what this study did not show is what would happen if progress were actually being made. Given signs of progress, I predict that optimists would actually work longer before switching, if they switched at all. After all, the evidence reviewed in Chapter 2 shows that in real-life tasks for which progress is possible, optimists are well known to keep going longer than pessimists. Taken together, all this evidence indicates that optimists are wiser than pessimists about when to pursue and when to give up on goals.

LEARNING THE HARD WAY . . .
OR NOT AT ALL

An optimist is a guy
that has never had
much experience.
—*Poet Donald Robert Perry Marquis*

Even if optimists sometimes persist too long, that is a different kind of error from the kind made by pessimists, which is not persisting long enough. These two kinds of errors are not created equal, and optimistic errors might actually lead to better judgment about what the wise course of action really is in different kinds of situations.

For most endeavors in life, initial failure does not mean it's time to give up. Instead, there is a point at which it makes sense to keep trying, even if you've recently failed, and a point at which it makes sense to give up and try for something else. The first time Brian asks Kim out and she says no, there's still a decent chance that she will say yes the next time. Maybe she will reconsider, or maybe she's playing hard to get, or maybe her friends will convince her that he's a good guy. He should probably try again. After the seventh time he asks her out and she says no, however, his odds that she will say yes on the eighth try are not very good. Time to move on. In academia, it's not uncommon for an article to be rejected by the first journal to which it's submitted. The odds that it will be accepted by another journal, however, are still good, even without its being submitted to a less picky journal. I have had articles accepted by more prestigious journals that were rejected by less prestigious journals. After a few rejections, though, it might be time to consider that there's something really wrong with the article and no one is going to publish it. Another way of understanding this limit is to consider how many efforts you've made and the likelihood of succeeding on the next try. I imagine this relationship looks something like the following:

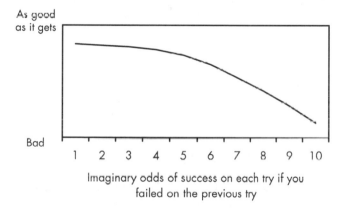

Imaginary odds of success on each try if you
failed on the previous try

The actual probabilities might change depending on what you're trying to do, but I think the shape of this graph is probably pretty accurate. With each failure, you learn something about your chances. One failure usually doesn't mean that you can't succeed on the next try, and your odds might even be just as good. Elective office is littered with first-time losers, including some who eventually made it all the way to the top. Bill Clinton lost his first bid for public office with an unsuccessful run for the House in 1974 but was elected attorney general in 1976. George Herbert Walker Bush lost his first race, for the Senate, in 1964, but was elected to the House in 1976. First-time losses were practically the norm among the founding fathers: Thomas Jefferson, John Adams, John Quincy Adams, and Andrew Jackson were all defeated in presidential elections before becoming president.

With a second failure, however, the odds drop off a little, since two failures mean you might have a project doomed to eventual failure on your hands. That's not certain, and if you try again, you might succeed. John Adams ran for president twice (1789 and 1792) before winning in 1796; Ronald Reagan lost bids for the Republican presidential nomination in 1968 and 1976 before winning it—and the presidency—in 1980.

However, with more and more failures, the odds that you will eventually succeed gradually drop off. After several failures, it becomes pretty clear that success (at least in that domain) is unlikely to come to you. Henry Clay ran for president five times from 1824 to 1848. He was unable to get the party nomination in his last bid, and even his home state of Kentucky went for his opponent, Zachary Taylor, in the Whig primary. The Whigs had figured out what Clay apparently had not: it was time to give up.

At some point, the odds of success become low enough that they aren't worth the costs of persistence. Knowing when you've reached that point is a matter of experience, not intelligence, and that experience comes from finding out what happens on the eighth, ninth, or tenth try. In other words, it comes from making optimistic mistakes. Knowing when to give up can be learned only from mapping the right-hand side of my made-up graph. Making pessimistic mistakes does not provide the kind of experience that leads to knowing when to give up. How long is long enough? Someone who gives up early never finds out. A few tries cannot tell you whether you worked long enough or give you a map of the world that helps you figure it out. That is, if Brian is optimistic when he pursues Kim, he is going to find out where the line is between persistence and stalking. He now has that knowledge to guide his behavior in the future, and he will know when it is wisest to quit and when it might just pay off to keep going. When the option to change course comes along (as it did in Lisa Aspinwall's experiment), Brian will be faster to recognize whether changing is the better option or not. A pessimistic counterpart, in unfamiliar territory, might actually waste more time in fruitless pursuit before recognizing that he is going down a blind alley.

I consider myself a persistent person, and although I believe in the wisdom that comes from persistence, there is one domain in which I can't stop even when it's time. Every time I start playing solitaire and (typically) lose, I think I was just on the verge of winning and firmly believe that if I can try just one more time, I'll win.[4] Gambling, solitaire, and similar activities are different from much of the real world, in that the number of times you've tried and your prior success often have very little to do with your future success. In true games of chance, your prior success has nothing to do with your future odds. Instead of producing the curve in the preceding graph, games of chance have functions that look like this:

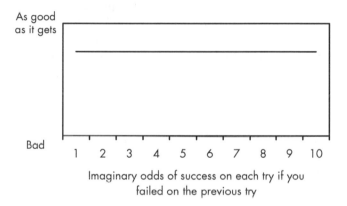

Imaginary odds of success on each try if you
failed on the previous try

Roll a die, with the goal of rolling 3. Your odds of rolling 3 are exactly 1 in 6, or about 17%, so the odds are that you failed. Roll again. Your odds of rolling 3 are still exactly 1 in 6. Roll again. 1 in 6. Roll again. 1 in 6. The difference between many real-life endeavors (getting a job, getting a date, getting a manuscript accepted, running for president) and games of chance is that in real life, persistence can teach you something about your odds as you go along, whereas in games of chance, the odds are known up front—persistence doesn't teach you anything useful.

This difference shouldn't matter much to pessimists: usually they try a couple of times, and if they don't succeed, they give up. On the other hand, optimists usually keep trying until the odds start to fall

---

[4]I'm a little bit tempted to stop writing and try again right now.

off. As long as the likelihood of winning is high enough to justify the effort, their kind of mistake—persistence—might keep them gambling longer than a pessimist because the odds never fall off in games of chance.

Furthermore, because optimists are more attentive than pessimists to positive signs of progress, they should be more vulnerable to "near misses." In a "near miss" you almost but not quite reach your goal. Not surprisingly, the people who design games of chance aren't insensitive to the effect of a "near miss." One of the most popular slot machines is called "Wheel of Fortune," which people feed upward of one billion dollars each year. When you play Wheel of Fortune, you can win in the usual slot machine way, by getting three cherries or whatever, but if you reach the "bonus round," you can also win *more* money when you electronically "spin" the "wheel" at the top of the machine. In the analog Wheel of Fortune on TV, you have equal odds of landing on any of the slices of pie on the wheel. In the digital, electronic Wheel of Fortune in Las Vegas, however, you don't. The machine is programmed to land on some pieces more than others. It doesn't take much thought to predict that it will land on smaller amounts of money more than on larger amounts, but it might surprise you to find out that the machine is also programmed to land frequently *next to* the largest amount. This slot machine essentially tells you, "Oooh, near miss. You were *so close*. Better put in another quarter and try again!"

I found another example in my grocery cart just last week. Someone had bought a lottery ticket called "Almost Lucky," scratched it, and abandoned it in the cart. The ticket has a tic-tac-toe pattern with numbers in it, and if you get three 3's in a row any direction, you win. The ticket I found had this pattern:

ALMOST
LUCKY
get three 3's
in a row
and today's
your lucky
day!

8	7	3
3	3	5
1	3	3

According to my calculations, the unlucky purchaser of this ticket nearly won (that is, had two of the three necessary 3's) in two of the three columns, two of the three rows, and two of the two diagonals. The point of this ticket is that the purchaser wasn't unlucky, but nearly lucky. Designers of games of chance know that an unlucky someone is less likely to try again than a nearly lucky someone.

Research shows that optimistic people are especially vulnerable to the near miss. In this study, people played a slot machine game that was manipulated by the experimenters (the same way the ones in Las Vegas are manipulated by the game designers). Optimists were definitely suckers for this game. First, they didn't stop betting just because they were losing. These optimists were like the optimists who worked on unsolvable anagrams: they kept persisting even in the face of failure. Second, optimists were more influenced by near misses, as indicated by more memories of "nearly winning" after the study was over (this was especially true if they were actually losing).

Optimism, like every other personality trait, is not adaptive in every situation, and here is a blind spot for optimists. Optimists are bigger suckers than pessimists when it comes to games of chance.[5] Their *modus operandi* seems to be to keep trying until the odds fall off, indicating that the smaller likelihood of succeeding is no longer worth their effort. Because the odds of games of chance never fall off, optimists gamble longer. They are also more susceptible to near misses, and if the game is able to manipulate those near misses to occur more often, optimists will be particularly drawn to that game.

On the other hand, cases in which there is no change in the odds of success over time seem to be the exception rather than the rule in life. Even endeavors we might call "gambles," like moving to Hollywood to get discovered and become a movie star, aren't really like gambling in that if you've been hanging out on Hollywood Boulevard for 10 years and no one's taken a second look (even to arrest you for soliciting, which would be the more likely outcome), that sends you a message about the likelihood that you will get discovered in the next

---

[5]Optimists are only one kind of sucker, however. Optimists gamble because "I believe I can make money in the long run." Other people gamble because "I like the 'rush' " or "I like the possibility of changing my life with a big win"—sensation seekers. Yet other people gamble because "it helps distract me from other problems I might be facing in my life"—avoidant copers. Optimists are not more likely to gamble for these reasons.

year (nearly nil). The advantage to making optimistic rather than pessimistic mistakes is that persistence is educational, even when it doesn't succeed. Giving up doesn't teach you anything, and you very often will miss the payoff.

GOAL VERSUS GOAL: CAN YOU STILL WIN?

A pessimist sees the difficulty in every opportunity; an optimist sees the opportunity in every difficulty.

—*Statesman Winston Churchill*

Imagine that you are highly engaged with two goals: that is, you have high expectations of achieving them both and you are highly committed to both. On the other hand, there are only 24 hours in a day, and you're only one person. If there were unlimited time, you could be in two places at once, and the goal to spend more time working in the garden and the goal to spend more time practicing your golf game would not conflict. Likewise, the goal to get a better grade in Biology 101 and the goal to get more involved in extracurricular activities would not conflict. Unfortunately, there are only so many hours in the day, and there is only so much energy, money, and other resources to spend pursuing goals. When two or more goals are competing for the same resources, *resource conflict* occurs. The bad news is that optimism and goal engagement are both associated with higher resource conflict. People who are more optimistic are more engaged with their goals, are less likely to give them up, and experience more conflict as a result.

Resource conflict involves two potential problems. First, there is the energy cost of pursuing conflicting goals. For the optimistic law students in Chapter 5, conflict between the desire to spend time and energy reaching law school goals and the desire to spend time and energy maintaining social relationships resulted in decreased immune function. Second, opportunity costs come into play. If two goals are competing for time and energy, then allocating most of those resources to one goal means less of those resources allocated to the other goal.

How can we best balance competing goals? It may be helpful to take a big step away from human goal pursuit and look at animal foragers. Foragers find their food by going out and looking for it, finding it, and consuming it. A forager could be a bird looking for seeds and berries or a fox looking for mice. To survive, foragers have to balance benefits and costs. The benefits of foraging come, of course, from the nutrition in the food found during foraging. Costs of foraging come from the time and energy spent looking for and consuming that food. An efficient forager spends little time and energy to find a calorie-rich food source that doesn't take a lot of time and energy to consume. An inefficient forager spends a lot of time and energy to find a calorie-poor food source that takes a lot of time to consume.

Time and energy are important because foragers, like pursuers of goals, incur opportunity costs with regard to these resources. Looking for berries uses resources that could also be spent looking someplace else for seeds. Looking for mice uses resources that could also be spent looking someplace else for stoats.[6] There's actually a formula that specifies the best foraging strategy. The formula[7] is:

$$R = \frac{\lambda e - s}{1 + \lambda h}$$

R is an index of how efficient the forager is. What this formula means is that efficiency increases when λ (the probability of finding a food source) is big, e (the energy obtained from that food source) is big, s (the cost of search, including opportunity cost) is small, and h (the time it takes to consume the food source) is small. That is, bigger values of R reflect good foraging strategy in that the strategy leads to a plentiful, rich food source that's easy to find and eat.

Goal pursuers are like foragers. They are efficient when they pursue achievable goals, analogous to plentiful food, that will bring a meaningful reward, analogous to nutrition. They are also efficient when resource conflict is low, meaning they aren't giving up resources that could also be applied to other goals. Optimists actually have higher values for all the components of the foraging equation, however, so it's not immediately obvious that they are doing the right

[6]Do foxes eat stoats? I don't know. It just sounded good. If I were a fox, I think I would eat a stoat, but it's getting pretty close to lunchtime now and the list of things I would eat is expanding accordingly.

[7]There will not be a quiz on this formula. I include it here for fellow formula geeks who are interested in this kind of thing.

thing. On the one hand, optimists have a higher likelihood of achieving their goals (λ) and expect more joy when the goals are achieved (e), so they are efficient when considering that part of the equation (λe). On the other hand, they also have more resource conflict, so they are less efficient when considering that part of the equation ($-s$). The question is, how well do they balance one against the other?

By substituting expectancy for probability of success, joy for energy obtained, and resource conflict for opportunity cost,[8] the foraging equation can illustrate whether optimists balance their costs and benefits better than pessimists do. In the everyday goals study, optimism clearly led to higher values of R, that is, more efficient goal pursuit and better balance of costs and benefits. The figure below shows the increase in R as you go from being highly pessimistic to being highly optimistic. Yes, optimism is associated with higher costs, but the association with benefits is so much higher that it more than makes up for the expenditure.

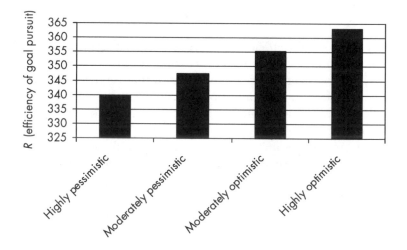

The relationship between optimism and R, the foraging function that weighs benefits and costs in goal pursuit.

[8]Consumption cost is assumed to be 0. Unlike eating a stoat, getting a good grade on an exam or spending more time with the family doesn't take extra time in achievement as opposed to pursuit. That is, once you've achieved a goal, you typically don't have to take a lot of extra time and effort to enjoy it.

Optimists and Their Vulnerabilities

> I became an optimist when I discovered that I wasn't going to win any more games by being anything else.
>
> —*Baseball manager Earl Weaver*

Lots of evidence shows that optimism benefits people and improves their well-being by engaging them with their goals and building their resources, but there are some drawbacks to being optimistic and doing as optimists do. These drawbacks are not the ones that people have typically proposed, such as vulnerability to disappointment and fruitless persistence. Rather, they seem to be well-defined Achilles' heels, such as the propensity to play roulette longer and the tendency to be spendthrift with energy to pursue competing goals (albeit in an efficient way).

How much do these vulnerabilities cost optimists? In the grand cost–benefit analysis, the proof is in the pudding. I concluded in Chapter 5 that the ultimate cost of immunosuppression due to pursuing conflicting goals could not be prohibitively high because, in the end, optimism didn't lead to higher rates of illness or mortality. Likewise, I conclude here that the ultimate cost of the circumscribed vulnerabilities associated with optimism cannot be prohibitively high because the long run shows a greater likelihood of optimists reaching goals and achieving higher well-being (Chapter 2) and satisfaction with life (Chapter 3). If optimistic vulnerabilities were fatal flaws, it just wouldn't happen that way. The benefits of optimism ultimately outweigh the costs.

CHAPTER SEVEN

Is an Optimist Born or Made?
The Optimistic Character Revisited

When it comes to the disposition to be optimistic, most people don't end up where they started out. Other personality characteristics have a good deal of basis in infant temperament; for example, relaxed babies tend to grow up into sociable children and adults, and tense babies tend to grow up into inhibited children and adults. Dispositional optimism, on the other hand, appears to develop in different ways for different people over their lifetimes, so that what an infant or child is like probably has only partially to do with how optimistic that person will be as an adult. If you aren't born optimistic, how do you end up there? Partly it's because of the world around you, but it's also a result of the world you create.

THE WORLD AROUND YOU:
CULTURES OF OPTIMISM

Most people in the United States are optimistic, but this is not true of people in many other countries of the world. Since 1976, the Gallup organization has been asking people in dozens of countries whether they think the next year will be better or worse than the present year. The United States is near the top of the list for the percentage of people who think the next year will be better rather than worse. Over a

10-year period, an average 50% of Americans thought the next year would be better (in one year, fully 70% of Americans thought the next year would be better).

Examining these lists, we find—consistent with the ideas first introduced in the Prologue—that being rich is not the answer. Some of the most optimistic countries are associated with national wealth and privilege (the United States, Canada, white South Africa), but so are some of the most pessimistic countries. Geographic location has something more to do with it, since the most optimistic countries have predominantly Western cultures. On the other hand, two of the top three—Asian South Korea and Mediterranean Greece—do not, and many of the most pessimistic countries are also Western.

Most optimistic and most pessimistic countries (with average percentage of people thinking that the next year will be better)

10 most optimistic countries	10 most pessimistic countries
South Korea (54%)	Austria (10%)
Argentina (51%)	Belgium (11%)
Greece (51%)	West Germany (17%)
USA (50%)	Japan (20%)
Brazil (48%)	Luxembourg (20%)
Australia (44%)	Netherlands (21%)
Uruguay (42%	France (22%)
Canada (38%)	Denmark (24%)
Chile (38%)	Portugal (25%)
South Africa (whites only) (35%)	Finland (26%)

South Korea, the most optimistic country, is an interesting exception to a rule that people in countries located in Asia, such as Japan, Singapore, and China, are more pessimistic than people in countries located in North America, such as Canada and the United States. This is a very robust cultural difference that is maintained even among ethnic groups living in the United States: Americans of Asian descent are more pessimistic than Americans of European descent, even though they are living in the same country. Even fairly homogeneous groups, like college students, show this difference.

Why is Asia more pessimistic than North America? Psychologists often think about the cultural differences among countries along a dimension of *individualism* to *collectivism*. Individualist countries include the United States, Canada, Australia, and (to a slightly lesser degree) Western Europe. Values in these countries emphasize the individual; most people are concerned with maximizing their individual well-being, standing out from the crowd, and being independent and self-sufficient. Each person is considered an entity unto himself. Collectivist countries include most Asian countries, as well as (to a somewhat lesser degree) Eastern and Mediterranean Europe. Values in these countries emphasize the group; most people are concerned with the well-being of the social groups to which they belong, fitting in with the crowd, and being interdependent and integrated into a social group. Each person is considered primarily to be a component of a larger social group, like a family or a workforce.

It can be hard, as a member of a fiercely individualist society, to understand what it would be like to live in a collectivist society. In the United States, we're so socialized to think of ourselves as entities unto ourselves that we see collectivism as alien, even literally so. On *Star Trek*, American suspicion of collectivism was taken to an extreme with the portrayal of the Borg—a group of individual alien entities whose brains were connected electronically so that they acted with eerie coordination to advance the cause of the collective. The reality of collectivist societies is less extreme, but it's true that in these societies people are more likely to define themselves as members of groups (the Star Trek crew, the Borg) rather than individual entities (like Captain Picard).

Collectivism is not eerie, just different. A helpful analogy to individualistic and collectivistic cultures is the difference between certain Olympic events. Living in an individualist culture is like running the 100-meter dash; living in a collectivist culture is like synchronized swimming. You "win" at individualism by running faster than other people and setting yourself apart from them, but you "win" at collectivism by fitting in with others. A synchronized swimmer who is faster than her teammates not only doesn't win but harms the team and thereby herself.

This difference affects how important it is that predictions about the future be personally motivating versus technically accurate. In the 100-meter dash, knowing exactly what all the other people in the race will do is less important than thinking about what you *might* do as an individual. Uncertainty in the race doesn't hurt you, and it might even help you (if the world champion gets a hangnail that slows her down by a fraction of a second). Runners would do well to think about what *might* be and to be less concerned with accuracy in predicting the outcome of the race than with motivating thoughts about the possibility of winning. In synchronized swimming, on the other hand, it's very important to know exactly what everyone else is going to do and when. Synchronized swimmers would do well to think about what *will* be, because accuracy is more important than individual motivation.

When you ask people from an individualist culture (which, like the sprinter, is tolerant of uncertainty) about the future, you are not likely to get their most accurate prediction; instead, you get a prediction based on the possibility that the future will be better. For them, as for the sprinter, it is most helpful to think about how their future *might* be better and how they could stand out. On the other hand, when you ask people from a collectivist culture (which, like the synchronized swimmer, is intolerant of uncertainty) about the future, you get a prediction based on the objective likelihood that the future will be better. For them, as for the synchronized swimmer, it is most helpful to think about how their futures *will* fit in with other people's futures. Consistent with this view, predictions are much more closely related to actual abilities in people from collectivist countries in Asia than they are in people from individualist countries in the Americas. In addition to the issue of accuracy, if you live in a collectivist culture, it does not benefit you to become more optimistic than the social group that makes up your identity.[1] It might even be a sign that you don't fit in and may have negative consequences for your adjustment.

---

[1]This idea (that you should be as optimistic as your culture) suggests why South Koreans can, as a group, be more optimistic than the Japanese, even though both cultures are collectivist. As long as the culture as a whole is optimistic, individuals can also be optimistic; on the other hand, if the culture as a whole is pessimistic, individuals probably do better to be equally pessimistic. Although no one has looked systematically at this issue (to my knowledge), one difference in individualist and collectivist societies might be the *spread* of optimism and pessimism scores. For example, South Korea might have a high average optimism with small differences between people, whereas the United States might have a high average optimism and large differences between people.

WILL AND GRACE: TWO ROUTES TO OPTIMISM

Within U.S. culture, black Americans have a somewhat more collectivist view of life than white Americans, but, like the South Koreans, they may also have somewhat more optimism than white Americans. What is particularly interesting is that black Americans get to be optimistic in a slightly different way than white Americans do, probably because of the experience of racism. Although institutionalized racism has been largely eliminated in America—black Americans no longer have to sit in the back of the bus, use different drinking fountains, and attend different schools—everyday racism, unfortunately, lives on. Black Americans may find themselves treated in subtly racist ways: a white woman takes a firmer grip on her handbag when she passes a black man, or a black guest at a formal party is mistaken for a waiter. The most important aspect of the experience of racism for understanding optimism, however, is the way in which racism intervenes between goal pursuit and achievement. As one group of researchers wrote, "racism erases at least some of the contingencies between hard work, personal action, and positive outcomes."

Most of this book is about how hard work and personal action are the ways optimism is put into action. Let's call this pathway "Will." "Will" is the way optimists achieve better lives than pessimists, as well as the way the less optimistic can achieve better lives and maybe become more optimistic in the process (coming up in Chapter 8). When racism blocks this pathway, however, there must be a different way for victims of racism to remain optimistic. I'm going to call this pathway "Grace."[2] The idea of grace is central to many religious beliefs. Divine grace means you'll attain a positive future (such as heaven) regardless of your own personal achievements. In fact, spiritual beliefs are the way around the roadblock of racism for many black Americans. Black Americans who report a loving, supporting, and empowering relationship with God and who believe their lives

---

[2]You probably noticed that my pathways have the same names as familiar TV characters from the show *Will and Grace*. I was driving through Delaware on my way to give a talk about optimism when a segment about TV's *Will and Grace* came on the radio. The fortuitous convergence of thinking about optimism and listening to the radio led to the realization that Will and Grace are also the two ways to a positive future: earn it yourself (Will) or have it given to you (Grace).

have a purpose, reason, and sense of direction given by God are also more optimistic. The same is not as true for white Americans (their spiritual beliefs are minimally related to their levels of optimism). Because racism blocks "Will" for many members of minority groups, they find their way to optimism through "Grace."

However, Grace may actually turn into Will.[3] That is, the optimism that black Americans and other minority groups achieve through Grace can empower their Will. One study examined what happens when optimists and pessimists were exposed to evidence of prejudice, in this case, sexism. Women read a "newspaper article" (actually written by the experimenters) about how women are discriminated against. The article claimed that female students were much more likely than male students to have sexist assumptions made about them, to be the target of sexist remarks, and to make less money after college. Essentially, this information said that women are less welcome in the university community (as indicated by sexist assumptions and remarks) and less valued by society (as indicated by lower wages), threatening both their social and status resources. As a consequence, after women read the article, their self-esteem dropped and they felt more depressed.

However, optimistic women were protected from this effect: their self-esteem and depression were pretty much the same as women who didn't read the article about prejudice. This protection came from their Will. To the degree that women thought they were able to deal with sexism, had the resources to handle sexism, and were prepared to rise up and meet the demands posed by sexism, they were protected against dents in their self-esteem and depression. In essence, they believed they could protect their social and status resources through effort, skill, and other strengths.

Optimism that comes from Grace may translate into the Will to deal with roadblocks, even those with a history as long as that of discrimination. This is important, because the good outcomes from optimism appear to come mainly from people's efforts to make those outcomes happen. Recall from Chapter 4 that optimism about marriage helped to effect a better marriage only when couples acted in a way to bring that future about. Likewise, when people confront prejudice,

---

[3]And this is where the parallels to the TV characters totally break down, unless a really major plot twist is in the offing.

they may turn to alternative fonts of optimism, like faith, which benefit them when that optimism helps them overcome the barriers that prejudice puts up.

THE EMERGING OPTIMIST: OPTIMISTIC FAMILIES

When looking for the cultural source of optimistic beliefs, researchers have not emphasized the effects of the broad culture of a nation or even subcultures within nations. Mostly, they have looked for the source of optimism in the small, idiosyncratic culture of the family. In part, this is based on the quarter of optimism that is genetically inherited from parents, but it's also based on other parental influences.

If you're an optimist today, it might be partly because your parents modeled optimism for you. Children learn a lot about the world by observing others (hence the concern about children's exposure to violent television shows and video games). They are particularly influenced by their observations and likely to mimic what they observe when they see someone rewarded for his actions. A parent who expresses positive beliefs about the future, is goal directed, and is apparently (to the child) rewarded for these thoughts and behaviors could influence that child to adopt similar views. Perhaps your parent launched a campaign to pass a new school bond or, perhaps more influentially, launched more than one campaign until the school bond passed (as he "knew it would"). Seeing your parent rewarded for positive beliefs and persistence could instigate your own optimism.

Second, parental relationships are important social resources for children. Think back to Chapter 4 and how important social relationships are to survival for adults. Now consider how much more important those relationships are to children, who require adults to provide for them. Parents who consistently provide the resource most important to children—parental acceptance and caring—could build their children's confidence in their ability to garner resources in general and support their optimism about the future. A child who finds that loving overtures to her father are returned in kind is more likely to make friendly overtures to other children and—via processes described in Chapter 4—build social resources both within and outside the family. It isn't a long stretch to hypothesize that the same child might take the confidence and positive expectancies built within the family and apply them to build resources that aren't necessarily social, such as sports, games, or school. A positive parental relationship that provides the child's most important early resource can initiate the upward spiral of positive expectancies and resource growth.

The differences in the way optimistic and pessimistic college students recall their childhoods supports these two routes of transmission: demonstrating optimism and providing social resources. Optimists are more likely than pessimists to remember their parents being optimistic, encouraging, and happy—that is, as role models for optimism. They also remember having more social resources in the family. Inside the home, they remember their relationships with their parents as warmer and less critical, hostile, or rejecting. They also had better relationships with their siblings, recalling less sibling rivalry.

Their answers to the question of whether they had ever wanted to trade places with one of their siblings are also revealing. Optimistic students are more likely to remember wanting to trade with an older sibling, whereas pessimistic students are more likely to remember wanting to trade with a younger sibling. Wanting to be more like an older sibling reflects a desire for more: more freedoms, more abilities, and more opportunities. Wanting to be more like a younger sibling reflects a desire for less: less pressure, lower expectations. This pattern recalls the social comparisons characteristic of optimists and pessimists: optimists look upward (in this case, literally) for inspiration, whereas pessimists look downward for solace.

A large group of almost 20,000 adult Finns recently provided even more compelling evidence for the relationship between optimism and resources in childhood. Adults who recalled warm, close relationships with their parents during childhood were also more optimistic. The importance of the parental resource was particularly evident when other family resources were threatened in childhood. Not surprisingly, these threats fall into the same familiar domains as goals and resources: social and status. The social integrity of the family—the primary social resource for a small child—is threatened by conflict within the family and by divorce. Finns who had experienced family conflict and divorce as children were less optimistic as adults. Likewise, the status of the family is threatened by financial problems, and those whose families had experienced financial problems when they were children were also less optimistic as adults. However, these threats were buffered by warm parental relationships. Suppose young Liisa's parents were unemployed and divorcing, but she had a good relationship with both of them. Her optimism as an adult would likely be higher than Katariina's,[4] who experienced neither conflict nor financial difficulty, but had a poor relationship with her mother. At least in early to middle childhood, the quality of child–parent relationships is the most important resource for a child and an important force in shaping that child's later optimism.

One problem with studies that ask people what their childhoods were like is that an optimistic person may *remember* childhood differently than a pessimistic person. Because optimists are more likely to pay attention to positive aspects of their environment, an optimistic child might have noticed more warmth from her mother than a pessimistic child. Childhood optimism could therefore cause both a positive perception of parents and adult optimism without the former necessarily causing the latter. Fortunately, another group of Finnish researchers has provided evidence that the mother's perception of her child at ages 3 and 6 accounts for that child's optimism at ages 24 and 27. Mothers who enjoyed being with their children more, who were more comfortable with their children, and who felt their children needed less strict discipline had more optimistic adult children. The warm and accepting mother–child relationship added an additional 5% of adult optimism to the 25% genetic endowment.

However, by the time children grow to young adulthood, it seems that relationships with parents have become less influential for a young adult's optimism. By the time children go off to college, parental warmth and approval is virtually unrelated to optimism. Developmental psychologist Erik Erikson pointed out that "there is no workable future [for a child] within the womb of his family." Just as much as a young antelope or baboon necessarily becomes less and less dependent on its mother or its natal troop as it develops, young humans evolve into independent adults and begin to locate their resources outside the nuclear family. It's very likely that social and status resources in young adulthood are more likely to be held by one's peers than one's parents. As they develop, children take more and more control over their own behavior, their resources, and therefore their optimism.

---

[4]If the Welsh ever go looking for their vowels, they might start with the Finns. (The Dutch are also likely culprits.)

THE WORLD YOU CREATE: OPTIMISM FROM THE BOTTOM UP

If you view optimism as coming only from your genes, your country, your culture, and your parents, you'll believe that optimism is largely out of your control, imposed on you rather than created by you. In personality psychology, this is considered a "top-down" definition: personality is an invisible quality that influences what you do. For example, having a hostile personality influences the way you see the world and how you behave in it. If another driver cuts you off, for example, you might think, "You a**! Learn to drive! Where do you get off?" and you might tailgate or blow your horn or make expressive hand gestures. On the other hand, if you have a conscientious personality, when you drive you probably use your turn signals, obey the speed limits, and eschew illegal U-turns.

This view of personality is called "top-down" because personality is at the top of the hierarchy, influencing what you think and do. From this perspective, you can't change your personality. You can act more or less in accordance with the dictates of your personality, but you won't really change who's at the top. Personality is king, and behavior is its vassal. Personality theorists who emphasize the influence of genes and temperament also endorse the top-down view of personality, because your innate neurological functioning is seen as influencing your ongoing thoughts, feelings, and behavior. Once again, however, this view doesn't apply as much to optimism as it does to other personality characteristics, because optimism is less genetically based than many other personality characteristics. Although some part of the well-being that comes from optimism can be attributed to its overlap with temperamental happiness or unhappiness (extraversion and neuroticism, as reviewed in Chapter 1), there's clearly more to optimism than happy and unhappy temperament.

In the 1960s almost everyone adopted the top-down perspective on how people behaved. Then, in 1968, a psychologist named Walter Mischel published a book called *Personality and Assessment*, the thesis of which sent a shock wave through personality psychology. Mischel argued that the idea that there are global personality traits that have broad influences on people's behavior (such as oral dependency, power motivation, or neuroticism, depending on your theoretical orientation) was nothing more than an illusion. Humans universally strive to predict and control their environments, and so we're motivated to see patterns and predictability wherever they might exist, and potentially some places where they do not. Mischel argued that one of these places was in other people's behavior as well as our own. He offered evidence that although we see ourselves as behaving in accordance with our character, we are actually highly changeable in our behavior depending on the situation. A friend of mine is married to a guy I would characterize as taciturn, but according to her, he talks her ear off every night when she comes home from work. Mischel argued that the idea that this guy has a "personality" that could be characterized as taciturn or talkative is absurd. Such ideas arise only from the fact that, when asked, both the subjects and the researchers are motivated to see the former as acting consistently.

You can only guess at the furor that this book caused among personality psychologists. I mentioned to an accomplished personality psychologist that I assign chapters from *Personality and Assessment* for a graduate seminar in personality, and you could see the steam coming out of this otherwise mild-mannered guy's ears. He was just finishing graduate school when Mischel's book came out, and he still blames Mischel for "practically killing personality psychology" just as he was getting started.

Personality wasn't dead, though. Instead of killing personality psychology, Mischel's arguments stimulated rebuttals and reconsiderations that changed the way we look at personality. One of these rebuttals was based on what we might call the law of reliability, which is similar to the law of averages. The law of reliability says you can't generalize from a single instance, and if you want to see an underlying pattern, you have to accumulate lots of different instances and take the average. How many times do you have to ask a person how she is feeling before you know whether you're dealing with a happy or unhappy person? A psychologist named Seymour Epstein set out to use the law of reliability to show that Mischel was wrong—that there are consistencies in behavior. He found that if you asked people on a couple of days, there wasn't very good evidence for happy or unhappy people. A small sample of days increases the probability that you will accidentally catch someone happy on an unhappy day (or vice versa), which makes them look unreliable. Increase the number of days to 10, however, and you find that people can be characterized reliably as happy or unhappy.

Emotion was not the only characteristic that provided this evidence for personality. The ways people behaved were reliable as well. Once you looked at a period of about 10 days, there were clear differences between people in the degree to which they affiliated with other people, solved problems, relaxed, or daydreamed. Some people were problem solvers, and other people were not; some people were daydreamers, and other people were not. Again, these people were not identified by a questionnaire like the Daydreaming Styles Questionnaire or genotyping (presence or absence of the daydreaming gene); they were defined by patterns in their own behavior.

This more democratic definition of personality is referred to as "bottom-up." In this view, the power to define personality lies in behavior much as the power of democratic government lies in the voters. Individual acts, like voters, combine to decide who will be at the top. From this perspective, how you behave *is* your personality. In fact, what you do from day to day, or even from hour to hour, defines the kind of person you are. Change the pattern of voting, and the leader is changed by definition. If you consider how you spend each day as "voting" for personality characteristics, you can easily imagine regime change. Even some influences that are traditionally considered top-down can be reconceptualized in this more democratic framework. For example, culture might define the acceptability or consequences of different behaviors, thereby shaping a pattern of behavior that is identified as personality. Imagine that you were born with the disposition to be emotionally demonstrative, but you were born into a culture that values emotional restraint. As a result, you learn to express little emotion in your day-to-day life. From a bottom-up perspective, you are an emotionally restrained person, because that is how you behave on an ongoing basis. You could imagine the opposite scenario, in which a dispositionally restrained person learns to be more expressive in his daily life to meet cultural expectations, becoming an emotionally expressive person from the bottom up.

The same principle is true for optimistic beliefs and behavior. In Chapter 6, I noted that even very optimistic people can have pessimistic expectations about a particular goal, like a happy person having an unhappy day. As a result, if you look only at one particular goal, like getting a good grade in a particular class, dispositional optimism doesn't seem to have much influence. If you look over a larger number of goals, though, dispositional optimism is strongly related to beliefs about particular goals. The question is, which came first? Does dispositional optimism cause people to be optimistic about particular goals (top-down), or does an aggregation of optimistic beliefs create dispositional optimism (bottom-up)?

Personally, I favor the bottom-up view because it reflects where optimism goes and where it came from better than the top-down view. If dispositional optimism is to have any meaning, it has to influence how people behave in real life, and global beliefs can't translate directly into specific behaviors. When people pursue goals, they don't pursue some kind of global goalness or goalitude; they pursue specific goals about which they have specific beliefs. Optimism as an aggregation of these specific beliefs makes more sense in terms of its day-to-day influence. What's more, the greater part of optimism, which is not a consequence of "nature," must come mainly from "nurture" or experience. Experience is not global; that is, your experience with goals was not an amorphous "success" or "failure" but rather an aggregation of the outcomes of specific goals. You have not succeeded or failed in life, but at individual goals such as getting good grades, getting a good job doing what you want to do, doing tasks within that job, meeting people, staying close to friends, making the team, winning the match, giving the speech, almost *ad infinitum.*

When I ask people to judge on an optimism questionnaire whether they believe that more good than bad things will happen to them, I am asking them to distill their beliefs about all the potentially important parts of their futures into their responses. Although there is some speculation about whether people do this accurately or not, they seem to do pretty well in this case. For example, our undergraduate goal pursuers responded to the dispositional optimism questionnaire in a way that reflected their aggregate attitudes toward their individual goals. If you turn the equation around, if I asked people about their attitudes about their individual goals, I would be asking them to apply their dispositional optimism to that specific response. Doesn't that seem backward? Bottom-up is a more sensible definition when it comes to optimism.

If I brought you into the lab 10 times and gave you difficult tasks, how would a pattern of persistence on those tasks define you? Using common trait labels, you might be identified as conscientious, and from the true bottom-up perspective a pattern of persistence needs no other label than persistent. Could you also be defined as optimistic? That's a more difficult question. Because the optimism label applies to beliefs rather than behavior, it might be inappropriate to use the term *optimism* to refer to your persistent behavior. On the other hand, it might be an appropriate *hypothesis* about you because optimism is so closely associated with persistence and because it is so unlikely for a truly pessimistic person to consistently keep trying. It might even turn out to be irrelevant to your well-being whether you are called conscientious, persistent, or optimistic because it is the pattern of behavior—the bottom-up process—that probably accounts for much of optimism's benefit (not to mention its costs, such as immunosuppression).

The bottom-up perspective on personality gives us reason to believe that if you are not at what you would consider to be an optimal level of optimism, you can still gain the benefits of being optimistic: you don't have to be inherently optimistic to live optimistically. The thesis of this book is that optimists are happy and healthy not because of who they are but because of how they act. Optimists have an advantage because their personalities lead them to do the optimistic thing naturally, but if you know what the optimistic thing is, you don't have to be an optimist to do it. You can stay the same person (thereby being recognizable to your family, friends, and coworkers— something that most people would want), just a more optimistic-acting version of yourself.

OPTIMISM'S DYNAMO

To get to the bottom of optimism, that is, the daily behaviors and experiences that add up to it, I want to return to the self-regulatory loop of Chapter 2. Recall that this is a negative feedback loop, in which a difference between your current state and goal state is closed by actions you take to get closer to your goal. Note on page 168, however, the new loop, which has some extra pieces. The first piece is a "success" box that gets activated when current state and goal state are the same. A second change is in the action oval. In the simpler loop, action was an automatic response to a discrepancy between your current state and your goal state. In the current loop, action is an option. You can *choose* either to take action to reduce a discrepancy, or to give up, which implies failure to reach your goal. This is an important part of self-regulation; without it you would be running around madly try-

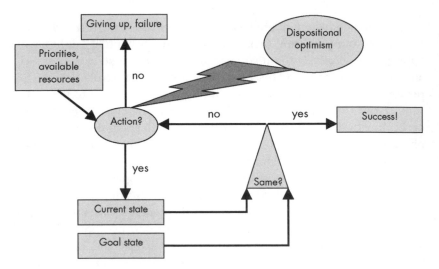

A self-regulatory loop that includes an action option and the optimism dynamo.

ing to reduce every gap between what you have and what you want at once. Generally we take goals one at a time, depending on which one takes priority at the moment. This brings us to the third change, which is a box that contains some of the determinants of whether you choose to take action or not. These include whether the goal is a high priority and whether the resources are available to reach the goal. In the simplest case, the question is, is there enough time and energy to take action? If it's the end of the day and you haven't practiced the piano yet, you can try to take action, but you might end up asleep on the keyboard. This is a bad idea because you likely aren't sleeping well, you certainly aren't practicing well, and you could drool on the keys, which is not good for them.

The fourth change, of course, is the addition of optimism. As we've seen repeatedly, one of the main things optimism does is to energize action to reach goals. It is at this action choice point that optimism influences daily behavior. When we start to look for optimistic personality in everyday life, therefore, we look for the propensity to keep taking action to reach goals. If you were to look at this figure with the eyes of a bottom-up personality theorist, you would say that the energetic essence—the dynamo—of optimism is action.

This, of course, brings us back to the previous definitional problem in which persistent behavior is called *persistence* and doesn't need a new name (*optimism*) that actually means "positive thoughts about the future." To solve this problem, let's add a few more pieces to the model. Let's add positive or negative expectations about goal accomplishment arising from success or failure. This addition does two very important things. It provides a home for a bottom-up perspective of optimism, and it closes the loop from optimism to self-regulation and back.

Without the loop closed, optimism had a top-down quality because it imposed its influence from above. With the loop closed, optimism becomes the bottom-up aggregate of individual beliefs that in turn are influenced by the outcomes of actions you choose to take or not to take. Optimism is embedded in this whole system, and although the label *optimism* is applied to a part of the system that has to do with beliefs, the phenomenon of optimism cannot be isolated from the system as a whole. Imagine that you took out the self-regulatory loop and drew arrows from *optimism* directly to *failure* or *success*. This is how many people think about optimism, but half the

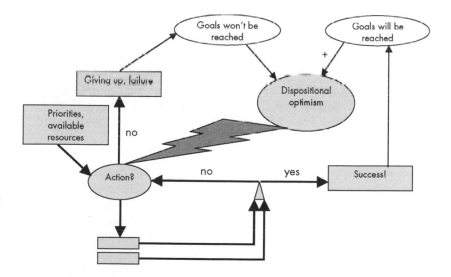

Closing the optimism loop by adding specific expectations. The original self-regulation loop is represented in miniature.

optimism system is gone! It would be like a car that has a frame, wheels, a great paint job, a leather interior, but no engine. You would probably still call it a car because it *looks* like a car, but it certainly wouldn't work like a car.

Unlike the initial self-regulatory loop, which is a negative feedback loop, the new, expanded loop that includes action, success, goal beliefs, and optimism is a positive feedback loop. The more action you take, the more likely you are to be successful, the more you will believe in succeeding at those goals, and the more optimistic you will be, which leads back to more action. Although the arrow isn't shown in the figure for the sake of simplicity, success will also build resources, which can also provide more fuel for action. This suggests an upward spiral over time.

The best data I have to show what happens to optimism over time are the 10-year follow-up questionnaires from the participants in my dissertation research. In Chapter 1, I told you that dispositional optimism was pretty stable over time, since about two-thirds of people changed by 10% or less. But what can we learn about the people who changed more than 10% and, in the case of one person, completely changed categories from pessimist to optimist?

First, average optimism increased over time for the sample as a whole. It was only a gradual increase, 5% over 10 years, but the group average did change toward the optimistic. If most people are optimistic (see Chapter 1), and optimism is a positive feedback loop, this is what you would expect: a generally optimistic group becoming a little more optimistic with each passing year. Another way of looking at this change is to compare the number of people who changed by 10% toward optimism versus pessimism: Three times as many changed toward optimism as toward pessimism.

Second, it was interesting to look at how the people whose optimism increased most were faring in terms of their resources 10 years later. If the system shown in the preceding figure is right, high levels of resources should go along with increases in optimism because both come out of the self-regulatory loop. One of the lawyers whose optimism increased quite a bit over 10 years provides an illustrative case. In terms of social resources and activities, she had a wide social network and activities including coworkers, family, friends, church, volunteering, and a club, and she rated her satisfaction with her relationships at the top of the scale. In terms of status resources, she had an excellent position within the legal field, as well as two other entrepreneurial endeavors on the side. The only area in which she was in the bottom half of the law student group: income. She made less than half as much as the top-earning lawyer in the group. On the other hand, she worked 40 hours a week, which was also below average for this group, and she was clearly using the rest of the time to build other kinds of resources that, not incidentally, add more to life than money does.

This illustrative case is supported by the pattern of change in the optimism of married working mothers. In a mirror image of the upward spiral enjoyed by many of the law students, loss of or threat to social and status resources among these women led to a loss of optimism over the subsequent year. In particular, problems in what is arguably an adult's most important relationship—with her spouse or partner—were associated with decreases in optimism over time, as were problems with her role as an employee. The cycle of optimism and resources rolls on.

When you look for evidence of your own personality, you have to look no further than your daily life. Your emotions, thoughts, goals, and behavior are dynamic, changing over the course of time, but across long periods of time, patterns emerge in the kinds of emotions, thoughts, goals, and behaviors that characterize you. Although the term *optimism* refers to thoughts, the entire system that includes optimism would consist of a tendency to think positive thoughts about the future and the likelihood of accomplishing goals, to be persistent in commitment to goals and goal-directed behavior, and to experience more positive mood and higher psychological well-being as a result. Furthermore, because this system is a positive feedback loop, gaining momentum one way or the other makes it possible for people who are optimistic to become pessimistic (if for some reason they stop engaging their goals and building their resources) and for people who are pessimistic to become optimistic (if they start engaging their goals and building their resources). This is not an easy proposition, because in a positive feedback loop, change is initially going to require swimming upstream against the momentum of one's history. On the other hand, it is possible to swim upstream, and in this case, the farther you swim, the more the current will change its direction and start to sweep you along.

CHAPTER EIGHT

Doing Optimism

Optimists, Pessimists,
and Their Potential for Change

I recently had cause to read some Web log ("blog") entries by people with broken legs (that cause being my own tibial plateau fracture and subsequent surgery to repair it), and I was struck by how many of the bloggers on the site struggled through recovery. Not incidentally, many of them were preoccupied with either underambitious or frankly pessimistic ideas about recovery from a broken leg. Many entries elaborated on how "old" they had become ("my doctor told me I had a 40-year-old knee before the accident and now I have a 60-year-old knee") or how long it took them to be able to drive, walk normally, and the like.

Now, a site like this is unlikely to attract people who are experiencing simple recoveries or have optimistic attitudes, because those people are less likely to be writing about their broken legs and more likely to be getting on with their lives. Optimistic people don't ruminate about what might have been; they act to bring about what might be. I was surprised to find so many bloggers who thought themselves ambitious to be driving again months after their accidents; one of the first things I did after my accident—in fact, at my first appointment with my orthopedic surgeon—was to get the paperwork completed for handicapped parking permits, because I was looking forward to getting around again and expected that I would be driving in short order.[1] Just over a week after my surgery, I am not quite ready to drive myself, but I do my physical therapy exercises religiously so that I will be flexible enough to get myself behind the wheel as soon as possible. I sometimes think about the long-term implications for my knee, but not as often as I think about when I will be able to start physical therapy in earnest and start rebuilding the muscles in my leg or about my ambition to be off crutches and use only a cane when my husband and I go on a second honeymoon later in the year.

Are pessimists with broken legs doing themselves a disservice with their blogs? Would they recover faster if they focused on the roadblocks to their recoveries less? I feel that they would. Furthermore, I have reason to believe that if they used their diaries somewhat differently, they could actually start to reverse the self-fulfilling prophecies of low expectations, and that the most pessimistic of them might even benefit the most.

Optimism can be defined from the bottom up as a collection of thoughts (positive expectations for the future) and behaviors (persistence, directing energy toward goals, and the like). The consequences of optimism arise from this collection of individual thoughts and acts: when people have positive thoughts about their futures, they are more likely to pursue goals that will make those futures come true. They are more likely to feel happy because they are making progress. They are more satisfied with themselves and their lives because they are building resources. They may even be healthier in the long run. I offer this reminder of what optimism in essence is and does because whether you can become more optimistic, happier, healthier, and the like depends on which statement is truer:

1. Optimism and happiness come primarily from genes, and although the leopard can get a dye job, it cannot change its spots.
2. Optimism and happiness come from your daily choices.

What if pessimism were nothing more than a habit that you could change?

---

[1] I was "lucky" enough to break my left leg, so having traded my standard-transmission car for my husband's automatic, all my driving limbs are functional.

Changing your thoughts, behaviors, and emotions just because you want to isn't all that easy. Ask anyone who's tried to get physically healthier by exercising more, eating better, or quitting smoking. Often people make several attempts at change before it sticks. Therapists who help people change their behavior, whether health behavior like exercise or emotional behavior like avoidance or passivity, know it's not just a matter of willpower, although being determined to change certainly helps.[2] Fortunately, psychologists have developed techniques that help people make difficult changes, and as it turns out, these methods can also be used to change pessimistic thoughts and behaviors. I'm not suggesting you change your essential nature to reap the benefits of optimism, however. It's like trying to teach a pig to sing: disappointing for you and frustrating for the pig. Nonetheless, there is evidence to suggest you can develop a more optimistic attitude, and if your "nature" is really just your habitual attitudes, changing your habits could actually change your nature.

THE HABIT OF OPTIMISTIC THINKING

Richard joined a study of whether people could increase their optimistic thoughts because he felt anxious and worried all the time. A decade away from retirement, he was already anticipating that it would be a personally and financially difficult transition. Certainly, attention to threats and defensive pessimism can be helpful (as considered in Chapter 6), but only when they initiate action, and in Richard's case, his vision of retirement was so pessimistic that there was no incentive to act. Perversely, although his pessimism did not motivate him to do anything about retirement, he *felt* that his worry and rumination were going to help him, and he was wary of more optimistic thoughts, claiming that such thinking created dangerous complacency and illusory hopes.

Richard was correct to be skeptical of fantasy. Fortunately, the research that he participated in was offering an experimental treatment to make people more optimistic, not one to get them to indulge in fantasy. In fact, he was encouraged *not* to fantasize. Research has

---

[2]How many psychologists does it take to change a light bulb? Only one, but the light bulb has to really *want* to change.

shown that fantasies have the opposite effect on motivation and action that optimism does. Fantasies encourage people to linger on a dream, whereas optimism encourages people to act to achieve it. Optimism involves consideration of the *contrast* between what is now and what could be: an optimistic Charlie Brown might think about the fact that he hasn't introduced himself to the little red-haired girl yet, the fact that he wants to meet her, and the odds of a successful meeting. Fantasy, on the other hand, involves immersion in an enjoyable but entirely simulated future world that doesn't admit the contrast between what is and what could be. If you're not aware of that discrepancy, you have no motivation to reduce it. As a consequence, when people only visualize already having what they want, they often disengage from actually trying to get it. If Charlie Brown wants to meet the cute little red-haired girl, sitting around imagining what it would be like to hold her hand or planning their wedding doesn't get him very far.

Beliefs such as "I'll just be disappointed if I think too positively," "I'll overlook something and fail," or "If I think too positively, I won't work hard" are not going to get you very far either. These beliefs are patently not true—optimists are not disappointed, they pay adequate attention to potential problems, and they work harder than pessimists—and they obviously inhibit attempts to have more optimistic thoughts. Richard's therapist suggested alternative thoughts about optimism, because until Richard let go of his optimism-suppressing beliefs, there was little possibility of actually starting to envision a more positive future. Once he substituted optimism-supportive beliefs, such as "optimism can decrease inertia" and "optimism can give you something to work toward," he was able to imagine his ideal retirement and consider the steps he would need to take to get there. Eventually, Richard admitted that "wishful thinking is not all undesirable." Faint praise, to be sure, but it reflected real change in psychological functioning: when tested at the end of the program, he and his fellow optimism trainees had more positive thoughts, felt more capable of solving problems, and generated more creative solutions to a real problem-solving task than people who had not been through the program.

In addition to undoing optimism-suppressing beliefs and learning to imagine a more positive future, good optimism training addresses automatic attention. The Stroop study discussed in Chapter 6 showed that optimists are automatically more attentive to positive aspects of the environment than are pessimists. Although *automatic* seems to imply "uncontrollable," automaticity is merely a function of practice. You can play a piece on the piano without thinking about where your fingers are or hit a tennis ball without thinking about what your elbow is doing only after consciously practicing the action over and over. If you have a bad habit, like biting your fingernails, the cure is to consciously substitute a better habit (even clenching your fists will do) until it automatically overrides the bad habit. When someone like Richard worries and ruminates, he is essentially practicing thinking about the negative aspects of his future and ignoring the positive. As a consequence, he develops the habit of pessimism. To undo this habit in pessimistic people, optimism training instructs people to deliberately focus on the positive, much as a nail-biter might deliberately clench his fists rather than bite his nails.

One simple way to train attention to the positive is to keep a log of three good things that happen each day. It's pretty safe to say that everyone experiences at least three good things—even if they are just little things—every day. Not everyone pays attention to them, though. Those who don't unfortunately miss the motivating and inspiring aspects of their lives, not to mention reminders of their progress and even their resources. Here are three positive things listed by an optimism trainee: seeing a pretty flower, being told he did a good job, and getting a good night's sleep. These are signs of a beautiful environment, professional progress, and energetic renewal, which are all resources that can lead to greater life satisfaction. Noticing these signs every day can help people to realize that they have more resources than they were aware of and to feel different about their lives.

In fact, this attentional change is one of the things that can lead to long-term changes in happiness, potentially allowing a person to escape the hedonic treadmill, psychological immune system, and other mechanisms that bring people back to their set points. A large study compared the effectiveness of several different 1-week exercises on happiness 6 months later. The exercises included thinking about a time in the past when you were at your best, identifying your personal strengths (such as gratitude, kindness, modesty, or curiosity), using strengths in new ways, expressing gratitude to someone you have never properly thanked, or writing down three good things that happened each day. All these exercises made people feel happier, but for the most part that happiness dissipated over time. The "three good things" exercise, though, actually increased happiness over time, so that people who did that exercise got happier and happier over 6 months. Why? First, people who did that exercise were more likely to keep doing it after their mandatory week ended. Second, as they did that, they probably got better at it. That is, over time, their attentional *habits* became more optimistic. Third, noticing the positive probably helped energize the loops shown in Chapter 7, leading to an upward spiral. A simple exercise, but one with complex, positive, and lasting effects.

OPTIMISM FOR EEYORE

For the true pessimist (or even the die-hard skeptic), changing thought habits from pessimistic to optimistic may not be as simple as retraining attitudes in the way Richard did. It's always easier to build on an existing foundation than to start from scratch, and so optimism training might be most effective for people who are already somewhat optimistic and want to expand or maximize that optimism and less effective for people who just don't feel that optimism is "them." I was in school with a couple of graduate students who were dedicated to being more positive in their attitudes, and I mean, they really worked at it. I'm sorry to say, however, that I don't think it ever really "took," because the positive veneer they put on seemed to be so easily shattered. One of them was on the verge of dropping out of graduate school whenever an obstacle or difficulty arose, which was—not atypically for difficult graduate study—about once a year. His friends and professors were pretty good at talking him down from the metaphorical ledge, but it was hard to see him as a positive or optimistic person down deep. Another problem both people had was that they were chronic giver-uppers who would start relationships or projects and abandon them a short while later. As a consequence, they failed to grow the kind of academic or social capital that you really need to keep you away from the ledge during graduate study.

Perhaps part of the problem is that being positive is not enough to get the entire optimism system working. Some evidence for the missing piece comes from studies that asked people to write journal entries about important situations in their lives. Many people think of a journal as a place to express their deepest thoughts and feelings, and there is interesting evidence that when people write about their deepest thoughts and feelings, a number of positive outcomes can ensue: better health, better immune function, better mood, and so on. Not all people improve through expressing their deepest thoughts and feelings, however, and emotional expression might not be good for people when their deepest thoughts and feelings are pessimistic. Instead of progressing toward a meaningful understanding of those thoughts and feelings, pessimists might get mired in rumination and depression. Rather than celebrating a return to weight bearing or appreciating lessons learned by breaking a leg,[3] pessimists are likely to dwell on the deficits they experience and dire predictions about their futures. Fortunately for pessimists, although it is the typical use of a journal, you don't have to use a journal to explore the deepest thoughts and feelings you already have. You can use a journal to create new habits of thinking.

One possibility is to use the journal to refocus on the possibility of a positive future, which is sort of the journal equivalent of noticing three good things because it gets you in the habit of thinking positively about the future. For example, one study asked HIV-infected women to write journal entries that focused on a future in which their treatment regimens were simple—one pill daily—which would be a significant improvement over the complex regimen currently available. Although very effective in reducing mortality, the currently available medication regimen involves taking a large number of pills on a strict schedule, some on an empty stomach, some on a full stomach, and so on. A simpler treatment regimen would significantly decrease the logistic burden of controlling HIV infection. Pessimistic women who focused on this possibility became more optimistic over the 4 weeks during which they were writing the entries.

You can also use a journal to better self-regulate, that is, to be aware of your goals, to behave in a way that is consistent with your goals, and to explore ways to overcome obstacles. Imagining not only what you want but also how you are going to get it—that is, substituting "mental simulation" (a mental practice of the steps you're going to follow) for fantasy—activates the self-regulatory loop and actually increases the odds that you'll get what you want. This way of using a journal should be particularly helpful for people who are not very

---

[3]I am already grateful for my competent and conscientious students and my culinary husband. It has been a joy to see them rise to the occasion of my sudden and unexpected disability.

optimistic and therefore don't already do this on their own and who might get mired in negative thoughts and feelings if they were to focus on expressing them. Another research study assigned college freshmen to (1) write about their deepest thoughts and feelings (expression), (2) write about their problems and challenges in college and ways they could cope with them (self-regulation), or (3) write about trivial aspects of college life (experimental control). As it turned out, the self-regulation task had the most beneficial effects. When it came to feeling better, people at all levels of optimism felt better if they did the self-regulation writing task rather than expressing their emotions or describing trivia. Optimists' health benefited from both self-regulation and expression, but pessimists' health benefited only from self-regulation and not from expression. Pessimists who expressed themselves had just as many visits to the doctor for illness as pessimists who focused on trivial topics.

The most interesting thing about these journal studies is that they were most effective for people who were the most pessimistic. On one level, this is unsurprising. After all, you wouldn't expect to dramatically influence the optimism level of someone who was already relatively optimistic. On another level, however, it's encouraging. Sometimes it's easier to build on an existing strength than to remedy a deficit—a new exercise program will be easier for a person who is already somewhat fit than for a person who is entirely sedentary. In the case of improving positive expectations and self-regulation, however, it appears to be possible to build from the ground up. By writing about their goals, ambitions, and plans to get there, the pessimistic bloggers might smooth the path to their own recovery and literally standing on their own two feet.

CHANGE YOUR LIFE
AND YOUR THOUGHTS WILL FOLLOW

The true diehard pessimist might still be skeptical that changing thoughts is possible for her. In fact, someone who is that pessimistic in general would be very likely to be pessimistic specifically about the possibility of change. Fortunately, you don't always have to believe in change for change to occur. I have seen a book entitled *Change Your Thoughts and Your Life Will Follow*. But what if the opposite were also possible? Can you change your life and have your thoughts—that is, optimism—follow?

Therapists who treat phobias see this all the time. People who have spent a lot of time and energy talking about their phobias without seeing any improvement can be especially pessimistic because they perceive themselves as untreatable. When I did my clinical internship, I treated a man named Jake who had developed an unusual phobia of hearing sirens. He worked in his home office near a busy thoroughfare, so he would hear sirens several times daily. Unlike those who fear dogs, spiders, or heights, he did not believe that the feared objects, the sirens, were going to hurt him, but he felt assailed by the noise. The more the sirens made him feel this way, the more upset he would be by subsequent sirens, which created an upward spiral of agitation. He took steps to eliminate the noise such as trying to soundproof his home office, but this only muffled the noise, and the failure to eliminate it made him feel more out of control. By the time he got to me, he had been to see several therapists and had tried our clinic only on the insistence of his family doctor, who had known another of his patients to improve there. As a consequence of his experiences, Jake felt quite pessimistic that I would be able to help him.

Fortunately for both Jake and me, I didn't need him to change the way he thought or felt about the sirens to help him get over his phobia. I only asked him to change the way he behaved. Instead of trying to avoid the sirens, I instructed him to try to hear as many sirens as loudly and as often as he could, even to the point of buying his daughter a toy ambulance with a siren (needless to say, siren toys had not been allowed in the house). That is, instead of avoiding sirens, he was now supposed to approach them.

Your thoughts, behaviors, and emotions are interrelated. The diagram on page 181 shows Jake's constellation of thoughts, feelings, and behaviors. The critical aspect of this constellation is that what you think, how you feel, and how you behave all influence each other. When Jake thought about how the sirens were both intolerable and uncontrollable, he naturally felt anxious and irritable. In turn, his anxious and irritable emotional state made him think and behave differently. Recall from Chapter 2 that emotions have signal value, and feelings of fear, anger, anxiety, and irritability signal threat. As a consequence, thoughts and attention will naturally be focused on potential threats in the environment. Left to their own devices, the thoughts and emotions will naturally spiral upward, as they had for Jake.

Now recall that Jake had also acted to reduce the impact of the sirens on his environment by soundproofing his office and forbidding toys with sirens in the house. This is not a surprising consequence of anxiety—after all, the point of feeling fearful of a saber-toothed tiger is not to induce you to go up and pet it (you might die trying). Unfortunately, however, the behaviors that arise from anxiety often either prolong or even create the feared outcome. For example, people who are insecure in their relationships often try to reassure themselves and cement their relationships by doing things like frequently asking their partners if they love them. This can, however, be perceived as nagging or clinging and can actually put the partner off. When the partner backs off, insecurity-driven behavior increases and the relationship gets on a downward spiral. Another example is the nervous speaker who tries so hard to look relaxed that she comes off as stilted. In both cases, the behavior that was intended to alleviate the problem actually creates it.

Unfortunately, the kind of behavior that Jake was pursuing to control his anxiety—avoidance of sirens—virtually eliminated the mechanisms that could actually change his anxious thoughts and alleviate his emotional distress. Getting him to pursue exposure to the very thing that made him anxious, done properly, could be an incredibly effective remedy. Why?

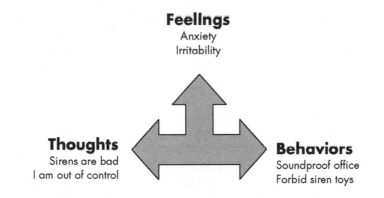

Feelings
Anxiety
Irritability

Thoughts
Sirens are bad
I am out of control

Behaviors
Soundproof office
Forbid siren toys

Thoughts, emotions, and behaviors are all interrelated.

On a very basic level, we might define it as effective because it undoes the problematic behavior. The definition of phobia includes avoidance of the feared situation that impairs the person's ability to live his life. If you can eliminate avoidance, impairment is decreased by definition: a person with social phobia is now talking to people at parties, a person with agoraphobia is now going to the grocery store. This is the psychopathology version of a bottom-up definition: What you do is the nature of your problem.

Exposure can, however, produce more benefit than behavioral change, because feelings and thoughts are linked to behaviors. The more experience people have with the situations they fear, the more they realize that the imagined consequences are not likely to come to pass and, if they do, they are not as catastrophic as feared. They become less anxious and fearful in those situations, which makes anxious thoughts and behaviors less likely. As thoughts and feelings change to be less anxious and anxiety provoking, exposure to the situations becomes easier, leading to greater cognitive and emotional change: an upward spiral that leads to overcoming fear.

In essence, when using exposure therapy, therapists are sending patients out into feared situations to collect data. If the sirens went all day, would you really go crazy? One of my favorite training experiences as a therapist was a workshop with the British psychologist Paul Salkovskis, an expert in treating anxiety disorders. In the workshop we watched a video of Salkovskis collecting data on the hypothesis of a patient with anxiety that any atypical behavior (like having a panic attack) would cause people to gather, sneer, point, and so on. Salkovskis did this by taking his patient to the mall. The patient gathered data by watching while Salkovskis did a Monty Pythonesque silly walk right through the middle of the mall. (How many people gathered, sneered, pointed, and so on? Try it for yourself sometime.)

Trying to change your feelings by changing your behavior has two advantages. First, behavior is easier to change than thoughts or emotions. Emotions are notoriously difficult to change through an act of willpower. In fact, if emotions have signal value, the ability to change them at will would actually be a pretty big design flaw in the human self-regulatory machine. What good would it be to voluntarily stop the hair on the back of your neck from prickling if, as a consequence, you missed the fact that a saber-toothed tiger was about an inch from said neck? Using the analogy between people and thermostats in Chapter 2, being able to change emotion at will would be something like being able to change the room temperature reading on the thermostat without actually changing the temperature in the room. This would be pretty stupid, because not only would you still be too hot (or too cold), but you would actually stop doing anything about it because the gauge said everything was okay.

If your therapist tells you, "Don't worry, be happy," find a new therapist (if for no other reason than that given in the very first point in the Prologue of this book, that trying to be happier can backfire on you). Find one who will teach you ways to change your behaviors to escape the downward spiral. Don't worry about the emotions. They will take care of themselves.

Second, when you target behavior, you don't have to believe in the possibility of cognitive and emotional change for change to occur. It helps, but it's not necessary. Over a period of weeks, Jake's attitude toward the sirens changed. By actively pursuing exposure, he found that just listening to the sirens was not intolerable after all; he could tolerate as much noise as they could produce. He felt more in control and able to cope, and his anxiety decreased. Jake reversed the downward spiral he had been on by taking control of the behavioral part of the spiral and letting thoughts and emotions come along for the ride.

Behavior change may also be the best route to the benefits of optimism because it does not require the adoption of thoughts that for some people may feel foreign. Furthermore, the loops in Chapter 7 suggest that the truest route to optimism is to act like an optimist until the positive feedback loop kicks in and starts growing optimism from the bottom up. That is, if you really want to develop optimism, "fake it till you make it." People can learn to be more optimistic by acting as if they were more optimistic. In this case, that means being more engaged with and persistent in the pursuit of goals. What are your goals? What is important to you?

Make a list of your goals or write a description of what you want yourself and your life to look like in a few months or years. Every once in a while, look at it. In the self-regulation study, students wrote in their journals on only three occasions. For only 5 minutes on each occasion, they listed three things that they could do to help them deal with the problems and challenges they were facing in the transition to college. Those 5 minutes, however, were critical to the benefit that accrued to their happiness and health. Even brief reminders about important goals and brief plans about how to go about reaching them can make a big difference. Get a little chalkboard or even a sticky note and write down three things you can do to help you get to your most important goal. Next week, evaluate whether any of them are working and whether they should be continued, modified, or replaced. This may be all the "journal" you need.

Behaving optimistically can also translate into trying one more time (or maybe more) when you feel like giving up, because that's what an optimist would do. Be ready for the possibility that you might succeed more than you expected. Also be ready for the possibility that you might not succeed even when you persist. See those as learning experiences: even if persistence doesn't pay off, you start to learn the signals that differentiate trying hard to get a date from stalking.[4] Next time, you will be wiser. Keep it up long enough and you're on your way to optimistic behavior and all that comes with it.

TAPPING YOUR INNER MOTIVATION

As Jennifer's and Marie's goals in Chapter 2 showed, optimists and pessimists don't necessarily have different kinds of goals. Nonetheless, I'd be remiss if I did not address the effects of the kinds of goals you have and where they came from, because both are very important for a goal's effect on well-being.

Each year my students and I interview each of the law students participating in our ongoing optimism–immunity research. The interview focuses on their perceptions of what has been challenging or difficult (stress processes from Chapter 3), whether they compared themselves with others (social comparison processes from Chapter 4), and so on. The interview opens with a "warm-up" question, which was

---

[4]A caveat: At each point, you have to weigh the benefit of accomplishing your goal against the potential cost. If the worst that can happen is that you get turned down for a date, it might be worth asking again later if you were turned down the first time. The potential cost to your ego may be rather small compared with the potential benefit of getting the date. On the other hand, if you have been threatened with a restraining order, you should really question whether the extremely small likelihood of actually getting the date is worth the financial and opportunity costs of going to jail.

originally intended to let the students relax and get used to talking on tape before the hard questions start. We begin this way: "Tell me about why you decided to go to law school."

As we've found, students go to law school for all kinds of different reasons. Some enjoy the intellectual challenge, some want to use a law degree as a means to a career in another field such as government, some are going into the family business (everyone else in the family is a lawyer), and some want to be able to help and protect others using the legal system. Some even go to law school as a default professional degree—medicine wasn't appealing (all those sick people), and a PhD takes too long. Although all these students were working toward the same goal—to graduate from law school—that goal had very different origins for different students.

When you think about *what* goals you have, be sure to think also about *why* you have them. Self-determination theory says that people have three basic psychological needs: competence (doing well), relatedness (connecting with others), and autonomy (acting freely). Well-being and healthy development arise from pursuits that meet these needs. When a goal arises from a person's own values and identity, it is called "self-determined" (hence, self-determination theory). Self-determined goals provide their own reward and motivation because they meet autonomy needs (you are acting freely in adopting the goal). That is, goals you choose yourself are inherently rewarding. Macaroni art is not a good money-making proposition but, when intrinsically motivated, offers an opportunity for the exercise of creativity and skill (forms of competence) and autonomy. Goal pursuits that are extrinsically motivated—that arise from the pursuit of external rewards or punishments, to avoid guilt or shame, or because of rules (real or imagined)—can never offer the same reward.

Furthermore, people make better progress toward intrinsically motivated goals than extrinsically motivated goals and feel better while doing it. Students who are intrinsically motivated learn better than students who are extrinsically motivated. Churchgoers who are intrinsically motivated have greater well-being than those who are extrinsically motivated. Among our law students, we would expect that those who went to law school for intrinsic reasons (they enjoy the law, they want to help people) to be better adjusted and more successful than those who went to law school for extrinsic reasons (my husband wants me to make more money, Grandpa always wanted me to be a lawyer).

Providing external reasons for doing something can even undermine existing intrinsic motivation. In one classic demonstration of this effect, when children who were interested in drawing were told they could get a certificate by doing more drawings, they eventually lost interest in drawing, spending about half as much free playtime drawing after the certificate offer as before. Children who were unexpectedly given a certificate or who did the extra drawings "for free" stayed interested in drawing. Once kids expected that they should get some kind of reward apart from their own enjoyment, they stopped being rewarded *by* their own enjoyment.[5]

In adulthood, cultural messages about the importance of extrinsic rewards may also undermine our best motivations. When students start law school, most of them pursue academic goals because they think those goals are important and they find them enjoyable and stimulating. As law school progresses, however, a number of messages, explicit and implicit, begin to take a toll on these students. Students start hearing more and more about money and status and not as much about public service, intellectual stimulation, or other personal reasons for studying the law. Consequently, they start to pursue certain goals and pathways because of the money or status, because other people think they should, or because they would feel guilty if they didn't. Intrinsic motivation falls as much as 25% in the first few months of law school, a change that leads to a loss of well-being and an increase in physical symptoms such as insomnia and headaches. When law students' intrinsic interest in the law is supplanted by expectation of extrinsic rewards, they suffer.

Unhappily for those who become absorbed in extrinsic motivators for their behavior, this change in motivation works against them, since extrinsic motivation also predicts lower grades in law school, and lower grades means less ability to pursue the "status" careers. The pursuit of extrinsically motivated goals may be self-defeating.

If you were to make a list of your goals, it might be tempting to idealize it:

---

[5]Note that extrinsic motivators are still extremely useful for increasing the likelihood that a kid will do something that is not intrinsically motivating, like taking out the trash, picking up toys, brushing teeth, feeding the dog, and so on.

Write a guaranteed best-seller novel
Run for Mrs. Jessamine County
Keep up correspondence with 300 best friends (reminder: buy
  more engraved notecards)
Have four perfect offspring
Teach four perfect offspring to play violin, viola, and cello for
  perfect offspring string quartet
Host elaborate dinners for 40 (reminder: dig wine cellar)

However, when you consider your goals, you do yourself a disservice if you edit yourself or try to limit yourself to what you think are good or admirable goals. If you want to learn macaroni art, don't leave it off the list. No one can tell you what your goals should be. Other people may have goals for you, but those are their goals and not necessarily yours. In fact, these two sets of goals are so distinct that people who study the self actually separate out two *possible selves*, which are people's views of what they might look like in the future: an "ideal" self that incorporates a wished-for future self based on one's own values and goals and an "ought" self that incorporates a future self based on other people's imposed wishes, values, and goals. The goals that drive you may be either your own or other people's. Maybe other people have very good ideas for what you should be like, but the research evidence suggests that when it comes to happiness, your goals are better for you than other people's goals.

Like goal engagement, intrinsic motivation is something you may be able to maintain through a simple process of reminding yourself. Psychologist Ken Sheldon and his colleagues have suggested some strategies for increasing intrinsic motivation that may help you:

1. *Own the goal.* Think back to the core value, important resource, or ideal self that the goal expresses. What does macaroni art do for you? Does it tap into your desire to create? Does it allow you to unleash your inner Impressionist?
2. *Make it fun.* Pursue the goal in a context you enjoy. Find people, times, or settings that maximize enjoyment. For example, while riding the stationary bike one day, I was reading an interesting book on self-regulation.[6] For perhaps a better

---

[6]For nongeeks: This made it more fun.

example, the author of that book wrote about how, when he lived in Europe, his morning jog seemed effortless because his route took him through a park known for topless sunbathing.
3. *Remember the big picture.* If you have a relatively narrow goal ("lose 10 pounds"), what broader purpose does it serve ("live a longer, healthier life")?

The first rule of doing optimism is pursuing goals. Optimism acts as a kind of permissive agent for all kinds of motivation, because the ability to see positive outcomes promotes all kinds of motivation. Pessimism can undermine intrinsic motivation via negative expectations for achieving competence, connectedness, and autonomy; likewise, pessimism can undermine extrinsic motivation, if the expectation is that external punishments are more likely than rewards. Because any motivation is clearly better than no motivation in terms of well-being and performance, optimism yields benefits in those areas. However, focusing the benefit of optimistic beliefs on self-determined, intrinsically motivated goals may further increase its power by channeling the resulting motivation into goals that will meet the basic needs of competence, connectedness, and autonomy.

RESOURCE GROWTH FROM DAY TO DAY

While I was working on this book, the 2005 New Year passed. Two days later, in the *New York Times*, I found the following headline:

Resolved: To Do More. Or Less. Or Something.

Guides to self-improvement can't agree on whether to go faster
or slower on the road to happiness.

Apparently self-improvement books fall into two camps: Those that claim you'll be happier when you do more (wake up early, set goals, make lists) and those that claim that you'll be happier when you do less (sleep late, relax, contemplate). I immediately thought of this book and whether, if it were a guide to self-improvement, it would fall into the former or the latter camp. It seemed likely, perhaps overwhelmingly so, that it would fall into the former group, the club of the do-mores, the back-to-works, the get-after-its. I was a little chagrined by this thought, because I don't necessarily believe people don't do enough. I do, however, believe sometimes people aren't doing the right things.

Just a month before the *New York Times* article, another article came out in the much less widely read, but equally if not more prestigious, publication *Science*. This article had the titillating title:

A Survey Method for Characterizing Daily Life Experience
The Day Reconstruction Method

The results of the survey were, fortunately, more interesting than the title of the article. The survey included 909 daily diaries kept by working women who recorded their activities, positive and negative feelings during those activities, and how many hours per day they engaged in those activities. Here are the most common activities in these women's daily lives and the average number of hours per day spent in each activity:[7]

Activity	Average hours/day	Activity	Average hours/day
Work	6.9	Prepare food	1.1
Talk on phone	2.5	Take care of children	1.1
Socialize	2.3	Housework	1.1
Relax	2.2	Nap	0.6
Eat	2.2	Pray/worship/meditate	0.4
Watch TV	2.2	Shop	0.4
Computer/ e-mail/Internet	1.6	Intimate relations	0.2
Commute	1.6	Exercise	0.2

[7]The totals add up to more than 24 hours per day because a person can engage in more than one activity at once; for example, eating and talking on the phone, socializing and working, and even napping and commuting (if you take the bus or train).

This seems like a very ordinary way to spend your day, and I would say my day often looks similar. What is extraordinary is to compare the relative amount of time spent in each activity with the relative amount of positive and negative mood experienced during that activity. If this is a typical day, then we all look a little bit like masochists, because the things we spend the *most* time on are often things that make us feel the most negative and least positive (commuting, computer) and the things we spend the *least* time on are mostly things that make us feel the most positive and least negative (exercise, intimate relations, prayer or meditation).

Recall from Chapters 2 and 3 that the best activities for happiness and well-being are those that lead to progress toward goals and building resources. This study was a nice demonstration of that principle, because the women in the study were happiest when they were engaged in exactly those kinds of activities. These women were at their happiest when they were building basic, energetic resources by relaxing, eating, or exercising; when they were building social resources by socializing or being intimate; or when they were building existential resources by praying.

How do the ways in which you expend time and energy resources in your daily life correspond to your goals? If you can't answer clearly, or the way you're spending resources doesn't correspond to your values, it might be time for you to revise your behaviors so they align with your goals. Furthermore, having established that you have to develop and believe in your *own* goals, I would now like to tell you what your goals should be. Not all goals are created equal in terms of their potential to do good or harm. First, intrinsically motivated goals are clearly better for you than extrinsically motivated goals. Second, goals that build resources are clearly better for you than goals that do not build resources.

Consider the following goals from our student goals study:

Stop biting fingernails
Save money
Be more patient with roommate
Make Mom proud
Be attractive
Strengthen religion

Get a degree
Keep good friendships

These goals obviously differ in the degree to which they're going to build resources. In general, goals that self-determination theory labels "intrinsic" (that is, they satisfy basic needs such as autonomy, competence, and relatedness) build better and more lasting resources than goals that are "extrinsic" (that is, they display worth to others but may have little worth in and of themselves). In this list, intrinsic goals include affiliation with others (for example, be more patient with roommate, keep good friendships), which builds social resources; achievement (for example, get a degree), which builds status resources; and personal growth (for example, strengthen religion), which builds existential resources. Extrinsic goals focus on attaining wealth, fame, or image (for example, be attractive). If they build any resources at all, extrinsic goals build status resources. However, self-determination theory would predict that some status resources are "empty"–they are not valid resource currency.[8] Although wealth, fame, and image may buy admiration, to be truly helpful they need to be convertible into other meaningful resources. When the famous fall, their fame may be converted into help and support, but it seems just as likely–if not more likely–that others will respond with the emotion of *schadenfreude*, which can best be described as a feeling of smugness, satisfaction, or even glee at another's downfall.

I believe it's fair to say that everyone needs all kinds of resources: basic resources, social resources, and status resources (especially certain status resources such as knowledge that help meet basic needs such as competence). In addition to the "why" of your goals, then, it's worthwhile to contemplate the "what" of your goals. What resources are you building and what is their value?

[8]Where some goals fall on the resource dimension isn't always immediately obvious from the goals themselves. If you stop biting your fingernails because you want to have 5-inch red talons that will impress your manicurist and associated fingernail fetishists, that extrinsic orientation isn't going to build important resources. On the other hand, if you stop biting your fingernails so that you can play classical guitar, that intrinsic orientation and the way the goal feeds into higher competence and autonomy needs means that your success may in fact help you build important resources. Either way, try the fist-clenching exercise suggested earlier.

REBUILDING YOUR DAY

Now, you're probably saying to yourself, HA! The reason I do things that don't necessarily pursue intrinsic goals that build my resources and make me happy is that I *have* to do things like commuting, and that doesn't leave me very much time to do other things like have intimate relations. You have a point. If you look at things that people have to do (food preparation, child care, housework, working, commuting), those things don't make them as happy as the things they don't have to do (socialize, watch TV, nap, have intimate relations). Using the difference between positive and negative mood from the study of women's daily lives as a "mood balance index," optional activities averaged 3.7, whereas mandatory activities averaged 3.0.[9] These numbers are calculated including eating with mandatory activities. Eating was the most pleasant mandatory activity by far, averaging 3.8, so if you don't include eating, the difference is even bigger.

On the other hand, if you include only optional activities in the analysis, the same relationship is revealed: we spend more time doing things that make us less happy and spend less time doing the alternatives that make us more happy. It's not a matter of doing more or doing less; it's a matter of picking the right thing to do.

I was very surprised when the media reports of this research focused on how watching TV was one of Americans' happiest activities, because that wasn't the usual relationship between TV and happiness. (I was also a little alarmed that I might have to go back and rewrite the prologue to this book.) When I looked at the original research report, though, I found that although people were generally happy when they were watching TV, this happiness was a little below average for optional activities. So, I started monkeying around with the typical day. First I took out TV and redistributed that time to activities that were more positive, the same ones that have the greatest

---

[9]Overall, people were much more likely to experience positive moods (happy, warm, friendly, enjoying myself) than negative moods (frustrated, annoyed, depressed, blue, hassled, pushed around, angry, hostile, worried, anxious, criticized, put down). This was true even in the least pleasant circumstance, commuting, which averaged 3.5 for positive feelings and 0.9 for negative feelings for a "mood balance index" of 2.6.

capacity to build resources.[10] As you might expect, mood balance improved, and the relationship between time spent on activities and mood balance became neutral, so that now a more pleasing activity was not associated with less time spent in that activity.

Then I went really crazy. I took time away from the computer (e-mail, Internet, computer games, and so on) and redistributed that time to the more positive activities. When I did that, mood balance increased even more, and without TV or computer, the relationship between time and mood finally went positive, so that more time was at last being spent on more pleasing activities. People are generally happy when watching TV or playing computer games, sending e-mail, and so on, but then again, they are mostly happy all the time. In *every* situation, on average, the women in this study had between 4 and 10 times as much positive mood as they had negative mood. Just because an activity is pleasing doesn't mean it's a good way to spend your time if you want to get the most out of your emotional life.

Interestingly, activities that tend to increase status resources were not those that yielded the most positive mood balance. They did, however, dramatically increase another feeling: competence. Another article, this one from the *Chicago Tribune*, questioned the value of activity that increases status—that is, work:

There's No Stopping Us: We Work Too Much . . . and Play Too Little . . . but Who Dares Step Off the Treadmill?

The thesis of the article, obviously, was that we work too much, and with increasing length of the workweek and electronic tethers such as cell phones and remote access to e-mail, we may not ever escape from work at all. But there was an antithesis, too: Work is

---

[10]These more positive activities included having intimate relations (4.7), socializing (4.0), relaxing (3.9), praying or meditating (3.8), and exercising (3.8). I gave each of them an extra 24–30 minutes per day to compensate for the 2.2 hours that used to be spent watching TV. Now, some of these activities may have already been simultaneous with TV watching (for example, relaxing), but for the sake of illustration, I'm assuming that not watching 2.2 hours of TV will free up 2.2 hours for doing something else that can be done without the TV on, such as any of the aforementioned activities. Without being too explicit, some of them may even be more enjoyable if not done with the TV on.

experienced as a rewarding and exciting experience. Compared with leisure, work is more likely to yield the opportunity to pursue goals, build resources, challenge ourselves, and develop a sense of purpose. It doesn't have to be white-collar work, either. Many people with blue-collar jobs, such as janitors, see their work as fulfilling and worthwhile, whereas others with white-collar jobs are only working for the money.

The writer of the *Tribune* article, Chris Jones, admitted,

> The most chaotic weekend of my life this past year was when I got stuck in the blackout in New York and had to keep working. Not only did I dine out on those stories for months—starring myself as the hardworking hero—but I also was strangely content at that time. So, I suspect, were the emergency workers and the power crews. We all stopped worrying about growing older, a loved one's health, or some perceived slight at work—all stuff that consumes me when idle. Instead, we felt needed, albeit in my case mainly in my own mind. In short, we were engaged.

Could the treadmill actually be the road to happiness? The problem with the treadmill analogy is that it mixes two ingredients together: working hard and doing the same thing over and over again. It's okay to step off the treadmill if you hit the running trail, doing the same work in a different context. After all, one thing we have to avoid if we want to maximize well-being is that other treadmill, the hedonic treadmill, and to do that we have to constantly strive for new and different accomplishments, new levels of performance, intimacy, or connection to the future.

As little as we like it, there is only so much time and energy available to each of us, and we can spend it as we wish. The study of optimism has inspired me to think more often about the time and energy available to me and whether I'm using it in ways that build me up. If I didn't watch *ER* on Thursday night, slept an extra hour, and had more energy to interact with my students on Friday, is that a better investment? If I spent an hour less on Friday surfing the Web and had a cocktail with my girlfriends, is that a better investment? It might build my social resources more than any other thing I do all week. How do you use your time and energy? Are you making the most of your optimism?

Epilogue
Confessions of a Reluctant Optimist

I have a confession to make: I am still not always eager to identify myself as an optimist.

I've already explained how I manage to weasel my way out of journalists' questions about whether I'm optimistic. In part, I couldn't identify with the stereotype of the happy-go-lucky optimist, but that's not the whole story. Another part was that saying out loud that you're optimistic is a little bit embarrassing. Once I tried to dodge the question by telling a reporter that I thought I was quite optimistic in some domains but not others. For example, I explained, I have very optimistic expectancies when it comes to my work, but more pessimistic expectancies in other domains, like (at that time) finding dates. What was the last line of the article when it came out? "'I'm a professional optimist,' Segerstrom says."

Do you think I took some ribbing for that? It sounded like I was claiming to make a living being optimistic! I was humiliated! And as I recall, at least one of my colleagues gave me serious grief about the quote, and that was a fellow optimism researcher. I can't imagine what my colleagues who study "serious" subjects like psychopathology or discrimination thought, but they didn't say anything. They probably were embarrassed to know me.

In part, I was embarrassed to be portrayed that way because the study of "positive" topics, like optimism or happiness, attracts a lot of skepticism from people who study "negative" topics. The stereotype of people who study positive topics is that they are not serious scientists. Unlike serious scientists, they are thought to have biases that influence the kind of work they do; for example, they are unwilling to believe that there is any downside to what they do and don't tolerate any dissent (actually, this wouldn't just disqualify you as a serious scientist; it would disqualify you as any kind of scientist). The stereotype portrays people who study these topics as interested only in Pollyannas and, worse, as Pollyannas themselves who refuse to see the negative side of anything.

Voltaire exploited this stereotype of optimism in his book *Candide*. The eponymous Candide, an open and naïve young man, has as his tutor Dr. Pangloss. Pangloss famously believes that all is (always) for the best, and, being a good pupil, so does Candide. Does Candide flourish because of his optimistic beliefs? Not at all. Voltaire rewards Candide for his optimism by consigning him to the Bulgar army, where he receives four thousand lashings. Through the rest of the book, Candide suffers through storm, shipwreck, earthquake, slavery, more floggings, war, near cannibalism (featuring Candide as dinner), thievery, deceit, and imprisonment. To top it off, when Candide finally is reunited with his beloved, for whom he has endured all these insults, she has turned into an ugly hag. This is considered a good joke on optimists.[1]

Ironically, in addition to being one of the purported Pollyannas or Panglosses, I am also one of the skeptics, which puts me in the awkward position of being suspicious of myself. A few years ago, a group of psychologists who study "positive psychology," topics like positive emotion, growth, and strength, started getting together. Spearheaded by Martin Seligman, whose research interests include optimistic explanatory style,[2] this group began holding an annual summit. I confess here that the first time I attended this summit, I sat near the

---

[1] I must point out that although Dr. Pangloss also flirts with death, first by syphilis and later by hanging, he ultimately survives—and with his optimism intact.

[2] The ways that people typically explain the events in their lives. Although this trait and dispositional optimism share the optimism label, they are actually fairly unrelated to each other. Whether you have an optimistic explanatory style has very little relation to whether you are also a dispositional optimist. This probably occurs because explanatory style is about things that have already happened to you, whereas dispositional optimism is about things that are going to happen to you. Those can be related, but they don't have to be.

door, poised to bolt at the first sign of Pangloss-ology. Instead, I found a serious and scientific consideration of the whos, whys, and hows of positive characteristics like happiness, including a presentation of the research discussed at the very beginning of this book that showed that trying to be happy may actually be a bad idea. Reassured that I wasn't getting into what some people (still) view as a happiness cult, I signed on. Good thing, too: one of the best intellectual experiences I have ever had was later attending a "think tank" for young positive psychologists. A few years later, I won the Templeton Positive Psychology Prize, which continues to fund some of the more innovative research in my lab, including studies that a larger, more established funding agency like the National Institutes of Health or the National Science Foundation might find too risky.

Although I was won over by the science, others' skepticism of positive psychology thrived. The Positive Psychology Prize was criticized for what was apparently perceived as bribery to entice young scientists to sign on with the positivity cult, like luring innocent children with candy. These critics apparently ignored the fact that I won the prize for work showing that optimism can be associated with suppression of the immune system. If positive psychologists were interested in only good news about optimism and the like, I never would have made it to the interview, much less won the prize.

I think a lot of skepticism about me and other "positive psychologists" (including my own skepticism) arises from the prominence of certain well-known advocates of positive thinking. I recently borrowed from my library a couple of examples from two such advocates, theologian Norman Vincent Peale and surgeon Bernie Siegel. Peale is, of course, the author of *The Power of Positive Thinking*, a 1950s volume that still sells well. The book I checked out was a 1976 follow-up called *The Positive Principle Today*. When I read the Foreword, I thought maybe I had been scooped by 30 years or so, because Peale wrote that his advice to people is to "Keep it going." That sounded a lot like what I have learned about optimism—that optimists' propensity to "keep it going" is responsible for many of the consequences of being optimistic. When I read further, however, I found that the book focused on the consequences of keeping a positive *attitude* going. In a series of tales about successful people, the miraculous consequences of positive thoughts were attributed to just having the thoughts. To wit: "That which we intensely image can and often does actualize in fact."

Even the chapter entitled "You Can Do Wonders If You Keep Trying" mainly advocated persistently visualizing those wonders, with less discussion of exactly how they were supposed to come about.

The book reminded me of another classmate I had in graduate school, a nurse who was enamored of the miraculous cure. At the beginning of class one day, she mentioned one of her patients who had been treated for cancer and was told that he would be infertile. He and his wife prayed and prayed for her to get pregnant, and she had finally conceived. Now, sometimes things come out of my mouth before I get a chance to put the brakes on, and I blurted out, "I'll bet they were doing a lot more than praying!" That was sort of an embarrassing thing to say in a graduate seminar, but the point is that the Norman Vincent Peale principle of letting God take care of everything may not be the whole solution. Remember too the Benjamin Franklin principle: God helps those who help themselves.

The Peale book was full of examples of people whose positive thoughts helped them achieve miraculous things. In this respect it was very similar to Bernie Siegel's book *Love, Medicine, and Miracles*, which was also full of examples of how positive patients and doctors effect miraculous cures and how negative patients and doctors cut life short. Notable by their absence were the examples of people whose positive visualizations were not realized. As a graduate student, I interviewed patients for a research project on adjustment to cancer. During the study, one of my assigned patients died. My last interview with her took place in the hospital, where she was fighting her disease and the side effects of treatment with the help of her family and friends, who brought all her meals in from outside (she decided she had too many other things to deal with to eat hospital food). She told me about the plans that she and her husband had to travel the world. Where was her miracle? Siegel's thesis implies that she had something wrong with her, that she didn't hope enough, that she didn't believe enough.

It's that kind of implication that makes researchers want to get as far from positivity gurus as they can. Scientists spend lifetimes trying to work out what is true and what is not about how humans work. I have spent the last 10 years of my life learning enough about optimism to be able to write this book, and it might be another 10 years (or longer) before I have accumulated enough scientific knowledge to fill another one. The research takes time, not least because scientists are usually not confident enough to promote their findings as fact until there is some convergence of evidence. Remember the sports analogy from Chapter 5? You wouldn't want to claim that the New Orleans Saints (who have never been to, much less won, the Super Bowl) are a better football team than the New England Patriots (who have been to three Super Bowls in the past 3 years and won two) on the basis that the former won the first game of their season and the latter lost theirs. To play out the season and find out who is really the better team takes a long time.

Doing research into the effects of optimism on health leaves a person feeling a little vulnerable to being lumped in with the children of *The Power of Positive Thinking* and *Love, Medicine, and Miracles*. Nonetheless, I have come to accept the fact that I am both an optimism scientist and an optimist myself. A few years ago, as part of my interactions with the other positive psychologists, I was inspired to take a questionnaire that measured my psychological strengths. Fortunately for me as an academician, my strengths included love of learning, appreciation of excellence, and curiosity about the world, not to mention humor, which helps me laugh at the vicissitudes of academic life. My final strength was optimism, as defined this way: "You expect the best in the future, and you work to achieve it. You believe that the future is something that you can control." I love that definition of optimism because it moves directly from positive thoughts about the future to their most important consequence: working to achieve that future.

So, I will face the cynics and admit here that I am an optimist. Rather than let this admission lead me to take steps to cure myself of optimism, I will instead offer a different 12 steps to confirm it:

1. Believed that good things were in my future.
2. Worked to make that future come true.
3. When encountering roadblocks, considered them carefully and worked to eliminate them.
4. Got off the hedonic treadmill by always having new goals to work toward.
5. Focused on goals that would build basic, social, status, and existential resources.
6. Prioritized goals that were important to me.

7. Believed the best of others and was inspired by them.
8. Spent basic resources to meet my goals, neither hoarding time and energy nor squandering them to no purpose.
9. Structured my day to make the most of my goals and resources.
10. Slept and ate well to replenish energy resources.
11. Accepted that optimism is not the answer to everything.
12. Stayed away from the roulette wheel.

Notes

PROLOGUE

Page 1

Happy people are more popular, successful, live longer: Danner, D. D., Snowdon, D. A., & Friesen, W. V. (2001). Positive emotions in early life and longevity: Findings from the Nun Study. *Journal of Personality and Social Psychology, 80*, 804–813. Diener, E., & Seligman, M. E. P. (2002). Very happy people. *Psychological Science, 13*, 81–84.

An experiment about the effects of trying to be happy: Schooler, J. W., Ariely, D., & Loewenstein, G. (2003). The pursuit and assessment of happiness can be self-defeating. In I. Brocas & J. D. Carrillo (Eds.), *The psychology of economic decisions* (Vol. 1, pp. 41–70). New York: Oxford University Press.

Page 2

Millennium celebrations: Schooler et al. (2003), op. cit.

Page 3

Americans are no happier today: Myers, D. G. (2000). The funds, friends, and faith of happy people. *American Psychologist, 55*, 56–67.

Number of votes, 2000 presidential election: www.census.gov

Page 5

Money doesn't buy happiness: Diener, E., & Seligman, M. E. P. (2004). Beyond money: Toward an economy of well-being. *Psychological Science in the Public Interest, 5.*

Notes

Page 6

Happiness for lottery winners versus accident victims: Brickman, P., Coates, D., & Janoff-Bulman, R. (1978). Lottery winners and accident victims: Is happiness relative? *Journal of Personality and Social Psychology, 36,* 917–927.

Page 10

Optimism 25% heritable: Plomin, R., Scheier, M. F., Bergeman, C. S., Pedersen, N. L., Nesselroade, J. R., & McClearn, G. E. (1992). Optimism, pessimism, and mental health: A twin/adoption analysis. *Personality and Individual Differences, 13,* 921–930.

Page 11

Forgiving of a number of cook errors: For a description of the Betty Crocker test kitchens and how they errorproof recipes, see Marks, S. (2004). *Finding Betty Crocker: The secret life of America's first lady of food.* New York: Simon & Schuster.

CHAPTER 1

Page 18

Optimism and pessimism in Alzheimer's caregivers: Robinson-Whelen, S., Kim, C., MacCallum, R. C., & Kiecolt-Glaser, J. K. (1997). Distinguishing optimism from pessimism in older adults: Is it more important to be optimistic or not to be pessimistic? *Journal of Personality and Social Psychology, 73,* 1345–1353.

Page 21

Optimism a significant predictor of well-being: Robinson-Whelen et al. (1997), op. cit., p. 1352.

Positive and negative expectancies in Navy recruits: Marshall, G. C., Wortman, C. B., Kusulas, J. W., Hervig, L. K., & Vickers, R. R. (1992). Distinguishing optimism from pessimism: Relations to fundamental dimensions of mood and personality. *Journal of Personality and Social Psychology, 62,* 1067–1074.

Page 23

A gene that carries the catchy title SLC6A4: Caspi, A., Sugden, K., Miffitt, T. E., Taylor, A., Craig, I. W., Harrington, H., et al. (2003). Influence of life stress on depression: Moderation by a polymorphism in the 5–HTT gene. *Science, 301,* 386–389.

Notes

Page 24

Heritability of optimism lower than for other personality dimensions: Plomin, R., Scheier, M. F., Bergeman, C. S., Pedersen, N. L., Nesselroade, J. R., & McClearn, G. E. (1992). Optimism, pessimism and mental health: A twin/adoption analysis. *Personality and Individual Differences, 13,* 921–930.

Abruptly stopping SSRIs results in a withdrawal syndrome: Black, K., Shea, C., Dursun, S., & Kutcher, S. (2000). Selective serotonin reuptake inhibitor discontinuation syndrome: Proposed diagnostic criteria. *Journal of Psychiatry and Neuroscience, 25,* 255–261.

Page 25

Heritability of extraversion and neuroticism: Bouchard, T. J. (2004). Genetic influence on human psychological traits: A survey. *Current Directions in Psychological Science, 13,* 148–151.

Beginning early in the 20th century, psychologists studied the effects of expectancies: An overview of expectancy theories can be found in many personality textbooks, for example, Carver, C. S., & Scheier, M. F. (2004). *Perspectives on personality* (5th ed.). Boston: Pearson.

Page 29

Eudaimonia means being your best self: Keyes, C. L. M., Shmotkin, D., & Ryff, C. D. (2002). Optimizing well-being: The empirical encounter of two traditions. *Journal of Personality and Social Psychology, 82,* 1007–1022. Ryan, R. M., & Deci, E. L. (2001). On happiness and human potentials: A review of research on hedonic and eudaimonic well-being. *Annual Review of Psychology, 52,* 141–166.

Page 30

Some theorists assert that eudaimonia doesn't feel good: Reviewed in Ryan & Deci (2001), op. cit.

Conscientiousness is also related to optimism: Bernard, L. C., Hutchison, S., Lavin, A., & Pennington, P. (1996). Ego-strength, hardiness, self-esteem, self-efficacy, optimism, and maladjustment: Health-related personality constructs and the "Big Five" model of personality. *Assessment, 3,* 115–131.

Page 31

Flow: Csikszentmihalyi, M. (1990). *Flow: The psychology of optimal experience.* New York: HarperCollins.

CHAPTER 2

Page 34

You would show significantly enhanced motivation and persistence: Carver, C. S., Blaney, P. H., & Scheier, M. F. (1979). Reassertion and giving up: The interactive role of self-directed attention and outcome expectancy. *Journal of Personality and Social Psychology, 37,* 1859–1870.

Page 35

If you were set up to actually perform well: Scheier, M. F., & Carver, C. S. (1982). Self-consciousness, outcome expectancy, and persistence. *Journal of Research in Personality, 16,* 409–418.

Page 36

In Lise's study, we measured their natural optimism: Solberg Nes, L., Segerstrom, S. C., & Sephton, S. E. (2005). Engagement and arousal: Optimism's effects during a brief stressor. *Personality and Social Psychology Bulletin, 31,* 111–120.

Page 43

Robert Sternberg has proposed that intelligence should be defined: Sternberg, R. J. (1997). The concept of intelligence and its role in lifelong learning and success. *American Psychologist, 52,* 1030–1037.

Page 44

You can feel happy if you're progressing at a satisfactory *rate*: Carver, C. S., & Scheier, M. F. (1990). Origins and functions of positive and negative affect: A control–process view. *Psychological Review, 97,* 19–35.

Page 45

Parenthood decreases marital satisfaction: Tsang, L. L. W., Harvey, C. D. H., Duncan, K. A., & Sommer, R. (2003). The effects of children, dual earner status, sex role traditionalism, and marital structure on marital happiness over time. *Journal of Family and Economic Issues, 24,* 5–26.

Goals aimed at achieving benefit do not increase happiness, purpose in life, or meaning: McGregor, I., & Little, B. R. (1998). Personal projects, happiness, and meaning: On doing well and being yourself. *Journal of Personality and Social Psychology, 74,* 494–512.

Notes

Page 46

Psychological research may be slightly distorted in its view: Sears, D. O. (1986). College sophomores in the laboratory: Influences of a narrow data base on psychology's view of human nature. *Journal of Personality and Social Psychology, 51,* 515–530.

Page 48

We could draw some conclusions about whether optimism was related to a person's "typical" day-to-day goal: Segerstrom, S. C., & Solberg Nes, L. (in press). When goals conflict but people prosper: The case of dispositional optimism. *Journal of Research in Personality.*

Page 52

Lack of action to overcome the roadblock maintains depression and preoccupation: Pyszczynski, T., & Greenberg, J. (1987). Self-regulatory perseveration and the depressive self-focusing style: A self-awareness theory of reactive depression. *Psychological Bulletin, 102,* 122–138.

Page 54

50% of new businesses fail within 4 years: U.S. Small Business Administration (2004, December 7). Frequently asked questions: What is the survival rate for new firms? Available at app1.sba.gov/faqs/faqindex.cfm?areaID=24.

Bezos on optimism: Bezos, J. (2004, April). Jeff Bezos, amazon.com: Because "optimism is essential." *Inc.: The Magazine for Growing Companies,* 148–150. Quote on p. 150.

Page 55

The optimist's superior ability to surmount the obstacles of fibromyalgia: Affleck, G., Tennen, H., Zautra, A., Urrows, S., Abeles, M., & Karoly, P. (2001). Women's pursuit of personal goals in daily life with fibromyalgia: A value-expectancy analysis. *Journal of Consulting and Clinical Psychology, 69,* 587–596. Quote on p. 593.

Page 56

Disruption is less severe for optimistic women with cancer: Carver, C. S., Lehman, J. M., & Antoni, M. H. (2003). Dispositional pessimism predicts illness-related disruption of social and recreational activities among breast cancer patients. *Journal of Personality and Social Psychology, 84,* 813–821.

Notes

Page 57

Optimism turned out to be a good predictor of whether older people remained engaged: Duke, J., Leventhal, H., Brownlee, S., & Leventhal, E. A. (2002). Giving up and replacing activities in response to illness. *Journal of Gerontology: Psychological Sciences, 57B*, P367–P376.

Page 58

Prescribed goals lose their positive punch: Sheldon, K. M., Ryan, R. M., Deci, E. L., & Kasser, T. (2004). The independent effects of goal contents and motives on well-being: It's both what you pursue and why you pursue it. *Personality and Social Psychology Bulletin, 30*, 475–486.

CHAPTER 3

Page 59

People thought they were better drivers than average: Svenson, O. (1981). Are we all less risky and more skillful than our fellow drivers? *Acta Psychologica, 47*, 143–148.

Page 60

One study tried self-enhancement to bolster self-esteem: Forsyth, D. R., & Kerr, N. A. (1999). *Are adaptive illusions adaptive?*, cited in Baumeister, R. F., Campbell, J. D., Krueger, J. I., & Vohs, K. D. (2003). Does high self-esteem cause better performance, interpersonal success, happiness, or healthier lifestyles? *Psychological Science in the Public Interest, 4*, 1–44.

Page 61

One emotion researcher pointed out: Tim Wilson, quoted in Gladwell, M. (2004, November 8). Getting over it: The Man in the Gray Flannel Suit put the war behind him. Why can't we? *The New Yorker,* p. 75 ff.

Resources lead people to judge their lives to be close to their ideals: Diener, E., & Fujita, F. (1995). Resources, personal strivings, and subjective well-being: A nomothetic and idiographic approach. *Journal of Personality and Social Psychology, 68*, 926–935.

Being chosen to be part of a group or being chosen the leader raises self-esteem: Leary, M. R., Cottrell, C. A., & Phillips, M. (2001). Deconfounding the effects of dominance and social acceptance on self-esteem. *Journal of Personality and Social Psychology, 81*, 898–909.

Notes

Page 64

Resource themes—particularly acceptance and status—surface across all domains of psychology: Bieling, P. J., Beck, A. T., & Brown, G. K. (2000). The sociotropy–autonomy scale: Structure and implications. *Cognitive Therapy and Research, 24,* 763–780. Helgeson, V. S. (1994). Relation of agency and communion to well-being: Evidence and potential explanations. *Psychological Bulletin, 116,* 412–428. McAdams, D. P. (1985). *Power, intimacy and the life story: Personological inquiries into identity.* New York: Morrow. Erik Erikson's developmental theory includes the stages of autonomy, industry, and generativity (related to status) as well as trust and intimacy (related to acceptance). That theory is described in most developmental and personality psychology textbooks, including Carver, C. S., & Scheier, M. F. (2004). *Perspectives on Personality* (5th ed.). Boston: Allyn & Bacon.

The kinds of goals that people were typically working toward: Emmons, R. A., & McAdams, D. P. (1991). Personal strivings and motive dispositions: Exploring the links. *Personality and Social Psychology Bulletin, 17,* 648–654.

Page 67

We are worse when we have fewer resources, a situation you will recognize as stress: My thinking about resources and stress initially arose from some immunological findings reviewed in Chapter 5 and was further influenced by Hobfoll, S. E. (1989). Conservation of resources: A new attempt at conceptualizing stress. *American Psychologist, 44,* 513–524. Also see Hobfoll, S. E. (1988). *The ecology of stress.* New York: Hemisphere, and Hobfoll, S. E. (1998). *Stress, culture, and community: The psychology and philosophy of stress.* New York: Plenum Press.

Profound negative consequences for mental and physical health: Kendler, K. S., Hettema, J. M., Butera, F., Gardner, C. O., & Prescott, C. A. (2003). Life event dimensions of loss, humiliation, entrapment, and danger in the prediction of onsets of major depression and generalized anxiety. *Archives of General Psychiatry, 60,* 789–796. Cohen, S., Frank, E., Doyle, W. J., Skoner, D. P., Rabin, B. S., & Gwaltney, J. M. (1998). Types of stressors that increase susceptibility to the common cold in healthy adults. *Health Psychology, 17,* 214–223. Matthews, K. A., & Gump, B. B. (2002). Chronic work stress and marital dissolution increase risk of post-trial mortality in men from the Multiple Risk Factor Intervention Trial. *Archives of Internal Medicine, 162,* 309–315; Li, J., Precht, D. H., Mortensen, P. B., & Olsen, J. (2003, February 1). Mortality in parents after death of a child in Denmark: A nationwide follow-up study. *Lancet, 361,* 363–367.

Page 69

One study followed hundreds of UCLA freshmen living in the residence halls: Aspinwall L. G., & Taylor, S. E. (1992). Modeling cognitive adaptation: A longitudinal investigation of the impact of individual differences and coping on college adjustment and performance. *Journal of Personality and Social Psychology, 63,* 989–1003.

Page 71

Cancer rates were 20% higher among those people living closest to the plant: Hatch, M. C., Wallenstein, S., Beyea, J., Nieves, J. W., & Susser, M. (1991). Cancer rates after the Three Mile Island nuclear accident and proximity of residence to the plant. *American Journal of Public Health, 81,* 719–724.

When residents were given a coping checklist: Collins, D. L., Baum, A., & Singer, J. E. (1983). Coping with chronic stress at Three Mile Island: Psychological and biochemical evidence. *Health Psychology, 2,* 149–166.

Optimistic rescue workers were most likely to cope by recruiting social resources: Dougall, A. L., Hyman, K. B., Hayward, M. C., McFeeley, S., & Baum, A. (2001). Optimism and traumatic stress: The importance of social support and coping. *Journal of Applied Social Psychology, 31,* 223–245.

Page 72

A study of women awaiting breast cancer diagnosis: Stanton, A. L., & Snider, P. R. (1993). Coping with a breast cancer diagnosis: A prospective study. *Health Psychology, 12,* 16–23.

Page 73

Combining the results of studies shows that optimistic coping is sensitive: Solberg Nes, L., & Segerstrom, S. C. (in press). Dispositional optimism and coping: A meta-analytic review. *Personality and Social Psychology Review.*

Trying not to think or feel something makes it prey on your mind: Wegner, D. M. (1989). *White bears and other unwanted thoughts: Suppression, obsession, and the psychology of mental control.* New York: Guilford Press.

Page 74

Emotion-focused strategies typical of optimists: Carver, C. S., Scheier, M. F., & Weintraub, J. K. (1989). Assessing coping strategies: A theoretically based approach. *Journal of Personality and Social Psychology, 56,* 267–183. Folkman, S., & Lazarus, R. S. (1988). *Manual for the Ways of Coping Questionnaire.* Palo Alto: Consulting Psychologists Press.

Page 75

Death provides motivation to attach ourselves to things that will outlive us: Pyszczynski, T., Greenberg, J., & Solomon, S. (1999). A dual-process model of defense against conscious and unconscious death-related thoughts: An extension of terror management theory. *Psychological Review, 106*, 835–845.

Page 76

"A person of value in an eternal world of meaning": Pyszczynski et al. (1999), op. cit., 838.

Page 77

People with high self-esteem did not show this increase in favoritism: Harmon-Jones, E., Simon, L., Greenberg, J., Pyszczynski, T., Solomon, S., & McGregor, H. (1997). Terror management theory and self-esteem: Evidence that increased self-esteem reduces mortality salience effects. *Journal of Personality and Social Psychology, 72*, 24–36.

Page 78

"Right after she was born, I remember having a revelation": Affleck, G., & Tennen, H. (1996). Construing benefits from adversity: Adaptational significance and dispositional underpinnings. *Journal of Personality, 64*, 899–922.

Optimists mentioned building or confirming social and existential resources: Davis, C. G., Nolen-Hoeksema, S., & Larson, J. (1998). Making sense of loss and benefiting from the experience: Two construals of meaning. *Journal of Personality and Social Psychology, 75*, 561–574.

Page 79

More optimistic patients and mothers saw the treatment as having more positive effects: Curbow, B., Somerfield, M. R., Baker, F., Wingard, J. R., & Legro, M. W. (1993). Personal changes, dispositional optimism, and psychological adjustment to bone marrow transplantation. *Journal of Behavioral Medicine, 16*, 423–443. Rini, C., Manne, S., DuHamel, K. N., Austin, J., Ostroff, J., Boulad, F., et al. (2004). Mothers' perceptions of benefit following pediatric stem cell transplantation: A longitudinal investigation of the roles of optimism, medical risk, and sociodemographic resources. *Annals of Behavioral Medicine, 28*, 132–141.

Many means of attaining generative and transcendent goals: Routledge, C., Arndt, J., & Sheldon, K. M. (2004). Task engagement after mortality salience: The effects of creativity, conformity, and connectedness on worldview defence. *European Journal of Social Psychology, 34*, 477–487.

Positive reinterpretation worked for the optimists but not for the pessimists: Stanton, A. L., Danoff-Burg, S., & Huggins, M. E. (2002). The first year after breast cancer diagnosis: Hope and coping strategies as predictors of adjustment. *Psycho-oncology, 11*, 93–102.

Only optimistic mothers felt better after they had initially looked for and found positive aspects: Rini et al. (2004), op. cit.

CHAPTER 4

Page 82

Maslow's "hierarchy of needs": Maslow, A. H. (1968). *Toward a psychology of being* (2nd ed.). New York: Harper & Row.

Page 83

Those who are isolated die sooner: House, J. S., Landis, K. R., & Umberson, D. (1988). Social relationships and health. *Science, 241,* 540–545.

Page 84

Resources associated with greater happiness and well-being: Diener, E., & Fujita, F. (1995). Resources, personal strivings, and subjective well-being: A nomothetic and idiographic approach. *Journal of Personality and Social Psychology, 68,* 926–935.

Getting married increases happiness for much longer: Lucas, R. E., Clark, A. E., Georgellis, Y., & Diener, E. (2003). Reexamining adaptation and the set point model of happiness: Reactions to changes in marital status. *Journal of Personality and Social Psychology, 84,* 527–539.

"You can't be yourself by yourself": Markus, H. (2005, January). *Branding social psychology.* Presentation to the Society for Personality and Social Psychology, New Orleans, LA.

People who have more social relationships have all kinds of better health outcomes: Cohen, S., Doyle, W. J., Skoner, D. P., Rabin, B. S., & Gwaltney, J. M. (1997). Social ties and susceptibility to the common cold. *Journal of the American Medical Association, 277,* 1940–1944. House et al. (1988), op. cit. Uchino, B. N. (2004). *Social support and physical health: Understanding the health consequences of relationships.* New Haven, CT: Yale University Press.

Page 85

One study of daily events logged the number of phone calls and letters participants received: Epstein, S. (1979). The stability of behavior: On predicting most of the people much of the time. *Journal of Personality and Social Psychology, 37,* 1097–1126.

A study of residents of university married-student housing: Gottlieb, B. H. (1981). Social support and social participation among residents of a married student housing complex. *Journal of College Student Personnel, January,* 46–52.

Notes

Page 86

Studies that subliminally present a name can increase commitment: Shah, J., (2003). Automatic for the people: How representations of significant others implicitly affect goal pursuit. *Journal of Personality and Social Psychology, 84,* 661–681.

Page 89

Finnish students who were socially optimistic were less lonely: Nurmi, J. E., Toivonen, S., Samela-Aro, K., & Eronen, S. (1996). Optimistic, approach-oriented, and avoidance strategies in social situations: Three studies on loneliness and peer relationships. *European Journal of Personality, 10,* 201–219.

Optimistic college freshmen had more friends at college: Brissette, I., Scheier, M. F., & Carver, C. S. (2002). The role of optimism in social network development, coping, and psychological adjustment during a life transition. *Journal of Personality and Social Psychology, 82,* 102–111.

Page 90

For each step of increasing pessimism, average friendship length dropped: Geers, A. L., Reilley, S. P., & Dember, W. N. (1998). Optimism, pessimism, and friendship. *Current Psychology, 17,* 3–19.

Page 91

They were more interested in interacting socially with the more optimistic "person": Carver, C. S., Kus, L. A., & Scheier, M. F. (1994). Effects of good versus bad mood and optimistic versus pessimistic outlook on social acceptance versus rejection. *Journal of Social and Clinical Psychology, 13,* 138–151.

Real social interactions with optimists are more positive: Raikkonen, K., Matthews, K. A., Flory, J. D., Owens, J. F., & Gump, B. B. (1999). Effects of optimism, pessimism, and trait anxiety on ambulatory blood pressure and mood during everyday life. *Journal of Personality and Social Psychology, 76,* 104–113.

Page 92

Beliefs about what someone is like actually *creates* those qualities: Snyder, M., Tanke, E. D., & Berscheid, E. (1977). Social perception and interpersonal behavior: On the self-fulfilling nature of stereotypes. *Journal of Personality and Social Psychology, 35,* 656–666.

Page 93

Prophetic effect occurs for all kinds of social relationships: McNulty, J. K., & Karney, B. R. (2002). Expectancy confirmation in appraisals of marital interactions. *Personality and Social Psychology Bulletin, 28,* 764–775. Miller, D. T., &

Notes

Turnbull, W. (1986). Expectancies and interpersonal processes. *Annual Review of Psychology, 37*, 233–256.

A study of newlyweds' satisfaction with their marriages: McNulty, J. K., & Karney, B. R. (2004). Positive expectations in the early years of marriage: Should couples expect the best or brace for the worst? *Journal of Personality and Social Psychology, 86*, 728–743.

Page 95

More optimistic college students expected more support: Brissette, I., Scheier, M. F., & Carver, C. S. (2002). The role of optimism in social network development, coping, and psychological adjustment during a life transition. *Journal of Personality and Social Psychology, 82*, 102–111. Conn, M. K., & Peterson, C. (1989). Social support: Seek and ye shall find. *Journal of Social and Personal Relationships, 6*, 345–358.

Emergency workers who were more optimistic perceived more support from close others: Dougall, A. L., Hyman, K. B., Hayward, M. C., McFeeley, S., & Baum, A. (2001). Optimism and traumatic stress: The importance of social support and coping. *Journal of Applied Social Psychology, 31*, 223–245.

Optimistic men caring for partners with HIV/AIDS perceived more social validation: Park, C. L., & Folkman, S. (1997). Stability and change in psychosocial resources during caregiving and bereavement in partners of men with AIDS. *Journal of Personality, 65*, 421–447.

Optimistic adults in cardiac rehabilitation perceived more support: Shen, B. J., McCreary, C. P., & Myers, H. F. (2004). Independent and mediated contributions of personality, coping, social support, and depressive symptoms to physical functioning outcome among patients in cardiac rehabilitation. *Journal of Behavioral Medicine, 27*, 39–62.

Optimistic women with breast cancer perceived more support: Abend, T. A., & Williamson, G. M. (2002). Feeling attractive in the wake of breast cancer: Optimism matters, and so do interpersonal relationships. *Personality and Social Psychology Bulletin, 28*, 427–436. Trunzo, J. J., & Pinto, B. M. (2003). Social support as a mediator of optimism and distress in breast cancer survivors. *Journal of Consulting and Clinical Psychology, 71*, 805–811.

Page 96

A large social network and a higher level of perceived support should predict using social support to cope: Conn & Peterson (1989), op. cit: Dougall et al. (2001), op. cit.

Page 97

Support given under the radar is the best kind of support to have: Bolger, N., Zuckerman, A., & Kessler, R. C. (2000). Invisible support and adjustment to stress. *Journal of Personality and Social Psychology, 79*, 953–961.

Page 98

People who gave more social support to others had a decrease in mortality risk; receiving social support had no effect: Brown, S. L., Nesse, R. M., Vinokur, A. D., & Smith, D. M. (2003). Providing social support may be more beneficial than receiving it: Results from a prospective study of mortality. *Psychological Science, 14*, 320–327.

Page 99

Those who thought about meaningful and supportive relationships felt less anxious and had lower heart rates and blood pressures: Smith, T. W., Ruiz, J. M., & Uchino, B. N. (2004). Mental activation of supportive ties, hostility, and cardiovascular reactivity to laboratory stress in young men and women. *Health Psychology, 23*, 476–485.

Page 100

Women with breast cancer generally prefer to compare themselves with others who are worse off: Taylor, S. E., & Lobel, M. (1989). Social comparison activity under threat: Downward evaluation and upward contacts. *Psychological Review, 96*, 569–575.

Page 102

Pessimistic college students with declining GPAs lowered their comparison levels: Gibbons, F. X., Blanton, H., Gerrard, M., Buunk, B., & Eggleston, T. (2000). Does social comparison make a difference? Optimism as a moderator of the relation between comparison level and academic performance. *Personality and Social Psychology Bulletin, 26*, 637–648.

Page 103

An experiment in which a student would work alongside a "peer" who did either much better or much worse: Lyubomirsky, S., & Ross, L. (1997). Hedonic consequences of social comparison: A contrast of unhappy and happy people. *Journal of Personality and Social Psychology, 73*, 1141–1157.

Optimistic MS patients were not depressed by downward comparisons: Hemphill, K. J., & Lehman, D. R. (1991). Social comparisons and their affective consequences: The importance of comparison dimension and individual difference variables. *Journal of Social and Clinical Psychology, 10,* 372–394.

CHAPTER 5

Page 108

Allostatic *load*: McEwen, B. S. (1998). Protective and damaging effects of stress mediators. *New England Journal of Medicine, 338,* 171–179.

Higher cortisol has negative consequences: Sapolsky, R. (1994). *Why zebras don't get ulcers.* New York: Freeman.

Page 109

Better-regulated cortisol predicts longer survival with breast cancer: Sephton, S. E., Sapolsky, R. M., Kraemer, H. C., & Spiegel, D. (2000). Diurnal cortisol rhythm as a predictor of breast cancer survival. *Journal of the National Cancer Institute, 92,* 994–1000.

One of the earliest studies tested whether optimism could predict recovery from surgery: Scheier, M. F., Matthews, K. A., Owens, J. F., Magovern, G. J., Lefebvre, R. C., Abbott, R. A., et al. (1989). Dispositional optimism and recovery from coronary artery bypass surgery: The beneficial effects on physical and psychological well-being. *Journal of Personality and Social Psychology, 57,* 1024–1040.

Page 110

A half-million CABG operations were performed in the United States in 2001: De Milto, L., & Odle, T. G. (2004). Coronary artery bypass graft surgery. Retrieved June 8, 2004, from www.healthatoz.com/healthatoz/atoz/ency/coronary_artery_bypass_graft_surgery.html.

Page 111

The most pessimistic quarter of CABG patients were more than three times more likely to be rehospitalized: Scheier, M. F., Matthews, K. A., Owens, J. F., Schulz, R., Bridges, M. W., Magovern, G. J., et al. (1999). Optimism and rehospitalization after coronary artery bypass graft surgery. *Archives of Internal Medicine, 159,* 829–835.

Optimistic patients had less pain, experienced less negative mood, and were more satisfied: Fitzgerald, T. E., Tennen, H., Affleck, G., & Pransky, G. S. (1993). The relative importance of dispositional optimism and control appraisals in quality of life after coronary artery bypass surgery. *Journal of Behavioral Medicine, 16,* 25–43.

Notes

Pessimists were three times more likely to have a new coronary event:
Helgeson, V. S., & Fritz, H. L. (1999). Cognitive adaptation as a predictor of new
coronary events after percutaneous transluminal coronary angioplasty. *Psychosomatic Medicine, 61,* 488–495.

Over 4 years, people who were more optimistic had fewer coronary events:
Helgeson, V. S. (2003). Cognitive adaptation, psychological adjustment, and disease progression among angioplasty patients: 4 years later. *Health Psychology, 22,*
30–38.

**Transplant recipients who were more optimistic recovered from their surgery
better:** Leedham, B., Meyerowitz, B. E., Muirhead, J., & Frist, W. H. (1995). Positive expectations predict health after heart transplantation. *Health Psychology, 14,*
74–79.

**Optimism was not associated with the length of hospital stay after CABG or
valve replacement:** Contrada, R. J., Goyal, T. M., Cather, C., Rafalson, L., Idler,
E. L., & Krause, T. J. (2004). Psychosocial factors in outcomes of heart surgery:
The impact of religious involvement and depressive symptoms. *Health Psychology,
23,* 227–238.

Page 112

**Mothers who were more optimistic had longer pregnancies, and their babies
were bigger:** Lobel, M., DeVincent, C. J., Kaminer, A., & Meyer, B. A. (2000).
The impact of prenatal maternal stress and optimistic disposition on birth outcomes in medically high-risk women. *Health Psychology, 19,* 544–553. Rini, C. K.,
Dunkel-Schetter, C., Wadhwa, P. D., & Sandman, C. A. (1999). Psychological
adaptation and birth outcomes: The role of personal resources, stress, and
social–cultural context in pregnancy. *Health Psychology, 18,* 333–345.

Page 113

**Optimism and stress levels didn't predict outcomes in early pregnancy as well
as they did in later pregnancy:** Solberg Nes, L., Segerstrom, S. C., Spencer, T.
E., Snedeker, J. L., & Miller, F. C. (2006, January). *Optimism and coping in early
pregnancy.* Poster presented at the meeting of the Society for Personality and
Social Psychology, Palm Springs, California.

**Among younger cancer patients, survivors were about two-thirds as pessimistic
as those who died:** Schulz, R., Bookwala, J., Knapp, J. E., Scheier, M., & Williamson, G. M. (1996). Pessimism, age, and cancer mortality. *Psychology and Aging, 11,*
304–309.

Page 114

**Survival rates in head and neck cancer indicate that pessimists were over 50%
more likely to die:** Allison, P. J., Guichard, C., Fung, K., & Gilain, L. (2003).

Dispositional optimism predicts survival status 1 year after diagnosis in head and neck cancer patients. *Journal of Clinical Oncology, 21,* 543–548.

Being optimistic did not confer an advantage over the long term in lung cancer: Schofield, P., Ball, D., Smith, J. G., Borland, R., O'Brien, P., Davis, S., et al. (2004). Optimism and survival in lung carcinoma patients. *Cancer, 100,* 1276–1282.

"Fighting Cancer with a Frown": Marcus, A. D. (2004, April 6). Fighting cancer with a frown: Research questions role of optimism in beating the disease: "The tyranny of positive thinking." *Wall Street Journal,* p. D1.

"The Trouble with Optimism": Fording, L. (2004). The trouble with optimism. Retrieved June 9, 2004, from msnbc.msn.com/id/4269238.

Page 116

Dispositional optimism was unrelated to how fast helper T cells declined: Tomakowsky, J., Lumley, M. A., Markowitz, N., & Frank, C. (2001). Optimistic explanatory style and dispositional optimism in HIV-infected men. *Journal of Psychosomatic Research, 51,* 577–587.

Dispositional optimism was unrelated to how long HIV-infected men survived: Reed, G. M., Kemeny, M. E., Taylor, S. E., Wang, H. Y. J., & Visscher, B. R. (1994). Realistic acceptance as a predictor of decreased survival time in gay men with AIDS. *Health Psychology, 13,* 299–307.

Lower pessimism predicted lower viral load and higher optimism predicted higher numbers of helper T cells: Milam, J. E., Richardson, J. L., Marks, G., Kemper, C. A., & McCutchan, A. (2004). The roles of dispositional optimism and pessimism in HIV disease progression. *Psychology and Health, 19,* 167–181.

Higher optimism predicted higher numbers of T cells in a diverse sample: Ironson, G., Balbin, E., Stuetzle, R., Fletcher, M. A., O'Cleirigh, C., Laurenceau, J. P., Schneiderman, N., & Solomon, G. (2005). Dispositional optimism and the mechanisms by which it predicts slower disease progression in HIV: Proactive behavior, avoidant coping, and depression. *International Journal of Behavioral Medicine, 12,* 86–97.

Page 117

Dispositional optimism predicted only slightly higher numbers of cytotoxic T cells: Segerstrom, S. C., Taylor, S. E., Kemeny, M. E., & Fahey, J. L. (1998). Optimism is associated with mood, coping, and immune change in response to stress. *Journal of Personality and Social Psychology, 74,* 1646–1655.

Page 119

Dispositionally optimistic students who stayed home had fewer helper T cells than pessimists, and the reverse was true of students who moved away:

Segerstrom, S. C. (2001). Optimism, goal conflict, and stressor-related immune change. *Journal of Behavioral Medicine, 24,* 441–467.

Page 120

Optimism was protective against noise stress's effect on the immune system, but only when dealing with the stress was easy: Sieber, W. J., Rodin, J., Larson, L., Ortega, S., & Cummings, N. (1992). Modulation of human natural killer cell activity by exposure to uncontrollable stress. *Brain,Behavior, and Immunity, 6,*141–156.

The effects of everyday stresses on women's T cell counts: Cohen, F., Kearney, K. A., Zegans, L. S., Kemeny, M. E., Neuhaus, J. M., & Stites, D. P. (1999). Differential immune system changes with acute and persistent stress for optimists vs. pessimists. *Brain, Behavior, and Immunity, 13,* 155–174.

Page 121

Optimistic people were *more* resilient when *in vitro* attempts failed: Litt, M. D., Tennen, H., Affleck, G., & Klock, S. (1992). Coping and cognitive factors in adaptation to *in vitro* fertilization failure. *Journal of Behavioral Medicine, 15,* 171–187.

Law School Top 7 Most Stressful Things list: Segerstrom, S. C. (1996). Perceptions of stress and control in the first semester of law school. *Willamette Law Review, 32,* 593–608.

Page 122

Scott Turow's account of his first year at Harvard Law: Turow, S. (1977). *One L.* New York: Warner. Quote on page 41.

Page 126

Animals suffer decreases in immune function when energy sources are low: Nelson, R. J., & Demas, G. E. (2004). Seasonal patterns of stress, disease, and sickness responses. *Current Directions in Psychological Science, 13,* 198–201.

Goals that would promote reproduction and survival can take priority over the immune system: Aubert, A., Goodall, G., Dantzer, R., & Gheusi, G. (1997). Differential effects of lipopolysaccharide on pup retrieving and nest building in lactating mice. *Brain, Behavior, and Immunity, 11,* 107–118. Barnard, C. J., Behnke, J. M., & Sewell, J. (1996). Environmental enrichment, immunocompetence, and resistance to *Babesia microti* in male mice. *Physiology and Behavior, 60,* 1223–1231. Smith, F. V., Barnard, C. J., & Behnke, J. M. (1996). Social odours, hormone modulation and resistance to disease in male laboratory mice, *Mus musculus. Animal Behavior, 52,* 141–153.

Notes

Higher cortisol production occurred after sleep restriction: Leproult, R., Copinschi, G., Buxton, O., & Van Cauter, E. (1997). Sleep loss results in an elevation of cortisol levels the next evening. *Sleep, 20*, 865–870. Also see Ekstedt, M., Akerstedt, T., & Soderstrom, M. (2004). Microarousals during sleep are associated with increased levels of lipids, cortisol, and blood pressure. *Psychosomatic Medicine, 66*, 925–931; and Williams, E., Magid, K., & Steptoe, A. (2005). The impact of time of waking and concurrent subjective stress on the cortisol response to awakening. *Psychoneuroendocrinology, 30*, 139–148.

An immunological cost to optimism in a laboratory study of law and medical students: Segerstrom, S. C., Castaneda, J. O., & Spencer, T. E. (2004). Optimism effects on cellular immunity: Testing the affective and persistence models. *Personality and Individual Differences, 35*, 1615–1624.

People who had shown more engagement with the anagram task also had elevated cortisol: Solberg Nes, L., Segerstrom, S. C., & Sephton, S. E. (2005). Engagement and arousal: Optimism's effects during a brief stressor. *Personality and Social Psychology Bulletin, 31*, 111–120.

CHAPTER 6

"To him this is the best of all possible worlds, and the best of all possible times": Hughes, G. R. (1984). *Emerson's demanding optimism.* Baton Rouge: Louisiana State University Press.

People are most optimistic about events that can be controlled by their own behavior: Weinstein, N. D. (1982). Unrealistic optimism about susceptibility to health problems. *Journal of Behavioral Medicine, 5*, 441–460.

People who feel least vulnerable to getting a disease are also least interested in getting written information: Kulik, J. A., & Mahler, H. I. M. (1987). Health status, perceptions of risk, and prevention interest for health and nonhealth problems. *Health Psychology, 6*, 15–27.

Notes

Page 135

The graph on page 136 shows my results: Segerstrom, S. C. (2001). Optimism and attentional bias for negative and positive stimuli. *Personality and Social Psychology Bulletin, 27,* 1334–1343.

Page 136

Pessimists tend to be worriers: Segerstrom, S. C., Stanton, A. L., Alden, L. E., & Shortridge, B. E. (2003). A multidimensional structure for repetitive thought: What's on your mind, and how, and how much? *Journal of Personality and Social Psychology, 85,* 909–921.

Page 137

A study that examined information about health risks: Aspinwall, L. G., & Brunhart, S. M. (1996). Distinguishing optimism from denial: Optimistic beliefs predict attention to health threats. *Personality and Social Psychology Bulletin, 22,* 993–1003.

Page 138

"When things go wrong in a big way, the optimist may be particularly vulnerable": Tennen, H., & Affleck, G. (1987). The costs and benefits of optimistic explanations and dispositional optimism. *Journal of Personality, 55,* 377–393.

Page 139

Dart throwers were told to prepare for a darts test: Spencer, S. M., & Norem, J. K. (1996). Reflection and distraction: Defensive pessimism, strategic optimism, and performance. *Personality and Social Psychology Bulletin, 22,* 354–365.

Thinking about the possibility of failure was associated with higher GPA for defensive pessimists: Cantor, N., & Norem, J. K. (1989). Defensive pessimism and stress and coping. *Social Cognition, 7,* 92–112.

Both dispositional optimists and defensive pessimists think about how to overcome the problem: Showers, C., & Ruben, C. (1990). Distinguishing defensive pessimism from depression: Negative expectations and positive coping mechanisms. *Cognitive Therapy and Research, 14,* 385–399.

Page 140

Both dispositional optimists and defensive pessimists have a history of success, whereas dispositional pessimists have a history of failure: Cantor and Norem (1989), op. cit.

Notes

Law students who did well on the LSAT had more confidence in and positive expectations for their success in law school: Segerstrom, S. C., Taylor, S. E., Kemeny, M. E., & Fahey, J. L. (1998). Optimism is associated with mood, coping, and immune change in response to stress. *Journal of Personality and Social Psychology, 74,* 1646–1655.

When students predict their grades in a specific course, dispositional optimism accounts for only 2.3%: Robbins, A. S., Spence, J. T., & Clark, H. (1991). Psychological determinants of health and performance: The tangled web of desirable and undesirable characteristics. *Journal of Personality and Social Psychology, 61,* 755–765.

Page 143

A study in which people could either keep working on the fruitless task or change: Aspinwall, L. G., & Richter, L. (1999). Optimism and self-mastery predict more rapid disengagement from unsolvable tasks in the presence of alternatives. *Motivation and Emotion, 23,* 221–245.

Page 148

One of the most popular slot machines is called "Wheel of Fortune": Rivlin, G. (2004, May 9). The chrome-shiny, lights-flashing, wheel-spinning, touch-screened, Drew-Carey-wisecracking, video-playing, "Sound Events"-packed, pulse-quickening bandit. *New York Times,* p. 42.

Page 149

Optimistic people are especially vulnerable to the near miss: Gibson, B., & Sanbonmatsu, D. M. (2004). Optimism, pessimism, and gambling: The downside of optimism. *Personality and Social Psychology Bulletin, 30,* 149–160.

Page 150

Animal foragers: Stephens, D. W., & Krebs, J. R. (1986). *Foraging theory.* Princeton, NJ: Princeton University Press.

Page 152

Optimism clearly led to higher values of *R*: Segerstrom, S. C., & Solberg Nes, L. (in press). When goals conflict but people prosper: The case of dispositional optimism. *Journal of Research in Personality*

Notes

CHAPTER 7

Page 153

The Gallup organization has been asking people in dozens of countries whether they think the next year will be better or worse: Michalos, A. C. (1988). Optimism in thirty countries over a decade. *Social Indicators Research, 20,* 177–180.

Page 155

People in countries located in Asia are more pessimistic than people in countries located in North America: Chang, E. C., Sanna, L. J., & Yang, K. M. (2002). Optimism, pessimism, affectivity, and psychological adjustment in the U.S. and Korea: A test of a mediation model. *Personality and Individual Differences, 31,* 1195–1208.

Americans of Asian descent are more pessimistic than Americans of European descent: Chang, E. C. (1996). Cultural differences in optimism, pessimism, and coping: Predictors of subsequent adjustment in Asian American and Caucasian American college students. *Journal of Counseling Psychology, 43,* 113–123. Chang, E. C. (1996). Evidence for the cultural specificity of pessimism in Asians vs. Caucasians: A test of a general negativity hypothesis. *Personality and Individual Differences, 21,* 819–822.

Page 156

The difference between collectivism and individualism affects how important it is that predictions about the future be personally motivating versus technically accurate: Shuper, P. A., Sorrentino, R. M., Hodson, G., & Walker, A. M. (2004). A theory of uncertainty orientation: Implications for the study of individual differences within and across cultures. *Journal of Cross-Cultural Psychology, 35,* 460–480.

Page 157

Predictions are much more closely related to actual abilities in people from collectivist countries: Klassen, R. M. (2004). Optimism and realism: A review of self-efficacy from a cross-cultural perspective. *International Journal of Psychology, 39,* 205–230.

Page 158

"Racism erases at least some of the contingencies between hard work, personal action, and positive outcomes": Mattis, J. S., Fontenot, D. L., & Hatcher-Kay, C. A. (2003). Religiosity, racism, and dispositional optimism among African

Notes

Americans. *Personality and Individual Differences, 34*, 1025–1038. Quote on page 1029.

Black Americans who report a loving, supporting, and empowering relationship with God are also more optimistic: Krause, N. (2003). Religious meaning and subjective well-being in late life. *Journal of Gerontology, 58B*, S160–S170.

Page 159

One study examined what happens when optimists and pessimists were exposed to evidence of prejudice: Kaiser, C.R., Major, B., & McCoy, S. K. (2004). Expectations about the future and the emotional consequences of perceiving prejudice. *Personality and Social Psychology Bulletin, 30*, 173–184.

Page 161

Optimists are more likely than pessimists to remember their parents being optimistic, encouraging, and happy: Dean, M., Klavens, B., & Peterson, C. (1989). The origins of optimism. Cited in C. Peterson & L. M. Bossio, *Health and Optimism*. New York: Free Press. Quote on p. 74. Hjelle, L. A., Busch, E. A., & Warren, J. E. (1996). Explanatory style, dispositional optimism, and reported parental behavior. *Journal of Genetic Psychology, 157*, 489–499.

A large group of almost 20,000 adult Finns recently provided even more compelling evidence: Korkeila, K., Kivelä, S. L., Suominen, S., Vahtera, J., Kivimäki, M., Sundell, J., et al. (2004). Childhood adversities, parent–child relationships and dispositional optimism in adulthood. *Social Psychiatry and Psychiatric Epidemiology, 39*, 286–292.

Page 162

The mother's perception of her child at ages 3 and 6 accounts for that child's optimism at ages 24 and 27: Heinonen, K., Räikkönen, K., & Keltikangas-Järvinen, L. (2005). Dispositional optimism: Development over 21 years from the perspectives of perceived temperament and mothering. *Personality and Individual Differences, 38*, 425–435.

By the time children go off to college, parental warmth and approval is virtually unrelated to optimism: Brewin, C.R., Andrews, B., & Furnham, A. (1996). Intergenerational links and positive self-cognitions: Parental correlates of optimism, learned resourcefulness, and self-evaluation. *Cognitive Therapy and Research, 20*, 247–263.

Social and status resources in young adulthood are more likely to be held by one's peers than one's parents: Harris, J. R. (1995). Where is the child's environment? A group socialization theory of development. *Psychological Review, 102*, 458–489. Erik Erikson quoted on page 477.

Notes

Page 164

If you asked people on a couple of days, there wasn't very good evidence for happy or unhappy people: Epstein, S. (1979). The stability of behavior: I. On predicting most of the people much of the time. *Journal of Personality and Social Psychology, 37*, 1097–1126.

Page 171

Loss of or threat to social and status resources among these women led to a loss of optimism: Atienza, A. A., Stephens, M. A. P., & Townsend, A. L. (2004). Role stressors as predictors of changes in women's optimistic expectations. *Personality and Individual Differences, 37*, 471–484.

CHAPTER 8

Page 175

Fantasies encourage people to linger on a dream, whereas optimism encourages people to act to achieve it: Oettingen, G., Pak, H., & Schnetter, K. (2001). Self-regulation of goal setting: Turning free fantasies about the future into binding goals. *Journal of Personality and Social Psychology, 80*, 736–753.

Optimism trainees had more positive thoughts, felt more capable of solving problems, and generated more creative solutions to a real problem-solving task: Riskind, J. H., Sarampote, C. S., & Mercier, M. A. (1996). For every malady a sovereign cure: Optimism training. *Journal of Cognitive Psychotherapy: An International Quarterly, 10*, 105–117.

Page 176

The "three good things" exercise actually increased happiness over time: Seligman, M. E. P., Steen, T. A., Park, N., & Peterson, C. (2005). Positive psychology progress: Empirical validation of interventions. *American Psychologist, 60*, 410–421.

Page 177

When people write about their deepest thoughts and feelings, a number of positive outcomes can ensue: Pennebaker, J. W. (1997). *Opening up: The healing power of expressing emotions.* New York: Guilford Press.

Page 178

One study asked HIV-infected women to write journal entries that focused on a future in which their treatment regimens were simple: Mann, T. (2001).

Effects of future writing and optimism on health behaviors in HIV-infected women. *Annals of Behavioral Medicine, 23,* 26–33.

"Mental simulation" activates the self-regulatory loop and actually increases the odds that you'll get what you want: Taylor, S. E., Pham, L. B., Rivkin, I. D., & Armor, D. A. (1998). Harnessing the imagination: Mental simulation, self-regulation, and coping. *American Psychologist, 53,* 429–439.

Page 179

People at all levels of optimism felt better if they did the self-regulation writing task: Cameron, L. D., & Nicholls, G. (1998). Expression of stressful experiences through writing: Effects of a self-regulation manipulation for pessimists and optimists. *Health Psychology, 17,* 84–92.

Page 185

Self-determination theory says that people have three basic psychological needs: Deci, E. L., & Ryan, R. M. (2000). The "what" and "why" of goal pursuits: Human needs and the self-determination of behavior. *Psychological Inquiry, 11,* 227–268.

Page 186

When children who were interested in drawing were told they could get a certificate by doing more drawings, they eventually lost interest: Lepper, M. R., Greene, D., & Nisbett, R. E. (1973). Undermining children's extrinsic interest with extrinsic rewards: A test of the overjustification hypothesis. *Journal of Personality and Social Psychology, 28,* 129–137.

Unhappily for those who become absorbed in extrinsic motivators for their behavior, this change in motivation works against them: Sheldon, K. M., & Krieger, L. S. (2004). Does legal education have undermining effects on law students? Evaluating changes in motivation, values, and well-being. *Behavioral Sciences and the Law, 22,* 261–286.

Page 187

People who study the self actually separate out two *possible selves:* Higgins, E. T. (1987). Self-discrepancy: A theory relating self and affect. *Psychological Review, 94,* 319–340.

Strategies for increasing intrinsic motivation: Sheldon, K. M., Kasser, T., Smith, K., & Share, T. (2002). Personal goals and psychological growth: Testing an intervention to enhance goal attainment and personality integration. *Journal of Personality, 70,* 5–31.

Notes

Page 188

"**Resolved: To Do More. Or Less. Or Something**": St. John, W. (2005, January 2). Resolved: To do more. Or less. Or something. *New York Times,* pp. 9.1 – 9.2.

Page 189

"**A Survey Method for Characterizing Daily Life Experience: The Day Reconstruction Method**": Kahneman, D., Krueger, A. B., Schkade, D.A., Schwarz, N., & Stone, A. A. (2004, December 3). A survey method for characterizing daily life experience: The day reconstruction method. *Science, 306,* 1776–1780.

Page 193

There's No Stopping Us: We Work Too Much . . . and Play Too Little . . . but Who Dares Step Off the Treadmill?: Jones, C. (2004, March 14). There's no stopping us. *Chicago Tribune Magazine,* p. 13.

Page 194

Many people with blue-collar jobs see their work as fulfilling and worthwhile, whereas others with white-collar jobs are only working for the money: Wrzesniewski, A., McCauley, C., Rozin, P., & Schwartz, B. (1997). Jobs, careers, and callings: People's relations to their work. *Journal of Research in Personality, 31,* 21–33.

EPILOGUE

Page 196

Voltaire exploited this stereotype of optimism in his book *Candide*: Voltaire (1947). *Candide, or Optimism* (J. Butt, Trans.). New York: Penguin Books.

Page 197

Skepticism of positive psychology thrived: See, for example, Lazarus, R. S. (2003). Does the positive psychology movement have legs? *Psychological Inquiry, 14,* 93–109.

The Positive Psychology Prize was criticized: Simon, C. C. (2002, December 24). The happy heretic: Martin Seligman thinks psychologists should help people be happy. Who could possibly have a problem with that? *Washington Post,* p. F1.

Notes

"That which we intensely image can and often does actualize in fact.": Peale, N. V. (1976). *The positive principle today: How to renew and sustain the power of positive thinking.* Englewood Cliffs, NJ: Prentice-Hall. Quote on page 15.

Page 198

Positive patients and doctors effect miraculous cures and negative patients and doctors cut life short: Siegel, B. S. (1986). *Love, medicine, and miracles.* New York: Harper & Row.

Index

Index

Index

Index

Index

About the Author

Suzanne C. Segerstrom, PhD, is an associate professor of Psychology at the University of Kentucky in Lexington. She has conducted extensive research on psychological influences on the immune system, and on the relationship between optimism and well-being. Dr. Segerstrom's work has been sponsored by the National Insitutes of Health, the Norman Cousins Program in Psychoneuroimmunology, and the Dana Foundation. She is also a winner of the prestigious Templeton Positive Psychology Prize, awarded in recognition of her work on optimism. She lives near Lexington, Kentucky, with her husband and their dogs.